Oracle Database 11g– Underground Advice for Database Administrators

Beyond the basics

A real-world DBA survival guide for Oracle 11g database implementations

April C. Sims

PUBLISHING

BIRMINGHAM - MUMBAI

Oracle Database 11g—Underground Advice for Database Administrators

Beyond the basics

First published: April 2010

Production Reference: 1010410

Published by Packt Publishing Ltd.
32 Lincoln Road
Olton
Birmingham, B27 6PA, UK.

ISBN 978-1-849680-00-4

www.packtpub.com

Cover Image by Tina Negus (tina_manthorpe@sky.com)

Credits

Author
April C. Sims

Reviewers
Philip Rice

Charles Schultz

Lei Zeng

Acquisition Editor
James Lumsden

Development Editor
Dhwani Devater

Technical Editors
Akash Johari

Pallavi Kachare

Ajay Shanker

Copy Editor
Lakshmi Menon

Editorial Team Leader
Akshara Aware

Project Team Leader
Lata Basantani

Project Coordinator
Jovita Pinto

Indexer
Hemangini Bari

Graphics
Geetanjali Sawant

Proofreader
Aaron Nash

Production Coordinator
Shantanu Zagade

Cover Work
Shantanu Zagade

About the author

April C. Sims, after many career changes, has finally found a field that inspires, frustrates, and enthralls her at the same time—administering Oracle Databases. A previous career as a teacher lead her to continue teaching others about Oracle, as she considers the first year as a DBA to be the most critical. April is an Oracle Certified Professional 8i, 9i, and 10g with an MBA from the University of Texas at Dallas. She is an active technical presenter at regional Oracle Events, IOUG COLLABORATE, and Oracle OpenWorld.

She is a lead DBA at Southern Utah University, a 4 year regional university based in Cedar City, UT. Also known as Festival City, USA, it is home to 17 major events, including the Utah Summer Games and the Utah Shakespearean Festival. It is a beautiful place surrounded by National Parks.

April is also a Contributing Editor for IOUG "SELECT" Journal, which is a quarterly technical magazine for the Independent Oracle Users Group. She is also a contributor to *ORACLE SECURITY Step-by-Step A Survival Guide for Oracle Security* Version 1.0 by SANS Press, 2003.

I want to thank the most inspiring person that I have ever met during my Oracle career—my boss Jeanette Ormond. A big thanks to John Kanagaraj and IOUG SELECT for getting me started on my publishing career. Thanks to my Mom, Dad, and the rest of the huge family as part of my upbringing. They were responsible for the competitive spirit and stick-to-it nature that allowed me to finish this book. Thanks to my husband Loyd for the nights spent in front of the computer instead of cooking dinner. Thanks to everyone at Packt Publishing and especially the team of technical reviewers who did their best to keep me from making a fool out of myself.

About the reviewers

Philip Rice has been in the computer field since 1980 and began working with Oracle in 1991. He is now an Oracle DBA for campus enterprise systems at the University of California Santa Cruz, where the school mascot is a banana slug. Philip has done presentations on the RMAN topic for User Groups at regional and national levels.

Charles Schultz has worked at the University of Illinois since 1998 as an Oracle Database Administrator supporting various central administration services, including the University-wide ERP, where he specializes in rooting out performance issues. While Charles's main focus is on Oracle, he has dabbled in Sybase, MySQL, and MS SQL Server. Charles values the rich resources of the user community and teaches Oracle classes at a community college.

When not logged into a server, Charles can be found on a volleyball court, eating up a Sci-fi book, playing with his family, or engaging the community on social issues, and he has been known to be up in the wee hours playing video games.

Lei Zeng is a seasoned DBA with over ten years of hands-on experience in Oracle database management and administration on various platforms. She has worked with many mission-critical databases, including both OLTP databases and data warehouses up to terabytes. She is an OCP in Oracle 8i, 9i, 10g, 11g, and also a certified system administrator on HP-UX, Sun Solaris platforms. She has special interests in areas such as RAC, Data Guard, Stream, database upgrade, migration, and performance tuning. For the recent years, Lei has become an active contributor to IOUG's SELECT journal. Currently, she works for Yahoo! and can be reached at `aleizeng2003@yahoo.com`.

I would like to thank the author, April C. Sims, who worked diligently on this book to present it to the Oracle DBA community. This book provides wonderful guidance which will ensure a more successful DBA career.

Table of Contents

Preface

Oracle Corporation has become one of the largest software companies in the world with its premier Relational Database Management System known as Oracle. Larry Ellison, the current CEO, founded the company back in the 1970s. The growth of technology over the last twenty years also fueled the implementation of large databases to maintain control of the explosive growth of data. Through many technical advances and superior design, Oracle rose to the top when companies were choosing the database technology for their enterprise systems.

The role of the **Database Administrator (DBA)** includes certain key responsibilities—disaster recovery, database architecture and design, as well as performance tuning. Specific tasks also include new installations, security administration, and proactively monitoring all systems at several levels. Because of the great responsibility associated with being a DBA, a concerted effort is required to integrate a constant stream of new knowledge within a locally customized environment. While the documentation and training classes provide some benefit for the basics, it is the advice that comes from experience that lays the real foundation for a career.

DBAs must work closely with other IT members to maintain a high level of dependability for enterprise applications that run on Oracle, often outlined in an official Service Level Agreement. That is what this book is all about—integrating old knowledge with new ideas, while interacting with all levels of expertise within the Oracle Enterprise.

What this book covers

Chapter 1, When to Step Away from the Keyboard, answers the question "What does a DBA do all day?" It contains a comprehensive list of prioritized tasks that the average DBA is responsible for. A common theme throughout the book is introduced in this chapter: Tools should be extensible, flexible, and ubiquitous. Included in this chapter is a list of commonly seen mistakes that can be easily avoided by adopting recommended practices. Emphasis is placed on the attitude and philosophy that a DBA should have while doing their job as a valuable team member.

Chapter 2, *Maintaining Oracle Standards,* discusses "standards" such as Oracle's Optimal Flexible Architecture, Unix shell scripting, code and configuration basics. This is meant to provide a solid foundation designed to reduce future maintenance. This is where your dedication to detail comes into play, as it takes work to enforce standards, especially when the personnel in your department change. A DBA should be comfortable with the fact that a migration to the next patch set, version, or hardware replacement will always be in progress. This requires multiple Oracle Homes with completely separate environments that can be easily switched; this chapter outlines how to accomplish this goal. The new 11g Automatic Diagnostic Repository features, for diagnosing and repairing certain types of failures, will be outlined in the chapter as well.

Chapter 3, Tracking the Bits and Bytes, covers how data moves from one database component to the next; the mechanics or essential architectural infrastructure at the block level; what the data in a datafile, redo, undo, or archivelog actually looks like; and how the database keeps up with SCN changes. Dumping database blocks provides the raw hexadecimal values that convert to the characters that the end user sees at the application level. Other utilities such as LogMiner can be used to access information from certain database components, as well as the very basic Unix command strings. These essential concepts will provide you with the confidence that you can survive any disaster that you may have to tackle. Corruption prevention and detection is covered because this is one of the real tests for excelling at your job. No one really wants to have to fix corruption when it happens, because the data becomes unrecoverable fast.

Chapter 4, Achieving Maximum Uptime, covers redundancy at all levels: hardware, software, databases, ASM, SAN(s), and load balancers. Databases become redundant with Data Guard and RAC. This chapter offers an introduction to network and SQL*Net tuning for all types of implementations. Achieve the smallest outage windows by moving to rolling upgrades, ensuring there is some sort of backup plan for important personnel as well as documenting configurations with Oracle Configuration Manager. There are always single points of failure in every organization; identifying them is the first step on the path to a fully documented disaster recovery plan.

Chapter 5, Data Guard and Flashback, explains that the combination of Oracle's Flashback and Data Guard makes recovery scenarios, stress testing, and hot fix patching on a physical standby possible by making the database read and write temporarily. Using both Data Guard and Flashback in tandem can reduce or eliminate downtime for the primary database in certain types of recovery situations. It may reduce or eliminate the need for duplication of hardware for testing purposes. Several scenarios are outlined in detail, along with recommendations for implementations that fulfill disaster recovery goals.

Chapter 6, Extended RMAN, covers the essential tool for DBAs—RMAN, which is just complicated enough to warrant its own chapter. In this chapter, we will provide the foundations for writing your own scripts to get you started using this utility today. While the previous standard backups consisted of either a basic cold or hot version, RMAN does that and also adds even more flexibility when automating backup (and even recovery) routines. RMAN is the basic utility behind several types of disaster recovery and migration tasks such as: Creating Physical and Logical Standby(s). You can restore between different versions and migrate to new hardware using Transportable Tablespaces. RMAN is also involved with 11g's ADR Detected Failure Repairs, as well as duplication across the network (both local and remote).

Chapter 7, Migrating to 11g: A Step-Ordered Approach, talks about how migrating to a newer Oracle Database version doesn't have to be confined to a single outage period. Several interim steps can be done ahead of time to certain compatible components, saving valuable time. In a general sense, Oracle is backwards compatible for making that transition from an earlier version to a later one. The following components can be upgraded while still remaining compatible with earlier versions of Oracle:

- Oracle Net Services
- Clients
- RMAN binary, Virtual Private, and Normal Catalog Database
- Grid Control Repository Database
- Grid Control Management Agents
- Automatic Storage Management and Clusterware

This is an essential guide for upgrading to 11g using a multiple home environment: Cloning Oracle homes, Oracle Universal Installer (interactive, silent, and suppressed modes), RMAN catalog, and SQL Net. All of the options for performing upgrades are touched on in this book: DBUA, Manual Method, Export/Import, Data pump, TTS, RMAN, Physical Standbys, and the newer Transient Logical Standby.

Chapter 8, 11g Tuning Tools, covers ORION, TRCANLZR, and Statspack utilities. While it is easy to show someone how to use a tool, it takes experience to correctly interpret the results you get. This chapter will also cover different free-source, load-testing tools for forecasting trends of CPU utilization and I/O; in other words predicting the approximate time to purchase new hardware before the end user experiences degraded performance. 11g features such as SQL Plan Management will be covered along with Oracle's own Enterprise Manager tuning tools. A large portion of this chapter is dedicated to the migration path for upgrading the query optimizer using SQL Plan Management from 10g to 11g. Start a new paragraph from here, you might still be overwhelmed with all of the work set before you, and that's is why you've bought this book in the first place. This is a book you will keep for a long time, referring back again and again for each new project. It will be especially handy to show management when they start altering your job description. It is our hope that this is only a starting place for your career as a DBA and that by reading this book, you will share the knowledge with your peers as an active participant in Oracle User Groups.

What you need for this book

It would be helpful if you have some knowledge of SQL and are comfortable with the Unix operating system, but this is not absolutely essential. For those new to these technologies, keep the documentation nearby to use as a reference. This book is written for the Unix operating system, but you may only have access to a Windows operating system such as a desktop for testing purposes. There are tools, such as Cygwin (for Windows), which enable many of the same operating system commands to work on both Unix and Windows.

This book focuses on 11g Release 2 version with a reference to general Unix operating system commands. Previous versions of Oracle are also referenced when it applies to migration or upgrading to 11g as the topic. The Oracle Database Installation Guide for the version you are installing will have the prerequisite hardware requirements. The best place to start for the latest documentation and Oracle software downloads is the **Oracle Technology Network (OTN)** website: `http://otn.oracle.com`.

Who this book is for

This is for you if you find yourself in charge of an Oracle Database (understanding the full responsibility that goes with such a position), but are unsure of what tasks you need to perform. It can be easy to feel overwhelmed, so this reference is designed as a sanity check, whether you are a single employee or the DBA manager of several employees, or whether you are taking over an existing position or taking up a newly created one.

You are a person that wants to be proactively preventing disasters instead of simply keeping ahead of the next problem. In doing so, you'll help counter one of the major causes of professional burnout. This book is meant to make your technical transition to a DBA career easier and more efficient while educating you on how to reduce some of the most common mistakes.

You may be someone who needs guidance for migrating to 11g or implementing Oracle's Maximum Availability Architecture. This book is also meant to map out the migration options available when purchasing new hardware, giving you the opportunity to change the way your Oracle software is implemented, and to make it more Optimal Flexible Architecture compliant. This book will be useful when you are assigned the responsibility of making any sort of change in your Oracle environment—installations, migrations, upgrades, as well as patching. Take a few moments to read through the recommendations and suggestions for automating the maintenance tasks required for your applications to make them more redundant, flexible, and tolerant of future changes.

Conventions

In this book, you will find a number of styles of text that distinguish between different kinds of information. Here are some examples of these styles and an explanation of their meaning.

Code words in text are shown as follows: "We can include other contexts through the use of the `include` directive."

A block of code is set as follows:

```
run {

SET CONTROLFILE AUTOBACKUP FORMAT FOR DEVICE TYPE DISK TO '/
backuplocation/%F';

restore controlfile from autobackup;

alter database mount;

}
```

New terms and **important words** are shown in bold. Words that you see on the screen, in menus or dialog boxes for example, appear in the text like this: "clicking the **Next** button moves you to the next screen".

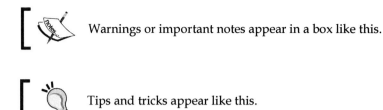

Warnings or important notes appear in a box like this.

Tips and tricks appear like this.

Reader feedback

Feedback from our readers is always welcome. Let us know what you think about this book—what you liked or may have disliked. Reader feedback is important for us to develop titles that you really get the most out of.

To send us general feedback, simply send an e-mail to feedback@packtpub.com, and mention the book title via the subject of your message.

If there is a book that you need and would like to see us publish, please send us a note in the **SUGGEST A TITLE** form on www.packtpub.com or e-mail to suggest@packtpub.com.

If there is a topic that you have expertise in and you are interested in either writing or contributing to a book on, see our author guide on www.packtpub.com/authors.

Customer support

Now that you are the proud owner of a Packt book, we have a number of things to help you to get the most from your purchase.

Downloading the example code for the book

Visit http://www.packtpub.com/files/code/0004_Code.zip to directly download the example code.

The downloadable files contain instructions on how to use them.

Errata

Although we have taken every care to ensure the accuracy of our content, mistakes do happen. If you find a mistake in one of our books—maybe a mistake in the text or the code—we would be grateful if you would report this to us. By doing so, you can save other readers from frustration and help us improve subsequent versions of this book. If you find any errata, please report them by visiting `http://www.packtpub.com/support`, selecting your book, clicking on the **let us know** link, and entering the details of your errata. Once your errata are verified, your submission will be accepted and the errata will be uploaded on our website, or added to any list of existing errata, under the Errata section of that title. Any existing errata can be viewed by selecting your title from `http://www.packtpub.com/support`.

Piracy

Piracy of copyright material on the Internet is an ongoing problem across all media. At Packt, we take the protection of our copyright and licenses very seriously. If you come across any illegal copies of our works, in any form, on the Internet, please provide us with the location address or website name immediately so that we can pursue a remedy.

Please contact us at `copyright@packtpub.com` with a link to the suspected pirated material.

We appreciate your help in protecting our authors and our ability to bring you valuable content.

Questions

You can contact us at `questions@packtpub.com` if you are having a problem with any aspect of the book, and we will do our best to address it.

1

When to Step Away from the Keyboard

Once, while attending an Oracle conference, I overheard a heated cell phone conversation with the phrase "Step away from the keyboard!" Things were not going well back at their office: the backup **Database Administrator (DBA)** was attempting to fix a problem and there was a debate about what to do next. The database was down and the less-experienced DBA was attempting to bring it up without investigating why it was down in the first place. Just taking an extra minute to look at the database alert log before attempting to bring up the database might prevent the need to do a time-intensive restore process from a backup. In this chapter, we shall take on the philosophy as well as the motivation behind the DBA's role in the Enterprise, which can make or break a technical career.

A DBA will not know exactly how to fix every problem or issue that arises, but they should be well-versed in the tools available for diagnosing and eventual resolution. Attention to detail while not losing sight of the big picture is an important attribute to have. Focusing too much on the smaller, less essential items would be a waste of valuable time. All tasks and accomplishments should be centered on improving service to the client, so it makes sense that maximizing availability is a primary objective for a DBA. This chapter also includes a list of tips to avoid making a major blunder or a possible career-ending mistake such as the example above.

Protecting and defending

The story above shows that protecting the database is considered one of the ongoing responsibilities of a DBA. So, how does one accomplish this goal? You do it with the right knowledge and tools. At the same time you can't make everyone else an enemy while staunchly protecting the database. There are security decisions that you will have to stick to, but you should try not to stand in the way of getting the work done. It is a position of respect that you are striving for, not a position based on fear.

How does one gain this knowledge? Obviously, one of the first answers is to read the supplied documentation, but that isn't enough. Other less obvious ways are interacting with your peers at conferences, joining Oracle User Groups, conversations with other DBAs, office meetings with IT personnel, writing papers and giving presentations, interacting with technical support sites, and e-mailing lists. Try gathering information about a particular issue or problem from as many sources as possible before implementing a possible solution. Always take advice with a pinch of salt (including this book). You will be able to make a better and more informed decision by doing as much research and using as many resources as possible.

With that being said, acquiring information is only one of the initial steps to resolving a problem. These investigate different scenarios, as there will usually be more than one approach to fix a complex issue or problem. It is only by working through an issue with hands-on experience that a DBA gains the confidence along with the ability to survive a production-crisis situation. To accomplish this, you need adequate resources, such as the correct hardware, software, and most importantly, scheduled time to do a practice run through various scenarios.

A DBA needs a box that no one else is dependent on so that they can create and destroy databases at will. Adequate hardware for testing purposes is almost as important as the production hardware for database administration. The software side is significant as well and requires much more work to keep up with all the technological and security updates. Change is constant in the software industry. You will always be migrating to the next software version (Oracle software or operating system), patch set, **Critical Patch Update (CPU)**, **Patch Set Updates (PSU)**, one-off patch, or hardware replacements.

One of the questions most frequently asked by DBA managers is: what type of person should I hire to be the DBA? This usually means they weren't happy with the previous candidates. To be good at the job takes a tough but not mean attitude, getting it just right, and paying careful attention to the smallest of details without losing sight of the big picture. You must know everything about the Oracle software and if you are not able to find someone who does, step out of the office, communicate with other IT professionals, and pass on the information you learn to others who need help as well. Teaching someone else is the best test to see if you really know it well. Above all, don't be afraid to do the right thing when it comes to database security and privacy issues — in most situations, a DBA is all powerful, but needs a certain amount of self-restraint.

This book assumes that you could be any type of DBA, working on a single, small database, right up to many large databases. A **Very Large Database** (known as **VLDB**) will take several DBAs to run, so teamwork is important. Don't be surprised, as the newcomer, if you are relegated to minor duties for several years. Also, don't assume that if your database is not large, its tuning isn't as important: Oracle **Maximum Availability Architecture (MAA)** and **Optimal Flexible Architecture (OFA)** standards will apply to all Oracle customers, not just VLDBs. Both MAA and OFA are discussed later in this book.

There are general practitioners (GPs) who perform routine health exams and treat common, everyday problems such as the flu or a muscle strain. You go to a specialist when the GP has reached his or her limit of expertise. If your organization is large, then there will be an opportunity for you to become a specialist as you gain experience. For now you should become familiar with all aspects of the database as a generalist DBA. Don't ignore or discount certain areas of database administration as being unimportant; if you are responsible for this database, then all areas will be important. Your customers will often see their requirements as more important than yours, so adapting to meet everyone's needs will require flexibility on your part.

Choosing your tools

Your tools should be extensible, flexible, and ubiquitous. Now that you have some knowledge, what tools are needed? As you go through these chapters, there will be mention of what tools are available time and again. Reasons for choosing a certain tool will be provided: make your decisions based on availability, cost, and adaptation to your particular need or environment, and personal preferences. Be open and willing to change to a new tool because it may just make you more efficient. Don't let the flashy software with high price tags and marketing hype influence purchasing decisions. There are a lot of great open source tools that are available, which may require a little more investment in time to configure, install, or maintain, but which are well worth it. You will only be as good as the tools you pick for this job. It is time to pick the programs you will become best at—command line or GUI-based or command line-based Unix scripting in combination with SQL*Plus are excellent for manipulating both the database and operating system for almost any task that needs to be done. Graphic-based tools have their place, but there will be times that you will need to revert to command-line versions of those tools, especially for troubleshooting. Proficiency will be the only way to be effective, efficient (across the enterprise) and ubiquitous—common among all of the systems or databases you will have to administer.

Graphic-based, command-line Oracle tools and usage

Oracle Enterprise Manager (OEM — database control) is for a single database, and the Grid Control version of OEM is for the enterprise-deployed tool. The browser-based GUI tool has links to almost all of the other tools in this section of the chapter, and OEM database control has command-line equivalent `emca` and `emctl` with limited functionality for specific tasks. You can migrate from database control to grid control with the `db2gc` command-line utility.

These are all of the graphic-based, command-line Oracle tools:

- **Database Configuration Assistant (DBCA)**: This is used for database creation, templates, and installing/uninstalling database options. It can use a utility to create scripts that can be saved to the OS, edited, and run manually for database creation. It has no real command-line equivalent.

- **Oracle Universal Installer (OUI)**: This is used for the installation of Oracle software and options. Its command-line equivalent would be to use the installer in silent mode with a text-based input file.

- **Oracle Wallet Manager (OWM)**: This stores SSL credentials for database access and also for the Oracle Advanced Security Option. The command-line equivalent is `orapki`.

- **Network Configuration Assistant (NETCA)**: There isn't a command-line version of all the features of this utility. Most often the DBA edits the resulting network configuration files directly. The command-line equivalent to the Listener subcomponent of this utility is `lsnrctl`.

- **Recovery Manager (RMAN)**: This is the backup and recovery tool for Oracle databases. The GUI-based version is found in OEM. The command-line equivalent is `rman`.

- **DATA GUARD**: This is the utility for configuring standby databases. The command-line equivalent is `dgmgrl`. SQL*Plus can also be used to configure standbys without the GUI screens found in OEM.

- **Database Upgrade Assistant (DBUA)**: This is the utility for changing a database from one version to another; it will have specific compatibility requirements, and can do all commands manually using SQL*Plus and OS commands.

- **Database NEWID command-line utility** (`nid`): This has no GUI equivalent, and functionality can be duplicated (with more work) using SQL*Plus commands, `orapwd`, and OS commands.

- **EXPORT/IMPORT and DATA PUMP** (`exp`, `imp`, `expdp`, `impdp`): This is the logical backup of all database objects, and command-line tools with no graphic-based equivalent.

- **SQL*Plus, OEM GUI-based SQL worksheet**: `sqlplus` is the command-line equivalent. This is the workhorse of the DBA. Most commands within the GUI OEM console can also be done using SQL*Plus.

- **SQL*Loader** (`sqlldr`): This is just a command-line utility for inputting correctly-formatted data into a database.

- **Automatic Storage Management** (ASM): This is tightly coupled and managed with specific OS commands. It depends on the deployment method, and is controlled by the `asmcmd` command-line utility.

- **Oracle Environment** (`oraenv` **and** `coraenv` **depending on Unix shell**): These are the command-line utilities for configuring Oracle Environmental variables, and they work on entries located in the `oratab` file.

- **Character Set Scanner** (`csscan`): This is the command-line utility for character set conversions.

- **Oracle Internet Directory Configuration Assistant** (`oidca`): This is the command-line utility for Oracle's version of the LDAP directory. There are several LDAP-specific command-line utilities for use with Oracle that all start with `ldap`.

- **TKProf**: This is a command-line executable (`tkprof`) that parses Oracle trace files to produce a human-readable output.

- **Workload Replay and Capture** (`wrc`): This is the command-line utility as an extra-option license for extensive application testing.

- **Automatic Diagnostic Repository Control Interface** (`adrci`): This is the command-line utility for tracing, diagnostic packaging, and logging output for most of the utilities in this list. It is meant to be run in a single location for all Oracle products installed on a single server.

- **Trace Route Utility** (`trcroute`): This is for checking network connectivity between servers.

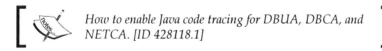

How to enable Java code tracing for DBUA, DBCA, and NETCA. [ID 428118.1]

For Unix shell scripting, install the open source terminal emulator Cygwin on the Windows systems, otherwise you will have to learn Windows scripting. But why learn two languages? Standardize across the enterprise because it is only a matter of time before you will be taking on new applications and databases, as the business needs change for your organization.

Staying away from dinosaurs

What is a dinosaur? It is someone who is stuck in their ways and too comfortable where they are to move (change things). You can spot a dinosaur if the answers to the following questions are positive.

- Do they only stay in their office, cubicle, or work area and rarely show up to meetings with other human beings?
- Are their questions and answers short, curt, and rarely reveal what really happened when things went awry?
- Do people wonder what they do all day?
- Do they go to conferences without any business cards to pass around?
- Do they just linger on technical e-mails, discussion lists, or forums?

Now that you know how to *spot* a dinosaur, the reasons for avoiding them may not be obvious. It is the sign of an insecure, cloistered individual who refuses to change because of fear of the unknown. Realize that there is no real way to know everything about Oracle and that you will need to be open and willing to change in order to keep ahead of the steep learning curve ahead of you.

Insisting on help

It is normal that you might be a bit overwhelmed as a new DBA for your first year. If this situation extends for much longer than that, then something is wrong and it is obviously time to ask for long-term help. This situation is especially true if you are the only DBA or the first Oracle DBA in your organization. Help can come in the form of changing your phone number to non-published within your organization, changing who you directly answer to, or adding another DBA (on-site, remote, or temporary consultant). Compare and evaluate the regular tasks you perform with other DBAs. It doesn't matter if you are only a backup or junior DBA at this point, it is the best time to learn these valuable concepts and still be protected from disrupting the production environment. Everyone wants you to succeed as a DBA because it is a position with a huge amount of responsibility, long hours, and it requires ongoing training to stay competent.

Are you barely able to answer requests as they pour in? Ask that those requests be filtered or first reviewed by a front-line tech support personnel. The exception would be if that is your job—a front-line DBA to serve as part of a tech support organization. On a side note, third-party vendors will put tech people in support positions who give DBA-like advice, but be very wary as they often have little to no actual experience. Remember, a lot of technical helpers only play with databases all day. They don't actually have to manage a live production one with your critical data in it. Learn to say no to these individuals.

A DBA is most often placed underneath the head of IT (most often the CIO) because the database is often central to the entire IT department. If you are one of the many DBAs, your organization will most often have an immediate DBA supervisor that you will answer to first, before the head of IT.

The DBA is not the sole source for any issue related to Oracle, especially if your entire IT department is new to Oracle. Their job is not to train everyone on the basics of Oracle—they don't have the time and probably aren't the best people for that job. Most DBAs don't have the experience of teaching others; they are usually best in a one-on-one situation training a backup or junior DBA. They also shouldn't be subjected to the whims of upper management when there is a technical issue that can't be resolved by the standard front-line personnel, or when the perception is that the issue won't be handled quickly enough.

After a year on the job, you should be proficient enough with **My Oracle Support** (**MOS**, Oracle's support site renamed from Metalink) to find out most of the answers on your own and be comfortable enough to implement the solution without help. Using an Internet search engine may be another source of information (beware that the information may not be timely, complete, or even accurate), but it is a source you turn to when other more dependable ones aren't productive.

When you create a MOS Service Request, don't expect an answer that day unless the severity level and contract agreement dictates that level of support. Oracle Engineer support help may be hours or even days from now. Reach out to the Oracle community for help at the same time you enter a Service Request, which often will get a quicker if not better answer than Oracle support, because these people will have encountered the same problem at some point. Not everyone will give reliable advice; learn to recognize those that do. Most often a test case with reproducible results is the best indicator of expertise, or at least a well-thought-out process. E-mail lists and forums have been known in the past for shooting down people who don't read the documentation first. The exception would be if you are at a total loss on how to fix a problem or are experiencing a disaster at a particular moment.

What does a DBA do all day?

Responsibilities include installing, configuring, and managing the database, and these responsibilities can be divided into tasks scheduled to occur at certain intervals. This is a generalized list and, depending on your environment, may or may not be applicable. Most of the outlined tasks will be investigated further in later chapters in the book.

Monitoring and Log Rotation tasks can be done with Enterprise Manager, Grid Control, Unix shell scripting, DBMS_Scheduler, Perl, third-party database tools, or a combination of any of these.

Prioritizing tasks—daily, weekly, monthly, quarterly, or yearly

Let's run through the priority tasks you need to cover. Scheduling will depend on your environment, application needs, and overall job priorities.

Daily

- Backups — these are usually incremental or cumulative, weekly fulls, and logs are archived and e-mailed to DBA upon failure
- Database Alert Logs — such as ORA-errors, automatic notifications through e-mail, pagers
- ADRCI — Automatic Repository Utility and Log Rotation
- Operating System File space, CPU and I/O statistics — depends on system admin support
- SQL Tuning Sets — Top 5 to 10 SQL statements
- Corruption — RMAN logs, export and/or datapump logs, dbverify, `v$database_block_corruption`
- Tablespace growth — Extension, Partition Management, Temporary Tablespace, Undo
- Data Guard — Log Shipping/Application in Synch
- SQL*NET Listener Logs — intrusion detection
- Audit trails and logs — intrusion detection, removal of unused accounts
- Core Dumps and User Dumps — file space, Oracle bugs
- New account creation — should be at least partially automated
- Personnel security changes — At least 24 hours notice
- Migrate schema and code changes or ad hoc SQL updates
- Large table growth, coalescing tablespace
- Keeping a log of daily changes to the database — publishing it for certain IT staff

Weekly

- Backups — usually full
- Cloning for non-production databases — automated or scripted
- Tablespace growth — daily rolled up to weekly
- Oracle upgrade or patch set Migration Projects — Milestone updates
- Data Guard site testing

- Check for updates from My Oracle Support—new patches, updates, or news releases
- Local Intranet updates on operational procedures

Monthly

- Cloning for non-production databases—automated or scripted
- Monitoring tablespace growth—weekly rolled up to monthly
- Trends and forecasts—CPU utilization, I/O stats, logons
- Password changes on production—sys, system, wallet, schema, grid control, OAS
- Oracle licensing usage and high water marks
- Practicing recovery scenarios

Quarterly

- Applying CPUs and PSUs into production with planned downtime. Applying CPUs, PSUs, one-offs into non-production instances
- Monitoring tablespace growth—monthly rolled up to yearly
- Oracle training updates—Oracle University (online or in-class), books, informal meetings
- Trends and forecast rollups

Yearly

- Tablespace growth—yearly report
- Trends and forecast rollups
- Attend Oracle-oriented conferences—regional or national Oracle user groups
- Oracle upgrades with planned downtime—version + patch sets + PSUs + one-offs
- Software licensing and warranty renewals
- Hardware evaluation and replacement
- SSL Certificate renewals, Oracle Wallets

Yes, these look like a daunting number of tasks that need to be accomplished, but you will have help in the form of tools such as OEM, Grid Control, third-party monitoring, or home-grown scripts. That is why I will reiterate that automating these tasks is of paramount importance.

SLAs: Why isn't the database down anymore?

A few years ago having the database down on a regular basis was normal and considered necessary just for backups. But it is no longer needed in these days of 24x7 IT operations and expanded **Service Level Agreements (SLAs)**.

The database most often will only have to be down for patches or upgrades, which can be either Oracle or application-specific. You should no longer need to have the database down to do backups. If cold backups are a norm at your workplace, then this is a sign of a dinosaur. Little to no downtime applies to production instances, but non-production should be mostly up during working hours with only intermittent outages.

Each organization has its own Outage Handling Procedures—depending on whether it is planned or unplanned downtime. Most DBAs are assigned a database to be the primary contact when there is an outage issue on call. Outage handling usually includes something similar to the following:

- **Initial troubleshooting to determine the type of outage**: Evaluate any automatic failover procedures to check for success.

- **Forecasting the amount of time before resolution**: This is the point for making the decision if a manual fail over is needed.

- **Bringing the application or database back online**: Not all failures are due to the database being down, even when that is what first appears to be the case.

- **Root cause analysis**: What was the real reason for the outage? This is not always evident at first glance.

- **Future preventive actions**: Evaluating and rewriting the outage procedures, reassigning team members for outage coverage.

Outage handling is an important process and includes quite a few non-DBA team members who must coordinate efforts, and not just point fingers to get this issue resolved. These types of procedures should be well documented (in both print and online form for disasters) with a definite line of authority as to who can execute the procedures with administrative approval.

There are many things that could cause the database to crash or become unavailable to end users:

- Hardware failure
- Corruption
- Operating system issues
- ASM or RAC specific problems
- Critical Oracle processes dying
- Certain ORA-600 errors
- Certain Oracle bugs
- Listener not running
- Human error

Speaking of the human side of things, the following list details how to avoid the really bad things that can happen to even experienced DBAs. Remember if you are a novice or new DBA, you shouldn't have access to certain servers or databases because your superior understands how easy it is to do the wrong thing at the wrong time. The following list may seem harsh, full of should and don't statements, but I felt it was important to state exactly what others have experienced or witnessed personally. Think of it as an experienced DBA giving someone under them some good advice about what to avoid.

Avoiding major blunders

- Don't use `rm -rf *.*` for any reason at anytime, do `rm *.log` or `*.lis` or `*.trc`: It is safer to back up a directory and use `rmdir` instead. It would be even better if you renamed the entire directory and left it in place renamed for a day or two.

- Assuming that all of the datafiles in a certain directory only pertain to one database is a recipe for disaster, those files can be created anywhere on the filesystem as long as Oracle has write access.

- Modifying access for a production instance at the SQL*Plus level is unusual and generally not granted to programming staff unless there is a single point of accountability, such as a lead programmer.

- It is best to use the Unix utility called `fuser` against a database file before using an `rm` or `mv` command because it checks if the file is actively being used. Another way would be to force a database checkpoint and check the timestamp before removing. If it is an active datafile, the timestamp would be current.

- Add the ORACLE_SID and user into the SQL prompt. This will prevent many a disaster by visually checking the prompt before running a script in what you think is a non-production database. Instructions on how to do this come later in the book.

- Use the extended Unix prompt that puts in the hostname, user, and ORACLE_SID. This will add more visual clues to ensure that you know exactly what you are modifying.

- Copying and pasting directly into a SQL*Plus or other command-line utility window can lead to the wrong code being executed. Copy and paste into a text file and run it instead. This double checks exactly what is in the copy/paste buffer.

- Type the word production into the command-line window after you finish using it. This will prevent disasters if you accidentally switch windows and run something you shouldn't have. It will only produce an error because there is no command called production.

- It is best to run recovery scenarios on a different server from any running production. Also, test operating system restores. Disaster recovery sites should also be located on a different server for true failover capabilities.

- Make sure you know how to use the command line for all of the Oracle utilities and Unix vi editor just in case you have nothing else at your disposal.

- It is suggested to make your production windows, application, or command-line utility like PuTTY a completely different color for production versus non-production, and the scrolling history as large as possible. Unix has a history capture utility called script.

- Tell someone else you are modifying something… just in case. Saying it aloud may give someone else time to stop you or at least give you a mental check on what you are doing.

- Log rotating scripts can play havoc with naming the online redo logs with a file extension of log. Using the letters rdo would be safer.

- Unknown outside consultants won't necessarily give the best advice. Be wary until you are sure of their expertise and ability. If at all possible, ask to do the work under their guidance so that you know what is actually occurring.

- Using the number *8* in any type of scripting, ORACLE_SID name, or the like can play havoc with scripting or command-line executions because the all-inclusive wild card character * is above the eight—it's too easy to type it accidentally.

- Double check by tracking the operating system's performance on a server, especially running out of file space.

- Beware the reuse clause when adding or altering a database file. This command can overwrite an existing datafile, which destroys any existing data.

- Be wary of scripts generated by third-party tools, they can be too powerful. A script to recreate an object usually drops it in the first line. This can be disastrous if the data has not been saved.

- You are responsible for backups. It is not wise to delegate this in any way.

- Be sure to investigate the addition of resource limits for any users that have ad hoc SQL access in production. Those types of users can easily hog CPU or I/O, which is needed more by the OLTP application.

- Make sure the system administrators know not to modify, move, or delete anything that belongs to the Oracle accounts.

- The Unix root account is not intended for everyday use and especially not suited for Oracle tasks. Investigate the use of `sudo` for tracking root-authorized activities.

- This is the most important blunder-avoiding tip—it is wisest not to do anything that you can't undo, reverse, or fix.

 Thanks to the Oracle-L e-mail list for their contributions.

Summary

As a new DBA, one of the hardest things to figure out is the philosophy behind the position. The best DBAs in the business seem to have an underlying sense or gut feeling when something is wrong, and when to speak up and say no.

Treat others as you would like to be treated with a certain amount of respect. There should be lines drawn based on your position in the organization. Those boundaries are there for a reason—responsibilities and duties are attributed to the team player based on those boundaries. You will be working closely with the team and you will depend on them doing their job. A database is dependent on a reliable framework of underlying software and hardware, which most often is not your responsibility; this makes your job very dependent on your fellow team members' expertise.

This chapter helped to show what a DBA does all day. All rules may need to be bent or modified to suit your organization's needs. Only experience and testing will allow your team to decide how best to proceed on any single rule or suggestion in this chapter.

2

Maintaining Oracle Standards

As a DBA you will be expected to draft and control different standards, as they pertain to an Oracle database. Some of the best standards are the ones that have a wide adoption rate, and which are easily understood and well-documented. Standards are intended to grease the various gears of a team so that they work together with less friction. Standards will also make a DBA's life easier in the long run, safer for all those involved, and more efficient, because time isn't spent reinventing or rewriting a process that wasn't based on a standard in the first place.

This chapter outlines several standards for the major tasks that most DBAs are expected to perform: installation, configuration, and the maintenance of Oracle software. Expect the standards that you adopt to change gradually over time as technology improves and to reflect changes within your organization.

Adapting to constant change

You can have more than one ORACLE_HOME for every node, primarily for migration projects that will be spread over an extended period of time. There is an inherent risk in running multiple ORACLE_HOMES, in that you may mistakenly use the wrong ones. It is my personal recommendation that the ongoing risk is worth it when using the Step-Ordered Approach to Migrating, because it reduces the overall downtime (see Chapter 7).

An ORACLE_HOME consists of installed binary files along with Oracle-supplied scripts. The database comprises memory structures, background processes, control files, parameter files, data files, and temporary and undo files. There are other types of ORACLE_HOME(s) that contain ORACLE installed software, as each of them is only an environmental variable pointing to a specific disk location. Other types will have other names like: CRS_HOME or AGENT_HOME that may be identified as an ORACLE_HOME in the Oracle documentation. This means you can have multiple ORACLE_HOMES on the same node running different versions of a database and/or different versions of other Oracle software.

Database concepts

You can have multiple instances of a single database. An instance consists of multiple background OS processes that are executed by the Oracle binary located in `$ORACLE_HOME/bin/oracle`. Multiple instances are known as **Real Application Clusters (RAC)** that can be deployed on a single server or distributed on multiple servers, but are associated with a single shared set of data files.

Refer to the installation guide for your operating system as well as the recommendations found on My Oracle Support. MOS also contains a Certifications Area, which you can use to determine if the operating system is compatible with the version you are installing, as well as to determine compatibility with other Oracle software that will be used with an Oracle database.

Database startup initialization Parameter files (`pfile`), as well as the new Server Parameter file (`spfile`), control each database instance, providing adjustable instructions. This flexibility allows for different instance parameters that are based on an application's need for distributing the available resources across multiple servers (also known as nodes).

A database control file connects all of the physical components found on a storage device with the correct database, tracking and synchronizing all changes. Since a database has its own controls, called a Relational Database Management System (RDBMS), making changes to the physical files at the operating system level can't be done when the database is open without incurring some sort of damage or data loss. Changes such as moving data files, renaming, or copying the physical components at an OS level may corrupt or make them otherwise unrecoverable.

Multiple ORACLE_HOME(s)

In this book, an `ORACLE_HOME` is the home that is currently in use. This may or may not be the production home. There is usually a different `ORACLE_HOME` that you are migrating to at any one point in time. This migration can happen on a production, test, or development server depending on which one you are working on at the time.

Oracle releases **Patch Set Updates (PSU)** and **Critical Patch Updates (CPU)** quarterly. CPU is the quarterly security release. Oracle recommends that clients use PSUs since a PSU is a superset of a CPU. There is continued ongoing debate on whether Oracle's recommendation should be followed because there are problems if you need to revert to applying CPUs. This is where it would be best to ask the Oracle community for feedback on this important decision.

When it is time to upgrade the Oracle database software, it is recommended not to upgrade the home that is currently in use, because that leaves you with a longer downtime should the upgrade process fail. It would be much faster as part of the downgrade process to shutdown the database and bring it back up in the previous ORACLE_HOME. This means you are only reversing any database changes rather than trying to reverse both software and database changes, which increases the length of downtime.

Keeping the environment clean

Multiple ORACLE_HOME(s) accessing different memory structures and background processes can cause the environment to become cloudy. Confusion as to which executables or scripts should be run can cause outages, core dumps, and human errors. There are some procedures and practices to adopt in order to keep the switching process as clean as possible.

How do you keep multiple installations independent of each other while reducing contention at all levels? Multiple operating system accounts are the cleanest way if implemented along with the **Optimal Flexible Architecture (OFA)** standards. Check out the installation guide as part of the documentation for your OS, which has quite a bit of information on how to run Oracle products with multiple accounts.

Here are a few notes about variations on the multi-user system of installing Oracle software on a single server:

- **One OS user account per database**, which would result in an increased complexity when shell scripting tasks run against a particular database. The script would need to verify the ORACLE_HOME and the correct database combination, as there is the possibility of several combinations. Each database would require their own ORACLE_HOME instead of sharing the same home between multiple databases. Setting environmental variables can be done with local customizations instead of using the Oracle-supplied oraenv file.

- **One OS user per Oracle release**, which would result in less ORACLE_HOME installs than one OS user account/database type. Running OS shell scripts against this type of database would more than likely be a combination of oraenv and custom environmental variables. It is easy to modify oraenv to source a custom variable, as shown later in this chapter.

While that may be the cleanest, most secure way to implement Oracle software installs, it is not necessarily the easiest method. There is more administrative overhead involved with configuring the operating system user and group accounts as well as the appropriate file permissions so that each is independent on a single server.

Oracle's Optimal Flexible Architecture (OFA)

In the following section, you will find a small summary of the OFA standard(s) that were written by Cary Millsap. His article titled *Oracle for Open Systems* was first published in 1995. It is still used today and is widely adopted on Unix systems by DBAs, no matter the database size. This standard that has been expanded and revised to embrace the newer hardware technologies, and the Automatic Diagnostic Repository found in 11g is in the installation guide of every operating system.

You can find the original 1995 version at the following location:
`http://method-r.com/downloads/doc_details/13-the-ofa-standardoracle-for-open-systems-cary-millsap.`

1. Name the Unix mount points with this pattern /mountpoint+numbered string and start numbering with a left-padded zero to keep the list in numerical order. For example, `/u01`, `/u02`, `/u03`.

2. The Oracle operating system account that owns `ORACLE_HOME` with a home directory of `/mountpoint/directory/user`. For example, `/u01/app/oracle`.

3. Remove all hardcoded references in shell scripts to exact path names except for the few key Unix files that require such an entry. Use environmental variables instead.

4. Each `ORACLE_HOME` is recommended to be installed with a pattern matching `/oracle_user_home_directory/product/version`. For example, `/u01/app/oracle/product/11.2.0/dbhome_1`.

5. In 11g, the Diagnosability Framework changes the older default location for `cdump`, `udump`, and `bdump` database parameters (see the next section *11g differences in the OFA standard*). It would be a recommended location for each of the following directories that are not part of the 11g Diagnosability Framework—`adump`, `create`, `logbook`, `pfile`, and `scripts`. There are other files related to archivelogs, data pump, or export files that are now Oracle-recommended to be put in the FLASH_RECOVERY_AREA (FRA). For example, `/u01/app/oracle/admin/newdb`.

6. Use the Unix profile and the Oracle-supplied files that set the environment—`oraenv`, `coraenv`, and `dbhome`. See later in this chapter for specific recommendations for these files, `ORACLE_SID` or just SID (System Identifier).

7. Identify an instance with the combination of $ORACLE_HOME, $ORACLE_SID and $HOSTNAME, which makes it unique and usually defaults to the database name.

8. Name data files with */mount point/specific_to_data/ORACLE_SID/control. ctl* (control files), *redo+number.log* (redo logs, change .log to .rdo, see Major Blunder list) and *tablespace_name+number.dbf* (data files). A personal recommendation includes adding the ORACLE_SID to a data filename. For example, /u01/oradata/newdb/contrl01_newdb.ctl.

9. Database objects that are backed up at the same time or that have a similar purpose or lifespan should be grouped in the same tablespace. For example, temporary segments should be in a temporary tablespace, read only objects should be in their own tablespace, system objects in the system tablespace, and so forth.

10. Limit tablespace names to eight characters with a matching data filename to simplify administrative tasks. For example, USERS tablespace with the data file: /u01/oradata/newdb/users01_newdb.dbf.

Steps 8, 9, and 10 will not be covered here (a lot has changed in data storage), as the original document refers to the obsolete Oracle Parallel Server and one data file per disk implementation.

11g differences in the OFA standard

The 10g release of the Oracle Database introduced the use of the new $ORACLE_BASE directory as the primary starting point for installations. ORACLE_BASE will be required in future installations, but it currently brings up a warning box during the GUI install if it is not set in 11g. It is highly recommended to go ahead and set ORACLE_BASE before installation in order to control the location of the new Diagnosability Framework components.

These details can be found in the *Oracle Database Pre-installation Requirements* section of the installation guide for your operating system. Oracle also recommends locating the Flash Recovery Area (FRA) and database files under $ORACLE_BASE. The FRA is meant for the storage of any type of backup, recovery, or flashback technologies when used in conjunction with an Oracle database. This type of implementation puts the majority of the files on a single originating mount point, such as /u01.

If you implement Oracle's Automatic Storage Management (ASM), then it would make sense to install all of the components in a single disk location or any other storage method for using multiple disks as a single unit of space. ASM is a logical volume manager on top of the physical disks; it presents those logical volumes as disk groups.

ASM is a volume management tool in that it simplifies data storage for a growing system. It gives you the ability to add additional storage, as the database needs it, without interruptions. While it provides additional flexibility in adding storage, most often it requires additional resources (time, personnel expertise) to install, configure, and maintain. There are also ASM-related changes to account for in most of the database maintenance tasks, backup and recovery routines, and Data Guard, among others.

XWINDOWS and GUI displays

Nowadays Unix hardware is more often headless in racks, and because of the missing components, there is no need to sit at the server anymore to run any type of GUI display such as the OUI, NETCA, or DBCA utilities. Simply run an XWindows display on your desktop or another server that has a GUI display. You must export the $DISPLAY variable to your desktop IP address to start Oracle's Universal Installer (OUI) or any other GUI Oracle utility. See your system administrator for assistance with XWindows issues.

Most Unix desktops such as the widely adopted Ubuntu will have XWindows built in, or packages are available for installation. XWindows software is needed for any GUI sessions if your desktop is Windows-based, because it will not have the X support built in. Other open source versions for Windows that are available include Cygwin/X, Xming, and WeirdX, and products that will require the purchase of a license include Xmanager, Exceed, MKS X/Server, Reflection X, and X-Win32.

System administrators will most often require the use of a secure shell (ssh) encrypted command-line utility to connect remotely to a server. PUTTY is a freeware telnet/ssh client and does this job very well; it can be downloaded from http://www.chiark.greenend.org.uk/~sgtatham/putty/.

Automating day-to-day tasks

Options to automate the DBA tasks mentioned in the previous chapter include some of the following:

- DBMS_SCHEDULER: Oracle-supplied PL/SQL package that comes preinstalled
- OS scheduling commands: Certain tasks such as monitoring file space usage and removing old trace/log files are often scheduled using something like Unix cron or the Windows at command. The best options include tasks that need to run no matter the database state—down, up, or mounted.

- OEM Grid Control Intelligent Agent: Requires installation and configuring to run OS type commands. A very useful Enterprise-wide monitoring tool but quite an investment in time to configure and maintain for multiple servers.

Let's look at an example task and apply it to each of the three types of automation mentioned above: **Monitoring the Database Alert Log**.

DBMS_SCHEDULER

DBMS_SCHEDULER, along with the power of PL/SQL, provides a mechanism for automating some of the daily tasks mentioned earlier in this chapter. Using a scheduler from within the database instead of an external scripting has some advantages as well as disadvantages.

Advantages of using DBMS_SCHEDULER:

- It is another tool to make your environment the same across the enterprise.
- Runs on any operating system that the database can.
- Capable to run a program, anonymous PL/SQL blocks, stored procedure, executables or even a chain of commands.
- It will execute operating system commands along with shell scripts, which can run external Oracle utilities, such as RMAN, export, adrci, or datapump.
- All of your tasks and PL/SQL (called metadata) associated with these scheduled jobs are backed up along with the database.
- Jobs run only when the database is up. There are many times when you have to disable certain jobs when the database is down if scheduled at the operating system level.
- It is relatively easy to grant or revoke access for each specific job to other users.
- It removes the need to store a password for job execution, as you have to do with scripting at the operating system level.

Disadvantages of DBMS_SCHEDULER:

- The fact that jobs only run when the database is open may be considered a disadvantage as well as an advantage of DBMS_SCHEDULER.
- It can be harder to manage due to the PL/SQL nature of the interface.
- Third-party interfaces to other applications, schedulers, assorted operating systems, or even databases can be challenging and hard to troubleshoot when things aren't working as expected.
- The OEM console is one GUI method of monitoring DBMS_SCHEDULER jobs, which takes quite a few clicks to determine status, failure, past runs, among others.

The following DBMS_SCHEDULER task will give you a critical piece of information for certain recovery situations (see *Chapter 6, Extended RMAN* for more information). See the downloaded code for this chapter for more examples of DBMS_SCHEDULER commands for certain DBA tasks.

Note how this job will be repeated on a daily basis. The following is an example of a recommended daily task, writing the database ID to the alert log:

```
BEGIN
sys.dbms_scheduler.create_job (
job_name => '"SYS"."DBID_TOALERT"',
job_type => 'PLSQL_BLOCK',
job_action => 'declare l_dbid number;
begin
select dbid into l_dbid from v$database;
dbms_system.ksdwrt (2, ''DBID='' || l_dbid);
end;
',
repeat_interval => 'FREQ=DAILY;BYHOUR=14',
start_date => to_timestamp_tz('2007-12-20 America/Denver', 'YYYY-MM-DD
TZR'),
job_class => '"DEFAULT_JOB_CLASS"',
comments => 'Write DBID to Alert Log for Recovery',
auto_drop => FALSE,
enabled => FALSE);
sys.dbms_scheduler.set_attribute( name => '"SYS"."DBID_TOALERT"',
attribute => 'job_weight', value => 1);
sys.dbms_scheduler.set_attribute( name => '"SYS"."DBID_TOALERT"',
attribute => 'restartable', value => TRUE);
sys.dbms_scheduler.enable( '"SYS"."DBID_TOALERT"' );
END;
/
```

OS cron utility executing a scheduled task on a Unix server

See the code provided for this chapter `dbid_toalert_os.ksh` Unix file for a complete script. The script includes the appropriate shell script commands to be able to run SQL code. The script also contains example code that contains suggestions on writing Unix shell scripting for DBAs found later in this chapter.

OEM Console plus the Intelligent Agent

To schedule the same job of writing the database ID to the alert log, see the following screenshot for details. This particular job is scheduled to run once daily with no expiration date.

If this job was resource intensive, it would be wise to use the following method: *How to Incorporate Pre-Defined jobs into your Resource Manager Plan [ID 971991.1]*. Resource Manager Plans would allow the DBA to control database jobs that need to run with certain priorities for allocating resources appropriately.

This basically takes the exact information as using the DBMS_SCHEDULER in the preceding section for utilizing a GUI screen to input the job information.

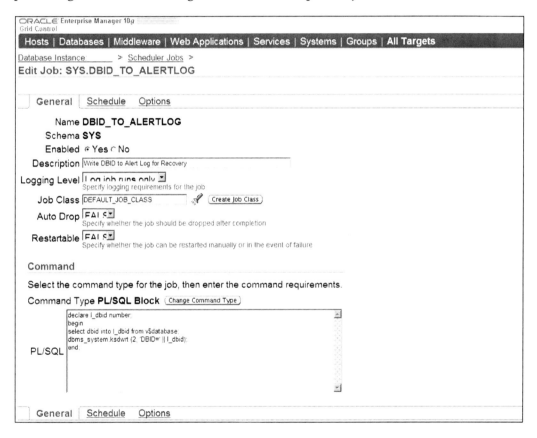

11g Diagnosability Framework

The Oracle 11g Database includes a full suite of diagnostic tools and advisors that are at least partially integrated with **My Oracle Support (MOS)**, automatically uploading metrics via the Oracle Configuration Manager. This new diagnosability infrastructure includes the monitoring of the RDBMS, Automatic Storage Management (ASM), Oracle Call Interface (OCI), SQL*Net, and Oracle Application Server 11.1 products.

This new version of Oracle introduces the Automatic Diagnostic Repository (ADR), which is a flat file structure containing all alert logs, core files, trace files, and incident information. The ADR_BASE = $ORACLE_BASE, which is controlled by the database diagnostic_dest parameter, replaces background_dump_dest, core_dump_dest, and user_dump_dest. The entire ADR repository can be moved to a different location than the initial install, at the same time resetting $ORACLE_BASE. Just removing or moving the directories will not disable the ADR. The TNS components can be disabled by following this document from MOS: *Using and Disabling the Automatic Diagnostic Repository (ADR) with Oracle Net for 11g [ID 454927.1]*.

A database parameter is used from the time a database is started. This parameter can be changed manually with what is known as a pfile or dynamically with an spfile. A database parameter is found by the following example query:

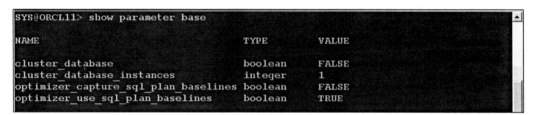

```
SYS@ORCL11> show parameter base

NAME                                     TYPE        VALUE
cluster_database                         boolean     FALSE
cluster_database_instances               integer     1
optimizer_capture_sql_plan_baselines     boolean     FALSE
optimizer_use_sql_plan_baselines         boolean     TRUE
```

Notice how it finds all parameters that contain the word base and also why $ORACLE_BASE is not here. It is an OS environmental variable, which is controlled outside the SQL*Plus prompt. The outside environment can be queried or manipulated by using host (use ! or the keyword host) commands within SQL*Plus. See the following query that uses the Unix echo command to determine where $ORACLE_BASE is set:

```
SYS@ORCL11> !echo $ORACLE_BASE
/u01/app/oracle
```

You will also see in the documentation that the combination of the following features is known as the Fault Diagnosability Infrastructure:

- ADR plus ADRCI (ADR Command Interpreter) command-line utility
- Alert Log
- Trace Files, Dumps, and Core Files
- Enterprise Manager Support Workbench

It is also important to evaluate the default database jobs and tasks that are created and enabled as of 11g. They are tightly coupled with the new Diagnosability Framework. See the MOS documents: *New 11g Default Jobs [ID 755838.1]* and *11g: Scheduler Maintenance Tasks or Autotasks [ID 756734.1]*. Become familiar with the new 11g Weekday Windows versus the 10g Weekend/Weeknight method of scheduling. This new method gives the DBA more flexibility in determining which day of the week is best for scheduling database maintenance tasks. Adjust the Resource Plan of each Window to allocate hardware and database resources as needed for prioritizing maintenance tasks.

Advisors and checkers

Tools within OEM (Oracle Enterprise Manager) known as advisors and checkers monitor and troubleshoot within the Diagnosability Framework. These tools include the Incident Packaging and Reporting, Support Workbench, and Health Monitor. There is a Trace Assistant for Oracle Net Services. Repair Advisors include the SQL Test Case Builder, SQL Repair, and one for Data Recovery used with RMAN.

While this entire new framework is a start towards diagnosing issues, will it really change the way in which Oracle supports and their customers interact? Oracle Configuration Manager, the software piece that uploads your local information to MOS, has been promised to make **Service Requests** (SR) easier to enter at the same time, resulting in Oracle's support personnel responding faster.

There are database packages that correspond to the diagnosability utilities available on the OEM dashboard. More information on the OEM GUI monitoring console can be found in *Chapter 4, Achieving Maximum Uptime* of this book. These are health check monitor and policies—DBMS_HM, V$HM_CHECK and Diagnostics—DBMS_SQLDIAG.

The screenshot below will only show a few components as part of the Diagnosability Framework, as each one is found on a different OEM tab. Several of these checkers were run in the example below to search for problems related to a missing temp file.

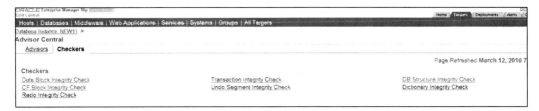

Out of the box OEM monitoring an 11.2.0.1 database could only partially detect what a DBA would consider a major error – missing temp files. A missing temp file would affect queries that need sort space. Initially, nothing in the OEM dashboard indicated anything was wrong; no alert log error entries appeared.

I knew there was a problem because I intentionally caused it by manually removing the actual temp file from the disk. Only after doing one of the workarounds mentioned in the following MOS document did the alert log error entries become viewable using OEM: *Monitoring 11g Database Alert Log Errors in Enterprise Manager [ID 949858.1]*. The step that was done was to copy (or create a softlink) the `ojdl.jar` file from `<AGENT_HOME>/diagnostics/lib` to the `<AGENT_HOME>/sysman/jlib`. See the document if this fix doesn't work for your environment.

Missing temp file resolution

Since Oracle Database Version 10g, temp files are automatically created on database startup and opened when they cannot be found. I verified that this behavior still exists in 11g by inspecting the alert log after opening the database (where I had removed the temp file), as seen in the following entry:

```
SMON: enabling cache recovery
Successfully onlined Undo Tablespace 2.
Verifying file header compatibility for 11g tablespace encryption..
Verifying 11g file header compatibility for tablespace encryption completed
SMON: enabling tx recovery
Re-creating tempfile /u01/oradata/orcl/temp01_orcl.dbf
```

This probably explains why the advisors and checkers didn't detect the missing files, as there is an automatic method of recreation. This makes me wonder: What else does Oracle consider not to be critical?

There were two possible solutions to this issue: recreate the missing temp files while the database was still open, or shut it down and have them automatically recreated on opening. I chose the latter in order to verify the automatic recreate functionality. In this case, the newer diagnosability features inserted an event in the Oracle database `spfile`, which prevented the database from even mounting, as seen in the following screenshot:

```
SYS@ORCL11> connect / as sysdba
Connected to an idle instance.
SYS@ORCL11> startup mount;
ORA-49104: [%s] is not a valid argument for %s [%s]
SYS@ORCL11> startup mount;
ORA-49100: Failed to process event statement [1110 incident(missing file)]
ORA-49101: Failed to parse action [INCIDENT]
ORA-49104: [MISSING] is not a valid argument for action [INCIDENT]
```

I entered a Support Request on MOS because the database would not open (or even mount). This problem was caused by the automatic insertion of an event into the corresponding `spfile` for the database. Once the following event was removed from the `spfile` (by creating a `pfile` and then editing to comment out the event), the database would then open normally:

```
*.event='1110 incident(missing file)'
```

When monitoring an 11g+ database with OEM Server and Agent Version 10.2.0.5+, the mechanism/metrics for monitoring the alert log have changed significantly. There are two different classes of error—incidents and operational errors:

- Operational errors include Data Block Corruption, Archiver Hung, or Media Failure.

- Incidents include Access Violation, Session Terminated, Out of Memory, Redo Log Corruption, Inconsistent DB State, Deadlock, File Access Error, and Internal SQL Error.

Be aware of these monitoring changes and how they might affect your current processes. At this point I would recommend holding on to any user-created monitoring (such as shell scripting or DBMS_SCHEDULER) that you currently have running.

An `alert_[ORACLE_SID].log` file and a `log.xml` file are written to the ADR location, but the `alert_[ORACLE_SID].log` file is now deprecated as of 11g. This means that there are plans to remove it in future releases.

See *Monitoring 11g Database Alert Log Errors in Enterprise Manager Doc [ID 949858.1]*

The following screenshot shows the alert log entries indicating the missing file, but running several of the checkers didn't cause alarms or create an incident (the missing file error ORA-01110 is a generic incident). I expected an incident to be automatically created and viewable by the Support Workbench. At this writing, an open SR had not been resolved to understand why no incident was produced.

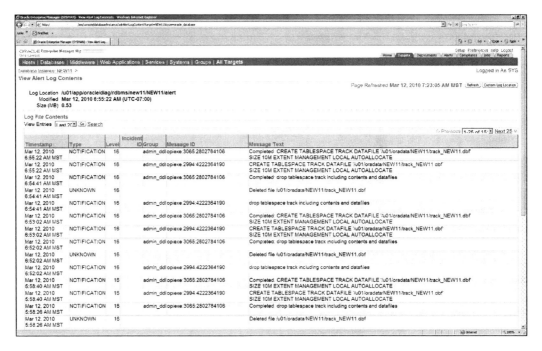

The MOS document 949858.1, which was mentioned earlier in this section, has more information on this problem and a couple of workarounds for non-detected events. You can create what is known as a User-Defined Metric for OEM monitoring or set a system-wide event to make sure incidents are created for specific errors raised in the alert log. Both of these workarounds add up to more work for you, but think of them as a change to the baseline functionality. Changing baseline functionality is a configuration change that you will have to track and maintain over time.

The Diagnosability Framework is meant to make the interactions with MOS and entering Service Requests for critical errors easier. For incidents to be tracked automatically, you must configure OEM using Oracle Configuration Manager (OCM) to package and upload the results to Oracle support. Incidents can be manually packaged and uploaded using OEM's Support Workbench or the adrci command-line utility.

In the past, MOS depended on customers running an RDA (Remote Diagnostic Agent) to upload system information for each Service Request. Now MOS is moving towards the model of daily updated configurations from a locally installed collector, so it is purported that RDAs won't be used as often.

Oracle service personnel will still ask for the output from an RDA for troubleshooting complex problems. Its basic job is to gather extensive environment information. Running an RDA before entering an SR would give insight into what information the Service Engineer from MOS would be looking at, and might even allow you to solve the problem without entering an SR. See the following MOS document: *Subject: Remote Diagnostic Agent (RDA) 4 – Getting Started [Doc ID: 314422.1 and Doc ID: 330760.1]*. Most DBAs don't know about the more advanced features of the RDA utility.

Anytime in this book that you see a Doc ID it is a document only found on the MOS website and available to customers who have a current licensing and/or support agreement from Oracle: `http://support.oracle.com`

Some of the most underused features of RDA include:

1. RDA report files are viewable by using a browser on the following file:
   `<rda_directory>output_directory>/report_group>__start.htm`

2. Security filtering is available to remove sensitive information such as IP addresses, domain names, and user names. This information is not really needed for most Service Requests.

3. Oracle Configuration Manager and RDA can be installed together at the same time.

4. There is a Testing Option (-T) available for certain modules. See the *Remote Diagnostic Agent (RDA) 4 – Content Modules Man Page [ID 330760.1]* document for specifics.

5. RDA profiles are provided, which may or may not fit your needs. It basically keeps you from having to answer the long list of yes/no questions. A more viable option would be to customize an RDA profile for future use, which can be transferred from one server to another.

6. User Defined Collection is available and it will collect custom files that you can add.

7. An RAC Cluster Guide is available for collecting multi-instance RDAs.

Don't forget to occasionally check for the newest release, as MOS constantly improves this utility.

If you use any of the 11g products, including the client, be sure to set the environment variable $ORACLE_BASE. This will control where the alert, trace, and log files are located. Utilize the built-in environmental variable within your own scripts and maintenance routines to become used to the new adrci command-line utility. If you don't set the variable, the log files will appear in $ORACLE_HOME/log even for client installations.

The default editor for adrci is vi and since a standard Windows install won't have the editor vi, make a copy of notepad.exe or wordpad.exe. Move that copy to a location in the Windows $PATH renaming that exe file to vi.exe. The adrci command-line utility has a set editor command but may yield unexpected results in Windows.

To script an automatic purging of date-aged logs, use adrci in a shell script with a text file that contains the commands as below. You will need to substitute the ORACLE_SID for all of the sid entries in the following parameter file:

```
#adrci_commands.par
#Change the nodename and listener_sid for your environment
set echo on
set homepath diag/tnslsnr/nodename/listener_sid
purge -age 10080 -type alert
purge -age 10080 -type incident
purge -age 10080 -type trace
purge -age 10080 -type cdump
set homepath diag/rdbms/sid/SID
purge -age 10080 -type alert
purge -age 10080 -type incident
purge -age 10080 -type trace
purge -age 10080 -type cdump
quit
```

See the file adrci_maint.ksh in the code provided for this chapter on the shell script that calls the adrci_commands.par found earlier.

As a side note, since the ADRCI interface (adrci command-line utility) will only change the XML-formatted alert file (log.xml), you will need to manually schedule log rotation, archiving, and eventual removal of the text-based alert logs. This behavior is similar to the older, manual method where files are put according to the database parameters *dump directories as mentioned earlier.

Environmental variables and scripting

Unix scripting will be one of the most powerful tools in your arsenal and only with constant use will you become proficient. Your standards for scripting need to produce code that is robust, modular, consistent, and scalable. This book won't cover everything you need to know about scripting. There are many excellent lessons available from your operating system vendor. See the following documents for more information specific to how Oracle products behave in a Unix environment:

- *Note: 131207.1 Subject: How to Set Unix Environment Variables*
- *Note: 1011994.6 Subject: How do Applications Act in Different Unix Shells.*
- *How to Integrate the Shell, SQL*Plus Scripts and PL/SQL in any Permutation? [ID 400195.1]* (Excellent document)

Usually `cron` is used for scheduling in Unix and the `AT` command with Windows.

For Oracle utilities that run outside the database (or which must only run when the database is down), Unix shell scripting is best used. A well-written script would parse `/etc/oratab` for a list of `ORACLE_SID`s on a single server for tasks such as parsing log files, consistent backups, exports, dbverify, and RMAN. If you have a solitary database, then DBMS_SCHEDULER can be used with a combination of SQL and PL/SQL integrated with OS commands.

Occasionally, DBAs rename the `oraenv` located in `$ORACLE_HOME/bin` when they have added custom code to the `/usr/local/bin/oraenv` (default location on Linux), so that they can make sure they know exactly which one is executed at run time. If you have any problems related to running a modified `oraenv` file, check which one is being executed and adjust the `$PATH` variable as needed.

The following is a list of some of the Oracle-provided Unix commands with a quick synopsis of their purpose. Most of them are located in `$ORACLE_HOME/bin`:

- `wrap` — encrypts stored procedures for advanced use
- `oerr` — displays oracle errors. Syntax: oerr ora 12154
- `Sysresv` — instance and shared memory segments
- `Tkprof` — formats output trace file into readable format
- `Dbshut` — shell script to shut down all instances
- `dbstart` — shell script to start up all instances at boot
- `Dbhome` — sets `ORACLE_HOME`
- `Oraenv` — sets environmental variables for `ORACLE_SID`
- `trcasst` — trace assistant

Guidelines for scripting

These are general suggestions for someone with some experience with a Unix operating system. You will need more background information than what is covered in this book to understand this section. The best sources of information will be the software vendor of your operating system, because there are small differences between the different versions and flavors of Unix. As with any code, you must test on a non-production system first, as inexperience may lead to unexpected results.

Separating the configuration file

Use the OS-provided default profile for environmental variables, but use a separate configuration file to set the $ORACLE_SID variable. There are several key environmental variables that are commonly used with Oracle software, all of which are found in the documentation specific to the operating system. **Optimal Flexible Architecture (OFA)** mentions setting the ORACLE_SID in the profile, but if you have more than one database or Oracle product installed on a system, it is best done interactively. A default profile is loaded when you first log in to Unix. So if the ORACLE_SID is loaded when you log on, what happens when you want to change ORACLE_SID(s)? This is when the environment becomes mixed. It just keeps appending the $PATH variable each time you execute the oraenv script. Which set of executables will you find first? It will be those executables for which you ran oraenv the first time.

At this point I wanted to execute SQL*Plus out of the 11g directory, but was able to determine that the 10gR2 client was first in the $PATH. How did I know that? Use the which Unix command to find out.

```
oracle@yournode.domain:/u01/app/oracle[orcl]
> which sqlplus
/u03/banjobs/product/10gR2client/bin/sqlplus
```

It is also a good practice to use a separate terminal window for each ORACLE_HOME. Normally, you will operate with multiple windows open, one for each ORACLE_HOME or ORACLE_SID in different colors to visually remind you which one is production.

The example profile is provided in the code section for this chapter: `example_profile.txt`. The profile sets the entire user environment at first logon. This one is specific to the `ksh` or `korn` shell on the Linux operating system and will also work for `bash`. Differences in `bash` include that the line history is scrollable with the up and down arrows instead of `vi` commands.

To set the `ORACLE_SID` and activate all of the variables located in `profile`, *source* the file `oraenv` (bash, Bourne, or korn shell) or `coraenv` (C shell). Source means the variables will be in effect for the entire session and not just the current line in the command window. You indicate source by putting a '.' (dot) in front of the file. As the `oraenv` file is located in `/usr/local/bin` (on Linux) and this location is in the `$PATH`, typing it at the command line works. Putting key Oracle files, such as `oraenv`, `oratab`, and `oraInst.loc`, in locations that will not be affected by standard Oracle installations is also part of the OFA. The `oraenv` script is installed into `/usr/local/bin/` automatically when running `.runInstaller` for the first time. Notice the prompt that you will see if you use the command as in the profile listed above:

```
oracle@nodename.domain:/u01/app/oracle[]
> .   oraenv

oracle@nodename.domain:/u01/app/oracle[newdb]
> .   oraenv
```

A note about prompts: Every person will want to customize their own prompt so; look around for various versions that tickle your fancy. This one is better than most examples to compare to. Notice the small difference in the prompt before and after? `ORACLE_SID` is now defined because `oraenv` is executed, which also runs `dbhome` (also located in `/usr/local/bin`), but these scripts require a valid entry in `/etc/oratab`. If you type the `ORACLE_SID` incorrectly on Unix, this will be case sensitive. It will ask where the `ORACLE_HOME` is if there is no entry in `oratab`. Making an `ORACLE_SID` lowercase conforms to the OFA standard (see the install guide for your OS for more information). Some DBAs use an uppercase `ORACLE_SID` because it makes it more prominent for any type of naming convention and is meant to reduce human error.

You can use an ORACLE_SID entry in the oratab file to reference other Oracle products such as the Grid Control Intelligent Agent. The ea, which is an ORACLE_SID in the following oratab example, is what I use to indicate the Enterprise Manager Agent. The third letter after the ORACLE_HOME (N) indicates when Oracle-supplied utilities (like db_shut and db_start) are *not* to execute against this ORACLE_HOME. I personally use the N for my own scripting to indicate which utilities shouldn't run against this ORACLE_HOME. What this does is take advantage of Oracle-provided files — oratab and oraenv — to accomplish other types of tasks. This is only a suggested use. There are other ways of setting environmental variables for non-database products.

```
#/etc/oratab
# This file is used by ORACLE utilities.  It is created by #root.sh
# and updated by the Database Configuration Assistant when creating
# a database.
# A colon, ':', is used as the field terminator.  A new line #terminates
# the entry.  Lines beginning with a pound sign, '#', are #comments.
# Entries are of the form:
# $ORACLE_SID:$ORACLE_HOME:<N|Y>:
# The first and second fields are the system identifier and #home
# directory of the database respectively.  The third field #indicates
# to the dbstart utility that the database should , "Y",or #should not,
# "N", be brought up at system boot time.
#
# Multiple entries with the same $ORACLE_SID are not allowed.
#
newdb:/u01/app/oracle/product/11.2.0.1/db_home1:Y
ea:/u01/app/oracle/product/agent10g:N
new:/u01/app/oracle/product/10.2.0.5:N
```

You will need to create a test database to work through all of the examples and practice scenarios in this book. How should you create the test database? Use the Oracle-provided Database Configuration Assistant (DBCA) utility to create a test database. There are default templates provided that will work for most of the tasks outlined in this book. If you are interested in duplicating some of the advanced tasks (like Data Guard), then it will require the installation of the Enterprise Edition of Oracle Database. All tasks in this book were done with 11.1.0.7 version of Oracle Database with some references to 11.2.0.1, which had just been released.

Host commands relative location

This will be important as you begin scripting. Host commands are relative to the location of the executable. As a general rule, you should execute database-specific utilities (imp, exp, datapump, RMAN, and so forth) on the server where the database is located in the correct ORACLE_HOME. This reduces the amount of issues such as core dumps and version compatibilities. This is different from what is usually thought of as a client utilities such as SQL*Plus.

There are exceptions to this rule, for it is recommended to run a compiled code (C, C++, Cobol) on a separate server rather than a database. See the following document for setting the TWO_TASK variable when using a separate node for compiled programs. TWO_TASK is an environmental variable. *Subject: How to Customize Pro*C and Pro*Cobol Makefiles demo_proc.mk And demo_procob.mk On Linux/Unix [Doc ID: 602936.1].*

Another exception to running a utility on a different node is when you are performing migration to a different version or patchset, or running the DATAGUARD broker. Both of these situations are discussed later in this book in the *Chapter 7*, and *Chapter 5*.

Notice the *WARNING!* message that is set using the new 11g sqlnet.ora parameter SEC_USER_UNAUTHORIZED_ACCESS_BANNER. The sqlnet.ora file is part of the SQL*Net components of Oracle RDBMS, which handle the communication between clients and the database.

```
oracle@nodename:/u01/app/oracle/admin/newdb[newdb]
> sqlplus /nolog
SQL*Plus: Release 11.1.0.7.0 - Production on Thu Nov 5 19:00:29
2009
Copyright (c) 1982, 2008, Oracle.  All rights reserved.
@> connect / as sysdba
###############################################################
###
WARNING!  This computer system is the property of YOUR
ORGANIZATION
and may be accessed only by authorized users.
Unauthorized use of this system is strictly prohibited and may be
subject to criminal prosecution.
Connected.
SYS@newdb>
```

If you wanted to execute something that is available on the operating system level, then you would use a host command (either Windows or Unix), or on Unix the ! symbol. The output below shows that I am logged into the newdb as sys and lists (ls command) the files located in the $ORACLE_HOME/sqlplus/admin directory:

```
SYS@newdb> !ls $ORACLE_HOME/sqlplus/admin
glogin.sql  help  libsqlplus.def  plustrce.sql  pupbld.sql
SYS@newdb> !vi $ORACLE_HOME/sqlplus/admin/glogin.sql
```

Notice how the SQL prompt is populated with the `ORACLE_SID` and the username that is connected to the database. This is done by adding a line to the `glogin.sql` file, which can be done within SQL*Plus as shown below (I used the text editor `vi`):

```
--
-- Copyright (c) 1988, 2005, Oracle.  All Rights Reserved.
--
-- NAME
--   glogin.sql
--
-- DESCRIPTION
--   SQL*Plus global login "site profile" file
--
--   Add any SQL*Plus commands here that are to be executed when a
--   user starts SQL*Plus, or uses the SQL*Plus CONNECT command.
--
-- USAGE
--   This script is automatically run
--
set sqlprompt "_user'@'_connect_identifier> "
```

Host commands work based on the location of SQL*Plus. If you want to execute these same commands from a Windows desktop connecting to a remote Unix database, then it would require a Windows equivalent command like Notepad or another editor. If you have Cygwin installed and configured on the Windows desktop, then it would allow you to run Unix-equivalent commands like `vi`.

Separating the variable part of the script into its own configuration file

There are scripts that will need some variables set, but you don't necessarily want to use the `profile` to set a variable at every login. The variables may need to contain commands specific to applications such as RMAN, SQL*Plus or specific to certain tasks. This is where a configuration file comes in handy, which is a personal preference as to what you call them. Be sure not to use reserved keywords for variables, as that leads to unexpected results. In the example below, we use `emal` instead of the word `email`.

To call this configuration file, you source it starting with the prerequisite . (dot) within a script. This file can also be used in the custom code section of the `oraenv` file.

```
# newdb.conf
# Configuration File for running scripts against this database.
ORACLE_HOME=/u01/app/oracle/product/11.2.0.1/db_home1
MY_EXE_HOME=/u01/app/localapps/bin
MY_BACKUP_LOCATION=/backup/$ORACLE_SID
DBAEMAL=dba@yourdomain.com
export MY_EXE_HOME MY_BACKUP_LOCATION DBAEMAL
PATH=$MY_EXE_HOME:$MY_BACKUP_LOCATION:$ORACLE_HOME/bin:$PATH
ORACLE_SID=newdb
# The backtick on the following date command allows you can assign the result
# of the date command to a variable.
DAT=`date '+%Y%d%m%H%M'`
export ORACLE_SID ORACLE_HOME PATH DAT
```

Don't hardcode values; reference a configuration file and password file at runtime

Values include items such as a directory path, ORACLE_SID, e-mail, or file locations as shown in the above newdb.conf file. Passwords should be in a separate hidden file-protected location (chmod 400, which is only readable by Oracle) to be read at runtime by simply inserting a small piece of code and an appropriate variable in each script:

```
#.oracle.passwd
system/password

PASS=`grep system /u01/app/oracle/.oracle.passwd | cut -f 2`;
 export PASS
$ORACLE_HOME/bin/exp userid=$PASS parfile=$HOME/export$db.par
```

The following line actually pulls the ORACLE_SID out of the oratab file. This is useful for executing against multiple databases on a single node. See the script labeled coalesce_tablespace.ksh for a complete example.

```
cat /etc/oratab | while read LINE
do
  case $LINE in
  \#*)              ;;        #comment-line in oratab
  *)
  #       Proceed only if third field is 'Y'.
  if [ "`echo $LINE | awk -F: '{print $3}' -`" = "Y" ] ; then
    ORACLE_SID=`echo $LINE | awk -F: '{print $1}' -`
    export ORACLE_SID
    ORACLE_HOME=`echo $LINE | awk -F: '{print $2}' -`
    export ORACLE_HOME
```

This small script shows how a local script on a database node can be run without a password, as the database has a password file and the startup initialization parameter `remote_login_passwordfile=EXCLUSIVE`. A password file is created for a specific database with a default file name format usually found in `$ORACLE_HOME/dbs/orapw<SID>`.

```ksh
#!/bin/ksh
#Source the configuration file as follows.
. $OTILS/newdb.conf
$ORACLE_HOME/bin/sqlplus -s <<EOF
connect / as sysdba
  set pagesize 0 feedback off termout off linesize 200
  spool output.txtselect tablespace_name from dba_tablespaces;
  spool off
EOF
exit
```

Using a hidden password file for scripting is more secure than embedding clear text passwords in the script itself. There is also a relatively new feature in Oracle Database 10gR2 and above called the External Password Store. This component is also part of the Advanced Networking Option (options are always an additional license cost) and is another way to store passwords. If used for password functionality only, the External Password Store is free of charge.

 http://download.oracle.com/docs/cd/E11882_01/license.112/e10594/editions.htm#CJACGHEB: This document details the differences between the different editions of Oracle. Search for Secure External Password Store; it is included with the Enterprise Edition of Oracle.

It requires the creation of an Oracle Wallet that stores encrypted username and password combinations for batch jobs, scripts, and even application code. This is one of the most secure ways to connect to the database while providing a single location for changing passwords on a regular basis. See the Oracle Documentation, Oracle Database, and Security Guide for your release for instructions on creating and maintaining a password store. See the following white paper for instructions that don't require a MOS account:

http://www.oracle.com/technology/deploy/security/database-security/pdf/twp_db_security_secure_ext_pwd_store.pdf

Putting variables at the top of the script with curly braces

This makes it easier to spot for editing and troubleshooting. Mixed case would make them stand out even more. Curly braces will resolve to the value of a variable that had already been defined at the top of a particular script.

```
$ORACLE_HOME # variable at the top of a script
${ORACLE_HOME} # Refers back to the variable
```

Moving functions to a centralized file to be reused

All scripts can use any of the functions within by referencing the function name. The example below illustrates this:

```
#!/bin/ksh
# otils.fnc
                function verify_directories {
if [ ! -d ${MY_BASEDIR} ];then
                mkdir ${MY_BASEDIR}
fi

if [ ! -d ${MY_BASEDIR}/scripts ];then
                mkdir ${MY_BASEDIR}/scripts
fi

if [ ! -d ${MY_BASEDIR}/archive ];then
                mkdir ${MY_BASEDIR}/archive
fi
}
```

And an example shell script that will call the separate function is simply run and sourced by putting a dot in front of the filename. In this case, the otils.fnc file can be found in the $PATH environmental variable.

```
-------
#! /bin/ksh

. otils.fnc
```

Validating the use of the script

To validate a script that should only be run by a certain user ID or on a certain host, only use `whoami` and `uname`. See the *Move functions to a centralized file to be reused* section for the idea of a centralized function file, as this would be a good candidate.

```
if [ `whoami` != "oracle" ]; then
    echo "error. Must be oracle to run this script"
    exit 1
fi
```

```
if [ `uname -a | awk '{print $1}'` != "databasenode" ]; then
    echo "error. This script only to run on databasenode server"
    exit 1
fi
```

The `if-fi` part of this code is used to evaluate something. `If` it is true, then do the next step. The `fi` indicates where the end of this section of code should stop.

Using SQL to generate code

The script provided for this chapter called `cleanout.sql` generates a file that is then run by SQL*Plus, which demonstrates the capability to run certain host commands from within the database. This is done by using the keyword `host` within the script, and on Unix you can also use the exclamation point (!) to indicate host commands. The Oracle user will be limited to executables that are in the `$PATH` and have the appropriate file permissions.

This ability to use SQL*Plus to generate SQL commands as well as execute OS commands by embedding SQL syntax in a script is a powerful tool for a DBA. This type of execution will dynamically generate spooled SQL commands. The resulting spooled SQL file can then run in the same script or edit it as needed before running manually.

The following scripts are especially handy for one-time mass updates, such as switching users to a new profile or expiring passwords. The single ampersand symbol (&) will substitute the value for that variable you provide a single time; two ampersands will substitute every time that variable is found in a script.

The first script, `grant_table_role.sql`, grants all privileges for a list of tables to a role that belongs to a certain schema. The second script inserts a username into a table generated by pulling the first part of an e-mail address, that is, everything before the @ symbol. The `chr(10)` puts in a newline and the pipe symbols `||` append each item.

```
--grant_table_role.sql
set echo       off
set feedback   off
set heading    off
set pagesize   0
set timing     off
set trimspool  on
set verify     off
spool grant_table_&USERROLE.&TABLEOWNER..sql
select 'grant select,insert,update,delete,references on ' ||table_name
|| ' to &&USERROLE; '
from dba_tables where owner = '&&TABLEOWNER';
spool off
exit

--update_email.sql
set echo       off
set feedback   off
set heading    off
set pagesize   0
set timing     off
set trimspool  on
set verify     off
spool update_email_users.sql
select 'update table_name set table_name_pidm =' ||EMAIL_PIDM || ', '
||'table_name_username' ||' = ' || chr (10) ||
(select substr(email_address,1, instr(email_address,'@')-1) from
email_table)|| 'table_name_user_id= BATCH, table_name_activity_date
=sysdate;'
    from general_emal;
spool off
@ update_email_users.sql
exit
```

In the e-mail example above, the script that was created in the first step is automatically called after the spool-off command.

```
--This script is a generic create user script.
--create_users.sql
set echo        off
set feedback    off
set heading     off
set pagesize    0
set timing      off
set trimspool   on
set verify      off
spool create_mass_users.sql
select 'create user ' ||username || ' identified by '
||'"'||TO_CHAR(BIRTH_DATE,'MMDDYY')||'"'||' ;'|| chr(10)||
        'alter user '  || username   || chr (10) ||
          ' default tablespace USERS;'          || chr(10) ||
          'alter user '  || username   ||
          ' temporary tablespace TEMP;'  ||chr(10)||
        '  grant CONNECT to ' ||username || ';' ||chr (10)||
        'grant USR_ROLE to '||username|| ';' ||chr (10)||
        'grant USR_QUERY to '||username|| ';' ||chr (10)||
        'grant USR_STAFF to ' ||username|| ';' ||chr (10) ||
' alter user '||username||' default role CONNECT, USR_STAFF ;'
    from table_name, person_table
 where table_name_pidm=person_table_pidm;
spool off
-- commented out the last statement to double check before running.
-- @ create_mass_users.sql
exit
```

The only difficult part about this process is that the number of quotes needed depends on the data retrieved. If it is a literal string (data that has to have quotes to do the insert), then you will need a corresponding set of two single quotes to do this. See the example create_users.sql.

All of the queries used in these examples may not work for you, depending on the data you are trying to retrieve. They are intended to provide examples of how to use the embedded SQL technique for different types of DBA tasks.

It takes some practice, but this is a tool that will make your job easier. The various set commands are specific to SQL*Plus. These settings remove extra characters that end up in the final script. Removing those extra characters from the final script allows it to be run in SQL*Plus without editing the file first.

Unix "ps" Command Exposes Password When Using Export/Import, SQL*Plus, Tkprof [ID 372964.1] provides important information about concealing passwords, which is easily found with the Unix ps command when running scripts.

Helpful Unix commands

The following table lists some helpful Unix commands:

Tasks	Unix commands
Show files greater than (>) 2 GB	`find /u02/oradata -size +200000000c -ls`
Show files less than (<) 2 GB	`find /u02/oradata -size -200000000c -ls`
Remove trace files not modified in the last 30 days	`find /u01/app/oracle -name "*.trc" -mtime +30 -exec rm {} \;`
Find scripts where new users are created	`find $ORACLE_HOME -type f -exec grep -il "identified by" {} \;`
Find sqlplus scripts that might have passwords in them	`find /u01/app/oracle/admin -type f -exec grep -il "sqlplus" {} \;`
Find all files that are owned by Oracle	`find /u01 /u02 /u03 -user oracle -print`
Remove all export files that are larger than 1 MB and older than 30 days	`find $ADMIN -name "*.dmp" -size +1048576c -mtime +30 -exec rm {} \;`
Find linked files	`find /u01/app/oracle /u*/oradata -type l -ls`
Find files modified in the last 24 hours	`find /u01/app/oracle/admin/orcl -type f -mtime -1 -print`

Show total size of all subdirectories with Disk Usage command on a disk (sorted in reverse order)	`cd /u02/oradata`
	
	`du -s * | sort -nr`
	
	`du -sh will provide a shortened readout in gigabytes`

Show total size of all data files in directory	`cd /u02/oradata/orcl`
	
	`du -k * | sort -nr`

Run more than one command on a single line by using a semicolon between the commands	`date; who`

Tasks	Unix commands
To debug a script with sh or bash and display the environmental variables	`sh -vx script.sh` or `bash -vx script.bash`
Bash shell debugging set command, a negative in front turns it on, a plus sign turns it off	set-x: Display commands and their arguments as they are executed. `set-x set+x` set-v: Display shell input lines as they are read `.#!/bin/bash -xv`

 There is more on SQL Toolkit Free Command Line Utilities for Oracle SQL*Plus at: `http://www.runner technologies.com/downloads.html`.

Reducing operating system differences with common tools

When your enterprise environment contains several different operating systems and database versions, it is best to have tools that work across scopes. We have already mentioned scripting as well as using DBMS_SCHEDULER and PL/SQL. There are also several software packages that offer GUI interfaces for real-time monitoring capability.

Oracle has a product called Grid Control (GC); it is the Enterprise Manager for the Enterprise. You can install a standalone version of Enterprise Manager in each database (called Database Control) or use GC with a centralized repository for all of your Oracle products. Grid Control is a free product from Oracle, the Management Packs have an additional license cost. Most customers purchase the DIAGNOSTICS & TUNING to take advantage of the extensive performance tuning features found in the Automatic Workload Repository, and not just for the OEM Interface.

The trade-off is a superb enterprise-wide tool, but one that requires an additional repository database for the infrastructure components of GC. The database or repository is not completely self-managed, but has not shown itself to be a large burden in terms of overhead. GC is a complex product that is now maturing in terms of scalability and flexibility. Challenges include limited migration paths when moving the different components to new hardware and/or hardware platforms.

GC version 10.2.0.5 has some of the best features so far: mass deployment of the agent, and installing the software and configuring later options for several of the components. Both of these new features directly address past migration and deployment issues.

Other third-party vendors with widely adopted database monitoring tools include Veritas, Quest, EMC, Embarcadero, and CA. Each of them have their own positive and negative features. Each one should be available for a full trial testing period before investing.

Configuration management, release management, and change control

One of the largest changes to Oracle is the recent acquisition of several other software lines and technologies. Oracle has combined all of these technologies and customers under a single support site called My Oracle Support at `http://support.oracle.com`, effective from Fall 2009. Along the way, Oracle also completely redesigned the interface, making it flash-based in order to provide a personalized GUI.

To take full advantage of the personalization features, you will need to install a free utility on each node and each `ORACLE_HOME` you would like to monitor. The following paragraphs outline several reasons for use and suggestions for getting started. Please review and discuss with the management the security implications of uploading critical information to a support website before proceeding.

Configuration management

Are you the only Oracle DBA in your company? How do you provide disaster recovery and redundancy for personnel in that situation?

MOS has a tool that provides an *Automatic Document Repository* (my words) called Oracle Configuration Manager (OCM). This tool has been mentioned several times in this chapter, but its real purpose is to manage all of your configurations (different systems, servers, databases, application servers) when dealing with Oracle support.

It is automatic in the sense that if you are out of the office, temporarily or permanently, the system configurations are available for viewing by anyone with the same Oracle **Customer Support Identifier** (CSI) number. The information is also available to Oracle support personnel. The repository is located on My Oracle Support. The systems are for you to choose, whether you want to only include production and/or non-production systems.

What information does OCM collect and upload? It contains extensive hardware details, software installs (not just Oracle products), databases, and Oracle application servers. There is enough information to help in recreating your site if there is a complete disaster. The GUI interface allows managers and other IT personnel to see how nodes and applications are related and how they fit into your architectural framework. The information can only be updated by the upload process.

Using OCM in disconnected mode with masking

There is sensitive information being collected from the OCM tool. If you are employed by an organization that doesn't allow you to reveal such information or allow direct access by the servers to the Internet, there are steps to improve the security of this upload process. This section is highly recommended to be reviewed before enabling OCM. You must know what types of information are there and how that information is used before enabling uploading capabilities to a support website.

To disable the collection of IP and MAC addresses, you add the following entries to the `$ORACLE_HOME/ccr/config/collector.properties` file.

To disable the collection of network addresses, add the following entry:

```
ccr.metric.host.ecm_hw_nic.inet_address=false
```

To disable the collection of the MAC address, add the following entry:

```
ccr.metric.host.ecm_hw_nic.mac_address=false
```

The OCM collector collects the schema usernames for databases configured for configuration collections. The collection of this information is filtered or masked when `ccr.metric.oracle_database.db_users.username` is assigned the value of 'mask' in the `$ORACLE_HOME/ccr/config/collector.properties` file. The default behavior of the collector is to not mask this data.

MOS customers may request deletion of their configuration information by logging a Service Request (SR) indicating the specific configuration information and scope of the deletion request.

Disconnected mode is carried out with something called Oracle Support Hub, which is installed at your site. This hub is configured as a local secure site for direct uploads from your nodes, which the hub can then upload to MOS through the Internet. This protects each of your nodes from any type of direct Internet access.

Finally, there is a way to do a manual upload of a single node using the method outlined in the MOS document 763142.1: *How to upload the collection file* `ocmconfig.jar` *to My Oracle Support for Oracle Configuration Manager (OCM) running in Disconnected Mode.* This is probably the safest method to use for OCM. Run it for a specific purpose with appropriate masking built-in and then request the information to be deleted by entering a SR request.

These tips came from these locations as well as the OCM licensing agreement found on MOS:

`http://www.oracle.com/support/collateral/customer-support-security-practices.pdf`

`http://download.oracle.com/docs/html/E12881_01/toc.htm`

The Oracle Support Hub can by found on the OCM Companion Distribution Disk at: `http://www.oracle.com/technology/documentation/ocm.html`.

Each node with an installed OCM collector can be automated to upload any changes on a daily basis or interval of your choice. OCM is now an optional part of any of the 10.2.0.4+ Oracle Product GUI installs. The OCM collector is also found by logging into MOS and selecting the collector tab. It is recommended to use at least the 3.2 version for ease of installation across the enterprise.

Be aware! The collector install actually creates the Unix `cron` entry to automatically schedule the uploads.

Mass deployment utility

The OCM collector utility has been out for over a year, but a recent enhancement makes installation easier with a mass deployment utility. On the MOS collector tab, find **Configuration Manager Repeater & Mass Deployment Tools** and the OCM Companion Distribution Guide.

The template file required to install the collector on multiple servers is in `csv` format, which you may find difficult to edit using `vi` or `vim`. The template doesn't have an initial entry and the length is wider than the average session window. Once the first entry is filled out (try using desktop spreadsheet software), editing this file with a command-line tool is easier. It has a secure password feature so that no password is stored in clear text. You can enter a password at the prompt or allow the password utility to encrypt the open text passwords in the template file during the install run.

Running the utility runs very quickly from a single node that has SSH access to all entries in the template. It auto detects if OCM was already installed and bypasses any of those entries. You may encounter an issue where the required JAVA version is higher than what is installed. Other prerequisites include SSH on Linux or CYGWIN for Windows.

A downside is that all configuration information is available to everyone with the same CSI number. In a small IT shop, this isn't a problem as long as MOS access is maintained properly when personnel changes. Providing granular group access within a CSI number to your uploaded configurations is a highly anticipated feature.

Release management

As a DBA you must be consistent in the different aspects of administration. This takes dedication to keep all of your installed Oracle products up-to-date on critical patches. Most DBAs keep up-to-date with production down issues that require a patch install. But what about the quarterly security fixes? The operating systems that your system admin is in charge of will probably be patched more regularly than Oracle. Why is that the case? It seems to take an inordinate amount of effort to accomplish what appears to be a small task.

Newer versions of Oracle are associated with major enhancements—as shown by the differences between versions 11.1 and 11.2. Patch sets contain at least all the cumulative bug fixes for a particular version of Oracle and an occasional enhancement as shown in the version difference between 11.1.0.6 and 11.1.0.7. Oracle will stop supporting certain versions, indicating which is the most stable version (labeling it as the terminal release). For example, the terminal release of Oracle 10.1.x is 10.1.0.5, as that was the last patch set released. See the following document on MOS for further information on releases—*Oracle Server (RDBMS) Releases Support Status Summary [Doc ID: 161818.1]*.

In addition to applying patch sets on a regular basis (usually an annual event) to keep current with bug fixes, there are other types of patches released on a regular basis. Consider these to be post-patch set patches. There is some confusing information from MOS, with two different methods of patching on a quarterly basis (Jan, April, July, Oct.)—Patch Set Updates and Critical Patch Updates. CPUs only contain security bug fixes. The newer method of patching—PSU—includes not only the security fixes but other major bugs. These are tested as a single unit and contain bug fixes that have been applied in customers' production environments.

See the following for help in identifying a database version in relationship to PSUs:

MOS Doc ID 850471.1
1st digit — Major release number
2nd digit — Maintenance release
3rd digit — Application server release
4th digit — Release component specific
5th digit — Platform specific release
First PSU for Oracle Database Version — 10.2.0.4.1
Second PSU for Oracle Database Version — 10.2.0.4.2

While either PSUs or CPUs can be applied to a new or existing system, Oracle recommends that you stick to one type. If you have applied CPUs in the past and want to continue — that is one path. If you have applied CPUs in the past and now want to apply a PSU, you must now only apply PSUs from this point to prevent conflicts. Switching back and forth will cause problems and ongoing issues with further installs, and it requires significant effort to start down this path. You may need a merge patch when migrating from a current CPU environment, called a **Merge Request** on MOS.

Important information on differences between CPUs and PSUs can be found in the following locations. If there is a document number, then that is found on the MOS support site:

`http://blogs.oracle.com/gridautomation/`

`http://www.oracle/technology/deploy/security/alerts.htm`

Doc 864316.1 Application of PSU can be automated through Deployment Procedures

Doc 854428.1 Intro to Patch Set Updates

Doc 756388.1 Recommended Patches

Upgrade Companions 466181.1, 601807.1

Error Correction Policy 209768.1

Now to make things even more complicated for someone new to Oracle; let's discuss recommended patches. These are released between the quarterly PSUs and CPUs with common issues for *targeted* configurations. The following are targeted configurations:

- Generic — General database use
- Real Application Clusters and CRS — For running multiple instances on a single database with accompanying Oracle Clusterware software
- DataGuard (and/or Streams) — Oracle Redo Apply technology for moving data to a standby database or another read/write database
- Exadata — Vendor-specific HP hardware storage solution for Oracle
- Ebusiness Suite Certification — Oracle's version of Business Applications, which runs on an Oracle Database

Recommended patches are tested as a single combined unit, reducing some of the risk involved with multiple patches. They are meant to stabilize production environments, hopefully saving time and cost with known issues starting with Oracle Database Release 10.2.0.3 — see *Doc ID: 756671.1*.

DBA issues with patching

Here is a list of the most frequently experienced issues with the patching process for Oracle products:

- What patches should be applied?
- No advance notification if there is a conflict.
- Patch conflicts that cause rollbacks.
- Merge requests for patch conflicts.
- Troubleshooting patch application failure.
- Conflicting and resolving differences in CPUs and PSUs.
- Should I apply the recommended patches?
- Am I the first person to deploy this patch?
- Documenting versions and patches across all systems.

Oracle recently added a new functionality to their support website called Patch Plans. It requires the 3.2+ version of the MOS Configuration Manager Collector (which is the collector component of OCM). It was just mentioned a few sections earlier and is available for download from the My Oracle Support website. Once the collector is installed and your system configuration information is uploaded to MOS, you can create a patch plan.

The following screenshot contains my list of patch recommendations for all of the ORACLE_HOME(s) that have a collector installed and configured for uploading to Metalink.

> There is an alternate login page for non-flash users—
> http://supporthtml.oracle.com, but this will not include
> any of the personalization features such as Patch Plans or uploaded
> configuration details.

There is one patch plan associated with the patch number 8534378, as shown by the folder icon. I purposely moved the sliding components of this dashboard so that the sensitive information is covered. You can also right-click to select a patch to add to a new plan or existing plan, download, or suppress this patch. The existence of a patch plan is indicated by the folder icon next to a certain patch, as seen in the very first entry of the list of patch recommendations. If you don't have any configurations, you will not see a list of patch recommendations.

The next screenshot is the full screen of a selected patch 8534378, which is the CPU for July 2009. Notice on the right the *Coming Soon!* banner, which is reserved for the community functionality that wasn't available at the time this book was written. This area of MOS will include end users' feedback on this particular patch and will also list the number of times it was downloaded over the past few months.

Applying a patch without integrating MOS with OCM

Here are generic instructions for applying a patch without MOS and OCM:

1. Download the patch, PSU, CPU, or patch set.
2. Create a new ORACLE_HOME for testing if alternating between different ORACLE_HOMES. Otherwise, all Oracle software running in the home to be patched will have to be shut down.
3. Install if there aren't any conflicts. If there is a conflict, then the patch is rolled back.
4. Check if any key patches are also rolled back.
5. Submit a merge request on MOS for key patches.
6. Download the merge request to start the patch process again.

Using the new patch plan functionality with OCM installed and uploaded to MOS

1. Patch Plan automatically checks for missing prerequisites. This functionality has not been shown to be consistent across the board yet.
2. It checks any conflicts before downloading.
3. It request a merge if required before downloading.
4. It will also check recommended patches for your configuration.

The following documents from MOS contain the manual methods for determining whether a patch will conflict using the Oracle supplied `opatch` utility. More details about `opatch` use are outlined in *Chapter 7*. If your organization doesn't want to install or configure the OCM collector for security reasons, then the following is a viable option for determining patch conflicts.

Refer to *How to find whether the one of the patches will conflict or not? [Doc ID: 458485.1]*. Here are a couple of examples of how to use this command-line utility outlined in the document:

```
opatch prereq CheckConflictAmongPatchesWithDetail -phBaseDir $ORACLE_
HOME/patches
opatch prereq CheckConflictAgainstOHWithDetail -phBaseDir $ORACLE_
HOME/patches
```

Change control

To keep from constantly writing the same pieces of code over and over again and reconciling differences between servers, a common storage area for DBA code needs to be established. It is most likely that your programming staff already has access to a code repository. The two largest open source versions are CVS (Open Source Version Control) and Subversion (SVN). They are both equally efficient and powerful tools with slightly different features. If version control software is already deployed in your enterprise, then ask for a repository for database administration and limit the access to that repository.

> Do not store passwords in a repository that means 'currently in use' or 'previously used'. Find an enterprise-wide password utility such as KeePass that will store encrypted passwords for all of the servers and databases. Integrate SSH PUTTY with KeePass so that it launches a terminal window without having to type the password. See the following blog for additional information on other password utilities like KeePass: http://princessleia.com/journal/?p=1235.

One way to use version control software is to check out the repository on each node and use the command-line version on that node. While you can check out code on your desktop, you will still have to shuttle any code changes via SSH or SFTP between your desktop and the servers, which adds another step to the process. There are also issues when editing the files with a Windows utility; it inserts the carriage return character that has to be removed to run on a Unix box. The Unix utility that removes special Windows characters is called `dos2unix`.

dos2unix removes any links (symbolic or hard) that a file currently has. This will affect how the file is referenced in the $PATH, so the links must be recreated. See the Unix help pages for ln, which is done by issuing a man ln. This command opens up the OS documentation for the ln command on Unix.

There is a way to eliminate the extra shuttling of code while keeping the GUI interface by using the open source ECLIPSE on the server. It is most closely associated with Java programming as an Independent Development Environment (IDE). There are additional plugins, software extensions, and code additions for almost any programming you would need to accomplish. Check out the Data Tools Platform Project for downloads specific to database development.

Version Control Software will take some time to learn to use safely. It can easily overwrite or remove critical pieces of code. So work closely with the code repository system admin to make sure there are backups! A safer way to use the repository might be to check it out in a temporary staging area and migrate the code safely to a protected code tree.

Where, when, and who to call for help

Okay, now that you know the major responsibilities as a DBA, *when* should you ask for help? When would you know something is wrong? One issue that every DBA dreads is when end users complain that the database is slow. It doesn't matter if you are sitting in your office and the database seems to be running perfectly well. Every script you run reveals no issues or distinguishable slowness. So what are those end users talking about? If the end users have an issue, then you now have a problem. And that particular problem is called response time; this subject will be explored further in Chapter 8.

Components (at several levels of the technology stack) that slow things down for the database can include the network, operating system, application servers, and of course hardware-specific problems. Start an SQL trace to help come up with an error message that will give more clues to the problem. Please don't assume it is someone else's problem.

If you encounter corruption at any level, automatically open a Service Request, even if you solve it completely yourself. Unless you know exactly how extensive the corruption is, it is best to take the database offline while it is being fixed because you may have to restore from previous backups, possibly losing the current transactions being entered.

The best defense against corruption is preventing it in the first place. 11g has a new startup initialization parameter DB_ULTRA_SAFE. Certain types of database corruption can also be prevented by implementing DATAGUARD for failing over when something disastrous occurs to the primary production database. In earlier versions of Oracle, the two database parameters db_block_checksum and/or db_block_checking were used to help in corruption detection and prevention.

Now is the time to point you to Oracle's website for the Maximum Availability Architecture (MAA). They have worked extensively with vendors and Very Large Database (VLDB) customers to improve performance at every level of the technology stack. Most of the concepts, techniques, and tips will apply to any company that runs Oracle. You need to download all of the white papers from the Oracle Technology website, print them out, and go over all of the details thoroughly. There is additional information available on MOS about MAA. Only by testing with your data can you be assured that true performance improvement or failover capabilities from these recommendations are suitable for your environment.

Critical tuning information presented in Chapter 8 will come from the practices outlined in the MAA white papers. The following URL comes from the Oracle Technology Network site, which contains extensive forums, white papers, online documentation, and software downloads for Oracle products.

```
http://www.oracle.com/technology/deploy/availability/htdocs/maa.htm
```

My Oracle Support

As a new DBA, I would recommend starting a search for a problem or issue on the My Oracle Support website. As you gain experience in researching issues that other DBAs have helped with, then you may decide to start with an Internet search first. On MOS there are database administration scripts, documentation, customer-written articles as well as complete checklists for any migration project. Look for FAQs on most subjects as they often have the complete list of all current documents that are related. The new **Upgrade Companion** found on MOS should be shown to your DBA manager so that they can see the complex process needed just to upgrade the database—it will help and scare you at the same time.

Double check whether the licenses listed on your MOS profile are correct; contact your Oracle account representative if they aren't.

If there is an error message involved, even if it isn't a specific Oracle message, MOS also has answers to errors related to the operating system, desktop, network, client browsers, compilers, and even common programming issues. The trick is learning to do advanced searching within MOS and to find the information you need. If you use an Internet software search site they will strip any non-alphanumerical characters, but not MOS. It will do exact, error code type of searches like "ORA-00600".

Check out the code download for this chapter. It contains a small plugin for Mozilla and information on downloading a Microsoft Deskbar, making searches on MOS easier. `MOS_search_mozilla.txt` and `MOS_search_msdeskbar.txt` each contain the code source and credit to the author. It will ask for your MOS username and password to complete the search.

Remember that if you have an emergency, MOS may take hours (if not several days) to respond, depending on the level of support purchased. There is a phone number to call MOS, but that will result in waiting until there is someone available to help you at the time you call. In the past, fairly good results came from telephoning Oracle support but these days you are summarily directed back to the MOS website to enter a Service Request. If you have system configurations uploaded to MOS (see *Change Control, Release, and Configuration Management* section) that makes it easier to enter a Service Request, as it automatically preloads a lot of the required information.

Documentation library

Of course, the first place you should start when you have a question on migrating to a new release is the documentation. Be sure to match the version of the documentation to the database version! Download the entire library found on the Oracle Technology Network website—`http://otn.oracle.com`. You will notice that even the downloaded local copy will have the search box returning to the Oracle website. There are occasions when the website is not available.

If you only want to search using desktop search indexing capabilities (see information in the preceding paragraphs), then open up the `index.htm` and comment out the following lines that reference the Oracle website. This will disable the feature completely and will show it has already commented out by adding `!` in front and in the last line of the code just inside the `>` signs;

```
<!--div class="simple_search_form_container" style="margin-bottom:
5px;">
<div>
<form class="simple_search_form" action="http://www.oracle.com/pls/
db112/search" method="get">
<input type="hidden" name="remark" value="quick_search" />
```

```
<span>
<input type="text" id="s_word" name="word" value="" class="search_
field" />
</span>
<span class="text">
<label for="s_word">
<span style=" display: none; ">Search:</span>
</label>
<input type="submit" value="Search" class="text" />
</span>
</div>
<div class="shortcut_links">
<a href="http://www.oracle.com/pls/db112/ranked?advanced=1" target="_
top">Advanced Search</a> &#149;
<a href="nav/portal_3.htm" target="_top">Master Book List</a> &#149;
<a href="mix.112/b14387/toc.htm" target="_top">Master Index</a> &#149;
<a href="mix.112/b14388/toc.htm" target="_top">Master Glossary</a>
&#149;
<a href="server.112/e10880/toc.htm" target="_top">Error Messages</a>
</div--!>
```

The Oracle community is world-wide and most people are willing to help even
novice DBAs. One of the best ways to get a question answered is by knowing how
to ask the question in the first place. See the following for a few pointers:

- Searching the forum archives first before asking a question — most often
  novices are asking a question someone else has asked.

- If forum searching is not successful then use your favorite Internet search
  engine. Be careful that the information found may not actually apply to
  your situation, as Oracle problems are time-sensitive and/or version specific.

- There is the old standby — Oracle documentation or searching MOS.

- Frequently asked questions or FAQ's on MOS (use both forms of the words
  FAQ to search with) will be more specific and up-to-date as compared to
  the documentation.

- Once you have some preliminary information, try to figure out the answer on
  your own in a test environment.

- Ask someone you know for the answer, but try not too overwhelm them with
  too many questions, they may stop responding.

- The Oracle code (PL/SQL and executables) is wrapped, making the source non-viewable by any utility. Look within the Oracle-supplied DBA views for information. Search on the Internet for a free utility to learn these views. Descriptions for the columns for the data dictionary are included from the dba_col_comments view, but using a utility makes it easier to read.

- You should really make an effort to figure this out for yourself. Take an Oracle University class to get started. Every certified Oracle instructor that I have had the chance to meet has been excellent and the group as a whole comes highly recommended.

- Check out your local community college or university for Oracle classes. Taking any type of instruction will give you a pool of people to ask for help when you need it.

The following recommended URL list is not comprehensive. It is a jumping-off place to get you started. What it does is eliminate a lot of the bad websites that have incorrect information or are just strictly commercial:

```
http://asktom.oracle.com
http://www.orafaq.com
Oracle-L email lists, part of ORAFAQ
http://www.freelists.org/archive/oracle-l
http://www.eclipse.org
Usenet Groups
http://groups.google.com/groups/dir?sel=33583151&expand=1
http://support.oracle.com
http://forums.oracle.com
OraNA :: Oracle News Aggregator
http://orana.info
Google Directories
http://directory.google.com/Top/Computers/Software/Databases/Oracle/
http://www.oracletips.info/
```

Summary

We looked at many things related to implementing standards across the enterprise in this chapter. Let's take a moment to run through them.

Multiple ORACLE_HOME(s) and multiple databases on multiple servers can be kept under control by maintaining consistent standards across the enterprise. These standards include both OFA and the methods used to automate DBA tasks. Don't let small mistakes keep you squirreled away in your office manually fixing problems that can be avoided in the first place.

Start off by writing your own scripts. Feel free to search on My Oracle Support or the Internet when you need some inspiration. But don't just implement what someone else has written; change it slightly to make it yours. Keep working on scripting as and when you have time.

This chapter contained an introduction to all of the latest manageability features found in 11g Diagnosability Framework. Several of the newer features are an additional licensed option, which are available as a link on the OEM console, as a database package, or as a command-line utility.

Installing the Oracle Configuration Manager allows uploading configurations, which will open up an entire new world on the My Oracle Support website. Be aware that it does reveal information about your site to support personnel and to anyone else with the same CSI number.

Ask everyone when an issue can't be resolved quickly. Compare answers from different sources. Looking for similarity between the responses is one way to gauge credibility. Test several different scenarios before implementing the best solution. There are so many tools on the Internet to keep you connected with the large DBA community: user groups, Twitter, blogs, IT conferences, e-mail lists, and forums. Remember everyone is a novice at some point.

The next chapter takes us into the most detailed level of the database: the data block. You will see how to use special commands to *dump* the data in its hexadecimal format and convert back to a character. Understanding how data travels from one database structure to the next will give you a solid background of technical information to build on as a DBA. It will also give you more confidence in your troubleshooting abilities.

3
Tracking the Bits and Bytes

As a DBA it is essential to know how data moves from one database component to the next; that is, the essential architectural infrastructure at the transaction level. Before continuing with this chapter, you should read the Oracle Database Concepts 11g Release 2 (11.2) of the documentation, the book every DBA should start with. There is a large amount of material in the concepts guide you need to be familiar with, and you should refer back to Sections I-IV as you read through this chapter.

The following list is a recommended shorter version the items in the concepts manual that you need to start with. If a topic isn't listed (for example, Table Clusters), it isn't as essential for understanding as the rest of this book. Come back to advanced topics as you have time or develop a need for that technology in the future.

- Part I Relational Data Structures: Tables, Indexes, Views, Data Integrity, and the Data Dictionary
- Part II Data Access: SQL
- Part III Transaction Management: Transactions, Data Concurrency, and Consistency
- Part IV Database Storage Structures: Physical and Logical
- Part V Instance Architecture: Database, Memory, Process, Networking
- Part VI Database Administration: Concepts for Database Administrators

While the information in this chapter is considered advanced by most DBAs, I consider it essential for understanding Oracle at the very core. This information should reveal to you the importance of restricting all access at the operating system to the database files. It is just too easy to strip the binary components, revealing the actual data without a database username and password. So if someone can get to your data files, backups, exports, or archive logs and they aren't encrypted, you have been compromised.

Instead of just reading this chapter, work through the samples as you go along and also open up the Concepts Documentation Manual to clarify any details you have forgotten or don't really understand. It will solidify these important concepts that are essential to your success as a DBA. After carefully going through the information in this chapter, you will know the direct relationship between the physical components and the logical structures of the database. There will be critical times where you have to make quick decisions to minimize data loss and this information will help you make the best decision.

The use of four different utilities will be covered in this chapter:

- Oracle's RDBMS SQL command `dump block`
- Oracle's RDBMS Log Miner utility
- Flashback Transaction Query and Backout
- Unix `strings` command

Dump block

Dump block gives you the view of the data at the block level, the smallest piece of storage for the data. Working through this chapter allows you to apply concepts of how data moves, block by block, through the physical structures of the database, really solidifying how transaction integrity is maintained. You would only use `dump block` on a **production** system with an Oracle Support Engineer, which is usually done during advanced recovery situations. The `dump block` is often used to determine the level and extent of corruption and what data can be recovered. It can also be used to resolve some tuning and performance issues.

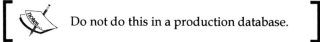 Do not do this in a production database.

Our examination of data blocks starts in *Section 12-6* of the Concepts Manual.

Data block format: *"Every Oracle data block has a format or internal structure that enables the database to track the data and free space in the block. This format is similar whether the data block contains table, index, or table cluster data."* A block is the smallest unit of logical storage that the **Relational Database Management System (RDBMS)** can manipulate. Block size is determined by the database parameter DB_BLOCK_SIZE. The logical storage of data blocks, extents, segments, and table spaces (from smallest to largest) map to the data files, which are stored in operating system blocks.

An undo block will store the undo transaction that is the actual SQL command needed to reverse the original SQL transaction statement. This undo is needed for read consistency for all read-only queries until you commit or rollback that transaction.

Read consistency within a changed block (transaction) is maintained for any of the following commands: `insert`, `update`, `delete`, `merge`, `select for update`, or `lock table`. Any of the previous changes are tracked until the command is issued to either `commit` or `rollback` a particular transaction. This consistency keeps the data view to each user the same, whether they are just doing queries or actually changing any other data.

A point in time or what is called the **System Change Number** (**SCN**) identifies each transaction, and transaction flags show the state of the transaction. The only end user that can see any changed data will be the one making the changes, no matter the application used until they commit that change.

The SCN advances for every change to the database as a sequential counter, which identifies a certain point in time. The SCN tracks more than just single transactions by end users. These transactions will be in **Data Definition Language** (**DDL**) or **Data Manipulation Language** (**DML**). DDL statements are associated with creating objects (`create table`) or what is also called metadata. DML are the other commands mentioned earlier (insert, update, delete, among others) that manipulate the data in some way. The RDBMS advances the SCN if another person logs in, reconnects, or alters their session as well as when Oracle background processes (which constantly check the state of activity inside of the database) take place.

It is undo that gives everyone a point-in-time consistent view of the data, which is called *Read Consistency*. There are controls created from business rules within the application called *triggers* and *integrity constraints* that validate the data entered by the user. Database locks control access to data during changes for exclusive access by the end user changing it.

During a delete or update statement:

- The data block is read, loading it into a memory structure called a buffer cache
- The redo log buffer will contain the corresponding `delete` or `update` statement
- An entry in the undo segment header block is created for this transaction
- It also copies the delete or update row into an undo block
- For a delete, the row is removed from the data block and that block is marked as dirty
- Locks keep exclusive use of that block until a commit or rollback occurs

Dirty is an internal designation where the block is identified as having changed data that has not been written to disk. The RDBMS needs to track this information for transactional integrity and consistency. The underlying dynamic performance view v$bh indicates when a particular block is `dirty`, as seen by the following query:

```
SYS@ORCL11>select file#, block# from v$bh where dirty='Y';
```

When a transaction is committed by the end user:

- The transaction SCN is updated in the data block and the undo segment header marks that statement as committed in the header section of the undo block.

- The logwriter process (LGWR) will flush the log buffer to the appropriate online redo log file.

- SCN is changed on the data block if it is still in the buffer cache (fast commit).

Delayed block cleanout can happen when all of the changed blocks don't have the updated SCN indicating the commit has occurred. This can cause problems with a transaction that is updating large numbers of rows if a rollback needs to occur. Symptoms include hanging onto an exclusive lock until that rollback is finished, and causing end users to wait.

The delayed block cleanout process does occasionally cause problems that would require opening an Oracle Support Request. Delayed block cleanout was implemented to save time by reducing the number of disk reads to update the SCN until the RDBMS needs to access data from that same block again. If the changed block has already been written to the physical disk and the Oracle background process encounters this same block (for any other query, DML, or DDL), it will also record the committed change at the same time. It does this by checking the transaction entry by SCN in the undo header, which indicates the changes that have been committed. That transaction entry is located in the transaction table, which keeps track of all active transactions for that undo segment.

Each transaction is uniquely identified by the assignment of a transaction ID (XID), which is found in the v$transaction view. This XID is written in the undo header block along with the Undo Byte Address (Uba), which consists of the file and block numbers UBAFIL data file and UBABLK data block, and columns found in the v$transaction view, respectively.

Please take the time to go through the following demonstration; it will solidify the complex concepts in this chapter.

Demonstration of data travel path

Dumping a block is one of the methods to show how data is stored. It will show the actual contents of the block, whether it is a Table or Index Block, and an actual address that includes the data file number and block number. Remember from the concepts manual that several blocks together make up an extent, and extents then make up segments. A single segment maps to a particular table or index. It is easy to see from the following simplified diagram how different extents can be stored in different physical locations in different data files but the same logical tablespace:

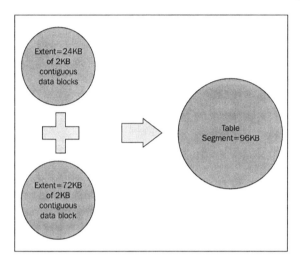

The data in the test case comes from creating a small table (segment) with minimum data in a tablespace with a single data file created just for this demonstration. **Automatic Segment Space Management (ASSM)** is the default in 11g. If you create a tablespace in 11g with none of the optional storage parameters, the RDBMS by default creates an ASSM segment with locally managed autoallocated extents.

It is possible to define the size of the extents at tablespace creation time that depends on the type of data to be stored. If all of the data is uniform and you need to maintain strict control over the amount of space used, then uniform extents are desirable.

Allowing the RDBMS to autoallocate extents is typical in situations where the data is not the same size for each extent, reducing the amount of time spent in allocating and maintaining space for database segments. Discussing the details, options, and differences for all of the ways to manage segment space in Oracle Database 11g is beyond the scope of this book.

For this example, we will be using race car track information as the sample data. For this demonstration, you will create a specific user with the minimum amount of privileges needed to complete this exercise; SQL is provided for that step in the script.

There are several key files in the zipped code for this chapter that you will need for this exercise, listed as follows:

- `dumpblock_sys.sql`
- `dumpblock_ttracker.sql`
- `dumpblocksys.lst`
- `dumpblockttracker.lst`
- `NEWDB_ora_8582_SYSDUMP1.rtf`
- `NEWDB_ora_8582_SYSDUMP1.txt`
- `NEWDB_ora_8621_SYSDUMP2.rtf`
- `NEWDB_ora_8621_SYSDUMP2.txt`
- `NEWDB_ora_8628_SYSDUMP3.rtf`
- `NEWDB_ora_8628_SYSDUMP3.txt`
- `NEWDB_ora_8635_SYSDUMP4.rtf`
- `NEWDB_ora_8635_SYSDUMP4.txt`

You will also need access to a conversion calculator to translate the hexadecimal to a number that is the first listing below—use hexadecimal input and decimal output. The second will allow you to look up Hex (Hexadecimal) equivalents for characters.

`http://calculators.mathwarehouse.com/binary-hexadecimal-calculator.php#hexadecimalBinaryCalculator`

`http://www.asciitable.com/`

Location of trace files

The dump block statement will create a trace file in the user dump (`udump`) directory on any version prior to 11gR1, which can be viewed by a text editor. Using 11gR1 and above, you will find it in the `diag` directory location. This example will demonstrate how to use the `adrci` command-line utility to view trace files. First we set the home path where the utility will find the files, then search with the most recent listed first—in this case, it is the `NEWDB_ora_9980.trc` file.

```
adrci> set homepath diag/rdbms/newdb/NEWDB
adrci> show tracefile -RT
   11-MAR-10 10:01:19   diag/rdbms/newdb/NEWDB/trace/NEWDB_ora_9980.trc
   11-MAR-10 10:00:46   diag/rdbms/newdb/NEWDB/trace/NEWDB_m001_28667.trc
   12-JAN-10 12:58:08   diag/rdbms/newdb/NEWDB/trace/alert_NEWDB.log
   12-JAN-10 12:58:05   diag/rdbms/newdb/NEWDB/trace/drcNEWDB.log
adrci>
```

Now that you know the location for the trace files, how do you determine which trace file was produced? The naming convention for trace files includes the actual process number associated with that session. Use the following command to produce trace files with a specific name, making it easier to identify a separate task:

```
SYS@NEWDB>ALTER SESSION SET TRACEFILE_IDENTIFIER = SYSDUMP_SESSION;
```

The topic of generating and formatting trace files will be covered again when we get to the *Chapter 8, 11g Tuning Tools*.

Running dump block SQL statements

Let's run through the test case demonstrating how transaction data moves from one component to the next. The first script dumpblock_sys.sql creates the tablespace and a user called TTRACKER with the minimum database privileges needed to perform this exercise. Please edit the script dumpblock_sys.sql to change the location of your data file in the test database. You could also leave it blank if the startup initialization database parameter db_create_file_dest is populated with a valid operating system location that Oracle has read and writes privileges to. Then, the database would create the data files in the db_create_file_dest and assign a system-generated name to them.

In this dump block exercise, you are going to need two different SQL*PLUS windows or sessions. You start by logging into the database as someone with sysdba privileges, which is usually the user sys on a small test database. In a production database, more often sysdba privileges are assigned to a DBA account, which can be more accurately tracked for auditing purposes. The SYS account is only used in this scenario to create the TTRACKER user and dump some of the blocks.

Run the dumpblock_sys.sql script first logged in as SYS, it will create the tablespace and table. Then pause and you'll see the following screenshots for the output:

```
SYS@NEWDB>@dumpblock_sys.sql
```

After the pause, log on as `ttracker` in the second window, as shown by the output below, and run the second script:

```
TTRACKER@NEWDB>@dumpblock_ttracker.sql
```

```
Session altered.

Table created.

1 row created.

FILENUMBER BLOCKNUMBER
---------- -----------
         8         135

CURRENT_SCN
-----------
    1583039

PROCESS
-----------------------------
8576
```

The second script will pause at a point and request that you run the first script again, but the first script needs some information from the `ttracker` session — the data file number and block number, in this example **8** and **135**. Your data file and block numbers will be different from any provided in the sample code. Return to the first window (sys), put in the correct numbers and press the *Enter* key until it says to CONTINUE DUMPBLOCK_TTRACKER.SQL IN PREVIOUS SESSION.

```
User altered.

CURRENT_SCN
-----------
    1583007

PROCESS
-----------------------------
8578

no rows selected

'IDENTIFYTHEFILENUMBERANDBLOCKNUMBERFROMTHETTRACKERSESSION'
-------------------------------------------------------------------------
Identify the file number and block number from the TTRACKER session

Enter value for dfnumber: 8
Enter value for bknumber: 135
```

When it pauses, return to the second window (`ttracker`) and hit the *Enter* key. There will be another pause where a request for the undo file number and undo block number is found by the `select` statement just above it on the SQL*PLUS command line. Go back and forth between the different windows at each pause until both scripts are done.

```
UNDOFILENUMBER UNDOBLOCKNUMBER UNDOSEQUENCE STATUS              NOU
-------------- --------------- ------------ ------------------- ---
TRANSACTIONID      START_SCN
---------------- ----------
             3             230          349 ACTIVE              NO
070002000C040000    1583038


CONTINUE DUMPBLOCK_SYS.SQL IN PREVIOUS SESSION and press RETURN WHEN FINISHED.


Commit complete.


CURRENT_SCN
-----------
    1583045


no rows selected

CONTINUE DUMPBLOCK_SYS.SQL IN PREVIOUS SESSION and press RETURN WHEN FINISHED.
```

What is happening is that you are dumping blocks with the `sys` login and manipulating data with the `ttracker` login (that is, `insert`, `update`, `commit`). At the same time, you are looking at how the SCN advances through the different transaction steps as well as matching the transaction with the corresponding undo SQL statement in the undo segment. We could have done this entire demonstration with a single logon, but I wanted you to visualize the read consistency view of a transaction.

What you should have when the script is finished is something similar to the following list in the trace directory. What will be different for your environment is the session number and ORACLE_SID. Notice that there are `rtf` versions of the following text files in the code section for this book, which are the highlighted sections mentioned in this chapter:

- `NEWDB_ora_8582_SYSDUMP1.rtf`
- `NEWDB_ora_8621_SYSDUMP2.rtf`
- `NEWDB_ora_8628_SYSDUMP3.rtf`
- `NEWDB_ora_8635_SYSDUMP4.rtf`

You should also have a couple of lst files in the directory you executed SQL*PLUS from, to review in case of an error. I have provided the same lst files from my session for you to review as well:

```
dumpblocksys.lst
dumpblockttracker.lst
```

If you choose to rerun these scripts on the same database, you will get an error on the create sections if you do not drop the user ttracker, tablespace, and the table named tracks. The easiest way to drop both the tablespace and table is:

```
sys@NEWDB> drop tablespace track including contents and datafiles;
```

and then follow this by dropping the user ttracker:

```
sys@NEWDB> drop user ttracker;
```

Identifying files and blocks

There is more than one way to identify the file number and block number of a particular segment. One way is with the dbms_rowid package. The Oracle-supplied package dbms_rowid will show the absolute block number and relative file number of a table extent. That information comes from both the data file header and the block header.

```
sys@NEWDB> select dbms_rowid.rowid_relative_fno(rowid) as filenumber,
    dbms_rowid.rowid_block_number(rowid) as blocknumber
    from tracks;
```

The next query will search for the data file where those segments or extents are stored. A tablespace is only a logical structure that actually maps to the data file. It is important to understand that only certain objects (extents) are mapped to a physical data file.

```
sys@NEWDB> select d.file_name, e.segment_name,  d.tablespace_name from
dba_data_files d, dba_extents e
  where d.tablespace_name=e.tablespace_name  and owner ='TTRACKER';
```

And finally, the following query will verify the file number for the tablespace TRACK data file. We are interested in manipulating the data in the TRACKS table only, which in this test database is file number 8 and block number 135. 135 is actually the starting block number for this table segment.

```
sys@NEWDB>select name, file# from v$datafile;
```

Each time you use the `dump block` command, it will create a trace file in order to track a single transaction across the database structures. This trace contains the following information that we are interested in for this demonstration:

- Contents of the block for a certain file number and block number
- List of the actual rows
- SCN of a particular block
- Transaction ID for a data block and the corresponding undo block
- Any locks being held for that transaction
- Flags indicating the state of the transaction
- Read Consistency, Fast Commit, and Delayed Block Cleanout behavior

The `dump block` command can be used in several different ways to extract information. See the following for a few examples as they apply in this test case:

```
sys@NEWDB> alter system dump datafile '/u01/oradata/NEWDB/track01_
NEWDB.dbf' block 135; -- one block at a time
sys@NEWDB> alter system dump datafile 8 block 135; -- one block at a
time
sys@NEWDB> alter system dump datafile 8 block min 135 block max 142;
--this dumps multiple blocks
```

There is much more information in these trace files than what we can cover in this book. For more information look for reference materials that refer to *Oracle Internals*. Refer to the following legend for the trace files.

Legend for Trace Files:
- Xid—Transaction ID
- Uba—Undo Byte Address
- Flag—Transaction flag
  - ° C--- Committed,
  - ° ---- Uncommitted
  - ° --U- Fast commit, delayed block cleanout has not happened
- Lck—Number of Rows locked
- Scn—System Change Number

 Not all of the transaction flags have been listed here and further research may be required.

Tracking the SCN through trace files

We will be going through four different trace files showing the transaction state at different points. It will be easier to switch from one to the other if you go ahead and open each one in its own window. Start with the output file called `dumpblocksys.lst` as that contains the starting database SCN number. That comes from the following query:

```
SYS@NEWDB>SELECT CURRENT_SCN FROM V$DATABASE;
```

The database SCN will always be ahead of a transaction SCN because the transaction event has already occurred. The transaction SCN is recorded in the accompanying trace file, while the database SCN is recorded in the `lst` output files.

Farther down in the file `dumpblocksys.lst`, there are no active transactions as shown by `no rows` returned when selecting from `v$transaction` the first time. At the first pause is the point where `ttracker` starts modifying the table, allowing us to actively track that transaction by dumping the block.

In the next section, different transaction types will be covered, actively demonstrating what is known as Oracle Internals, the undocumented internal structure of Oracle data.

Single Row Insert

Open up the first trace file called `NEWDB_ora_8582_SYSDUMP1_SESSION.rtf`, as this contains additional comments. The text version of this file (`trc`) is provided and contains the original trace data with any identifying or sensitive information removed. Note this transaction SCN number, which is then linked to the data from the `insert` statement as follows:

```
INSERT INTO TRACKS VALUES (1, 'ATLANTA'); --from dumpblock_ttracker.
sql
```

The hexadecimal number is converted to decimal format by using the calculator mentioned earlier.

SCN of block insert statement = hex scn: 0x0000.**001827be** = 1,583,038

Switch to the `dumpblockttracker.lst` output file. Note that the database `scn` has advanced past the original starting database value and past the first transaction `scn` (to `1583039`) due to the changes made; the tracks table was created and a single row has been inserted.

Switching back to the file NEWDB_ora_8582_SYSDUMP1_SESSION.rtf, farther down the Flag there are dash marks with a 1 in the Lck column. By referring back to the legend earlier in this chapter, this indicates that the transaction state is uncommitted and there is a single lock. This single lock is important, as the ttracker user can exclusively use this data block until a commit or rollback statement is issued.

```
Itl          Xid                 Uba            Flag  Lck
0x01   0x0007.002.0000040c  0x00c000e6.015d.04  ----   1
0x02   0x0000.000.00000000  0x00000000.0000.00  ----   0
```

Notice the Uba (Undo Byte Address) that ties this transaction to the matching SQL undo statement in an undo segment should the end user need to rollback this transaction. Also notice the Itl heading in the above list that stands for Interested Transaction List, which consists of all transactions currently active for that block. In this case, there is only the current single transaction.

The Xid found in NEWDB_ora_8582_SYSDUMP1_SESSION.rtf should match the query from the v$transaction table, as seen in the dumpblockttracker.lst file. The start_scn also matches the SCN found in the trace file NEWDB_ora_8582_SYSDUMP1_SESSION.rtf. Labeling the columns clearly specifies what each one represents. If the column labeled NOUNDO equals YES, then there would be no undo available. See the query as follows:

```
SYS@NEWDB>SELECT UBAFIL AS UNDOFILENUMBER,UBABLK AS UNDOBLOCKNUMBER,ST
ATUS,NOUNDO,XID AS TRANSACTIONID,START_SCN FROM V$TRANSACTION;
```

Farther down in the trace file is the section that contains the actual data. Look for the key words block row dump. The data found in the trackname column is in hexadecimal format, which is converted by referring to http://www.asciitable.com. Look up the Hex (hexadecimal) to find the Char (character) equivalent.

```
block_row_dump:
tab 0, row 0, @0x1f8a
tl: 14 fb: --H-FL-- lb: 0x1  cc: 2
col  0: [ 2]  c1 02
col  1: [ 7]   41 54 4c 41 4e 54 41   = A T L A N T A
```

Commit of a single row insert

What happens when we finally issue a commit statement? Looking at the NEWDB_ora_8621_SYSDUMP2_SESSION.rtf file, there are several items of interest. Notice the advancement of the SCN after the commit statement was issued from the previous insert statement:

```
scn: 0x0000.001827c3  --001827c3 = 1,583,043
```

The flag shown below is now showing as committed by *fast commit process*, which causes *delayed block cleanout* until this block is visited by another query, DDL, or DML statement.

Also see that the Uba is the same address as before the commit statement in the previous section (above), as excerpted from NEWDB_ora_8582_SYSDUMP1_SESSION.rtf:

```
Itl      Xid                    Uba                   Flag   Lck
0x01   0x0007.002.0000040c   0x00c000e6.015d.04   --U-   1
0x02   0x0000.000.00000000   0x00000000.0000.00   ----   0
```

The fast commit process is fast because it makes the minimal changes needed to indicate that a commit has occurred. This leaves the lock (see the Lck Flag of 1) even after the commit has finished! Delayed block cleanout happens when the next operation visits this block and refers back to the transaction table to find the details for finishing the cleanup process.

Single row update and corresponding undo block

Continuing with the demonstration, we are modifying the existing Atlanta entry in the tracks table to Daytona by issuing an update statement. In this case, we are dumping both the data block and the undo block in order to compare information across those two database structures. Taken from dumpblocksys.lst, the following information tells us several things.

The sys user only sees the previous data of Atlanta showing read consistency for everyone else; that information is coming from the undo segments. Ttracker sees the entry as Daytona, which has a lock (exclusive view) on the changed data. The select statement below returns the row ATLANTA:

```
SYS@NEWDB>SELECT * FROM TTRACKER.TRACKS;
```

There is an active transaction that shows how the undo file number, and undo block number can be determined. Just as we need the file number and block number of a table segment to explore the internals, we will need the file number and block number of the undo segment.

```
SYS@NEWDB>SELECT UBAFIL AS UNDOFILENUMBER,UBABLK AS UNDOBLOCKNUMBER,ST
ATUS,NOUNDO,XID AS TRANSACTIONID,START_SCN FROM V$TRANSACTION;
```

The SCN for this update statement is located in the file NEWDB_ora_8628_SYSDUMP3.rtf.

```
scn: 0x0000.001827cb        -- 001827cb = 1,583,051
```

Now that we have accessed the same block by issuing an update, the flag now shows as committed in the corresponding trace file. Also notice the lock (Lck) has been removed:

```
Itl             Xid              Uba            Flag   Lck
0x01    0x0007.002.0000040c  0x00c000e6.015d.04  C---    0
0x02    0x0000.000.00000000  0x00000000.0000.00  ----    0

col  0: [ 2]  c1 02
col  1: [ 7]  44 41 59 54 4f 4e 41  = D A Y T O N A
```

Comments in the file NEWDB_ora_8628_SYSDUMP3.rtf indicate where the data block dump stops and the undo block dump starts. Farther down in the same file, find the data section labeled as follows. This undo block dump contains the entry for Atlanta. Now, if the end user (ttracker in this case) rolled back the Daytona update, then the ATLANTA row would be restored as shown in the undo block dump:

```
col  1: [ 7]  41 54 4c 41 4e 54 41 = ATLANTA

frmt: 0x02 chkval: 0xa058 type: 0x02=KTU UNDO BLOCK
```

Let's continue with the demonstration to show the internal changes when the commit of an updated row in the tracks table occurs.

Commit of a single row update

The associated SCN for this transaction is listed in the trace file and converted as follows:

```
scn: 0x0000.001827d1     --  001827d1 = 1,583,057
```

Note that both transactions in the Itl are listed for this data block: first the commit and then the following update statement. Each statement is uniquely identified by its respective Uba and SCN. Just as before in *Commit of a single row insert*, the flag U indicates delayed block cleanout until this block is accessed again, and the lock is still at least partially present.

```
Itl             Xid              Uba            Flag   Lck      Scn/Fsc
0x01    0x0007.002.0000040c  0x00c000e6.015d.04  C---    0   scn
0x0000.001827c3
0x02    0x0008.010.000004cf  0x00c0056a.0112.14  --U-    1   fsc
0x0000.001827d1

col  0: [ 2]  c1 02
col  1: [ 7]  44 41 59 54 4f 4e 41 = D A Y T O N A
```

There is usually more than one way to accomplish a task, such as converting hexadecimal information to a readable character string. Earlier, this conversion task was outlined with reference to an online hex to ASCII calculator to do the work for you. There is an Oracle supplied package called `utl_raw` that can also do the same conversion with the word DAYTONA returned, as follows:

```
TTRACKER@NEWDB> SELECT utl_raw.cast_to_varchar2(HEXTORAW('444159544f4e
41')) FROM dual;
```

The last database SCN recorded in this exercise from the `dumpblocksys.lst` file is `1583062`.

We have traveled the SCN, changing from the initial value of 1583007 to the end value mentioned above as 1583062. By altering a small amount of data and looking at the associated changes within the trace files, we can clearly demonstrate database read consistency, locking mechanisms, and delayed block cleanout. While the concepts manual is a good place to start, a DBA needs to be able to prove what they have read (or heard) with an actual test case. The next section continues with other means of evaluating transactions within the database, for different reasons and with different utilities.

After accomplishing this task successfully, you should be more comfortable with the internal structures of the database. More advanced scenarios would be to work with more data, add indexes (index segments can be dumped), or multiple schemas. If this type of work really intrigues you, start asking around at conferences. There are lots of people that are used to working with Oracle at the block level. Truly geeky!

 Take this exercise a step further and create a database package to make dump blocks more readable. See: `http://dioncho.wordpress.com/2009/07/14/decoding-block-dump-using-utl_raw/`.

Oracle's RDBMS Log Miner utility

Log Miner can help when questions such as the following come up: What was changed? Who changed it? And in what order?

When unauthorized people change data, they may assume that the record does not retain all changes if that information isn't viewable at the application level. There is a record of all changes that are logged, but it takes time and trouble to find that information.

The tool most often used is the PL/SQL package DBMS_LOGMNR, but the GUI Interface called Log Miner Viewer has been added to the OEM. There are quite a few examples in the *Oracle Database Utilities Guide* of how to use this utility for both the browser-based and PL/SQL versions. We will concentrate on when and how to find the data to restore.

You already should have a good understanding of the database structures that include the undo and redo logs: undo is generated when an end user starts changing data and redo is generated after the commit. Each is written to their own set of files. While undo and redo are both online (database is open), archived redo is offline and written to a disk.

Archived redo logs are no longer needed for the transactions inside the database because they have been committed and written to disk. Archive logs are still important in order to restore the previously committed transactions in a recovery situation. Making an archive log offline allows backup procedures (RMAN, third-party backup software or OS utilities) to manipulate the files at the operating system level.

Recovery is a database process that will:

- Roll forward changes from redo logs and then rollback statements any end user used the rollback command for.
- Roll back any uncommitted changes found in the UNDO segments.

Look at *Chapter 6, Extended RMAN* for more information on how undo and redo is involved with transactional consistency for backups and recovery scenarios.

There are specific Oracle processes such as LGWR that write the redo to the online logs and then an archiver process (ARC) writes to the archived logs. The only way to ensure every transaction in a database has been logged for recovery purposes is to operate in ARCHIVELOG mode. There are special situations that will call for running in noarchivelog mode. It is assumed that any transactions lost between backups can be recreated. Archived redo logs can be used to restore transactions that occurred between regular backups. From the last exercise, you also have a good understanding of read consistency available from undo segments, which also contribute to redo entries.

The DBMS_LOGMNR package is used to find data in both the undo and redo database structures. It is also useful for analyzing patterns over time for specific tuning needs, schema changes, and forecasting the time for hardware upgrades. With the DBMS_LOGMNR package, you can extract data that populates the V$LOGMNR_CONTENTS view with the actual transactions that have been executed. These entries contain both the REDO and UNDO statements.

You can operate Log Miner on the original database that created the log entries or almost any other Oracle database of a higher version that is running the same character set, database block size, and operating system. This is why it is critical that you protect the online redo, undo, and archive logs—they can be mined for information. Most often a DBA will actually use a different database to do the mining so that it doesn't consume additional resources in a production database. If you use a different database than where the original transactions were created, you will have to rebuild the Log Miner data dictionary (online, offline, or a standalone flat file). The dictionary translates the internal object identifiers and types to table and column names that can be queried, but those object IDs will vary between databases, making the rebuild a requirement.

The Log Miner example task requires several preparatory steps to be completed first, with some additional discussion along the way. Discussion includes archiving, supplemental logging, and Flashback technologies. You won't get to an actual logminer example for quite a few pages. Since logminer has extensive documentation detailing all of the steps for various scenarios, it was decided to only include a lesser known method of using logminer in this book called Flashback Transaction Backout.

Turn on archivelog mode

Before we delve into the mining exercise, we will cover more information about SCNs, as they relate to checkpoints and log switches while turning on archiving for the database. Transactions in a database produce redo entries in the redo log buffer (in memory), but that is always being written to the online redo logs. That occurs according to different triggering events that can happen in the redo stream—a certain amount of data, commits, 3 seconds or 1/3 full redo log buffer. Whether these triggering events occur or not depends on the type and frequency of transactions.

A checkpoint synchronizes modified data blocks in the redo log buffer with the actual data files, keeping the data consistent. In the case of a database crash, this identifies the point where all outstanding data (transactions) have been written to disk. This checkpoint isn't synchronized with the SCN of a transaction commit and it does not behave like a log switch.

The files you will need as you work through this exercise are included in the code for this chapter as follows:

```
sys_archive.sql
sysarchive.lst
```

Open up the file `sysarchive.lst`. One of the most important views (anything labeled `v$` is called a dynamic view) in the database is `v$database`.

```
SYS@NEWDB> SELECT LOG_MODE, NAME, CURRENT_SCN, ARCHIVE_CHANGE#, OPEN_
MODE FROM V$DATABASE;
```

Find this section for the statement from `v$log_history` farther down in `sysarchive.lst`. What are all these entries if we aren't in `archivelog` mode? These are the log switches to the online redo logs. They are overwritten once that section of the redo log is no longer needed by a transaction to maintain consistency. This is where a checkpoint comes into play. It ensures that data is written to the disk and is independent of the ARC log switch process.

Once we switch to `archivelog` mode, the online redo will still be overwritten, but the ARC process will write a copy of that log to an archive destination. Below you will see that each log contains a range of database SCNs. This log contains database changes from the first SCN number to the next.

```
SYS@NEWDB>select first_change#, next_change# from v$log_history;
     3068574        3085227
     3085227        3085719
     3085719        3086405
     3086405        3088086
```

We have already covered what the `current_scn` means in the first section of this chapter, as it relates to transactions. Now we try to correlate `archive_change#` and `checkpoint_change#`. Also notice that the `checkpoint_change#` for each data file is consistent for normal database operations. I am showing only the partial output from the following command for the single data file created earlier in the chapter:

```
SYS@NEWDB> SELECT SUBSTR(NAME,1,50), CHECKPOINT_CHANGE# FROM V$DATAFILE_HEADER;

/u01/oradata/NEWDB/track_NEWDB.dbf 3087834
```

At this point, we have started the database in mount mode (the controlfile needs to be accessed, but the database is not opened for full use), turned on the archiving process, and verified that archiving has started and also verified the location of the archived logs. Making a log switch from one online redo to another doesn't sync the `checkpoint_change#` with what the controlfile has (`controlfile_change#` is what is also called a thread checkpoint).

```
SYS@NEWDB>SELECT CHECKPOINT_CHANGE#,CONTROLFILE_CHANGE# FROM V$DATABASE;

CHECKPOINT_CHANGE# CONTROLFILE_CHANGE#
------------------ -------------------
           3087837             3088086
```

Only when we do a manual checkpoint (instead of a database-activated checkpoint) do those numbers coincide. They can be verified with the dynamic view `v$datafile` as shown below:

```
SYS@NEWDB>ALTER SYSTEM CHECKPOINT;

System altered.

SYS@NEWDB>SELECT CHECKPOINT_CHANGE#, CONTROLFILE_CHANGE# FROM V$DATABASE;

CHECKPOINT_CHANGE# CONTROLFILE_CHANGE#
------------------ -------------------
           3088142             3088142

SYS@NEWDB>SELECT TO_CHAR(CHECKPOINT_TIME,'DD-MON-YY HH24:MI:SS'),CHECKPOINT_CHAN
GE# FROM V$DATAFILE;

TO_CHAR(CHECKPOINT_TIME,'DD CHECKPOINT_CHANGE#
-------------------------- -------------------
19-nov-09 09:42:22                     3088142
19-nov-09 09:42:22                     3088142
```

Additional information for troubleshooting archiving issues comes from another dynamic view, V$INSTANCE:

```
SYS@NEWDB> SELECT INSTANCE_NAME, ARCHIVER, LOG_SWITCH_WAIT FROM V$INSTANCE;

INSTANCE_NAME    ARCHIVER LOG_SWITCH_WAIT
---------------- -------- ---------------
NEWDB            STARTED
```

The `archiver` column can also indicate when the ARC process failed to switch logs with an automatic retry in another five minutes. The `log_switch_wait` will indicate the wait event the log switching process is waiting on—ARCHIVE LOG, CLEAR LOG, or CHECKPOINT.

All of the activity associated with log switches and checkpoints will influence database performance (which will be taken up in the last chapter of this book). We shall continue now with the further required setup steps to complete all of the tasks in this chapter.

Add supplemental logging

All undo and redo buffer entries are logged along with archiving redo log entries to disk. When would additional supplemental type logging be required? There are additional details needed that are not ordinarily included with undo or redo entries. The additional details make the transactions usable (identify the rows in the redo logs) by Log Miner. These are added to the redo stream by the following commands:

```
ALTER DATABASE ADD SUPPLEMENTAL LOG DATA; -- minimal
ALTER DATABASE ADD SUPPLEMENTAL LOG DATA (ALL, PRIMARY KEY, UNIQUE,
FOREIGN KEY) COLUMNS;  --Identification key logging
```

Identification key logging

Both the before and after images of the specified type of columns are captured in the redo log files. Both the **Foreign Key (FK)** logging and of course ALL would be very resource intensive, depending on the number of FK constraints involved with the transaction(s).

```
SYS@NEWDB> SELECT
  SUPPLEMENTAL_LOG_DATA_MIN MIN_LOG,
  SUPPLEMENTAL_LOG_DATA_PK PK_LOG,
  SUPPLEMENTAL_LOG_DATA_UI UI_LOG,
  SUPPLEMENTAL_LOG_DATA_FK FK_LOG,
  SUPPLEMENTAL_LOG_DATA_ALL ALL_LOG,
  FORCE_LOGGING FORCE_LOG
  from v$database;

MIN_LOG  PK_LOG  UI_LOG  FK_LOG  ALL_LOG  FORCE_LOG
-------  ------  ------  ------  -------  ---------
YES      YES     YES     YES     YES      NO
```

Table-level supplemental logging

Unconditional or Conditional Logging is tracked through log groups: Unconditional tracking would capture the before and after column images no matter what. Conditional tracking captures the before image only when the columns are updated; it always captures the after images. Table level logging would be involved with streams replication scenarios.

```
ALTER TABLE TABLENAME ADD SUPPLEMENTAL LOG DATA (PRIMARY
KEY,UNIQUE,FOREIGN,ALL) columns;
```

The following query can be used to check the table level log groups defined in the database:

```
SYS@NEWDB>  select * from DBA_LOG_GROUPS;
```

Since logging can be resource intensive, DBAs will need to turn it back off after certain tasks are finished. Turning off logging is done by stepping backwards, dropping the most restrictive logging first (key related), and then the generalized drop supplemental commands as shown below:

```
SYS@NEWDB> alter database drop  SUPPLEMENTAL LOG DATA (PRIMARY KEY,
UNIQUE INDEX, FOREIGN KEY, ALL) COLUMNS;
SYS@NEWDB> ALTER DATABASE DROP SUPPLEMENTAL LOG DATA;
```

Flash(back) Recovery Area (FRA)

You will see the FRA referred to as either the Flash Recovery Area (newer form) versus the older version called Flashback Recovery Area. They are the same thing, though Oracle decided to shift the emphasis so that the FRA should be used for all files associated with backup and recovery and not just Flashback logs.

If a mandatory archivelog destination becomes full at the disk level, it can cause the database to hang, as there is no room to write the archived log. FRA as an archivelog or flashback log destination can hang if you fail to accurately predict the amount of space needed to implement it. There are several recommendations from Oracle as what to store in this area, because it is primarily meant for backup and recovery files:

- Current control file
- Online redo logs
- Archived redo logs
- Control file autobackups
- Data file and control file copies
- Backup pieces
- Foreign archived redo log (logical standby database in continuous Log Miner mode. See MAA, Chapter 4)

Space issues with the type of files in the list above are mostly easily regulated by a competent RMAN backup policy. If you decide to implement the Flashback Database Feature, which requires Flashback logs, then running out of space due to a miscalculation or even a runaway process is a definite possibility. The number of logs produced is regulated by the `startup database initialization` parameter `DB_FLASHBACK_RETENTION_TARGET`. It is recommended that you start with an FRA at least three times the size of the database.

The MOS document "What is a Flash Recovery Area and how to configure it?" (Doc ID 305648.1) has a formula for estimating the size specific to your environment, as well as actively monitoring changes in the following query:

```
SYS@NEWDB> SELECT ESTIMATED_FLASHBACK_SIZE FROM V$FLASHBACK_DATABASE_
LOG;
```

Normal database processes ensure that the flashback recovery area is kept within certain space limits by deleting the logs under space pressure in two different situations:

- When archive logs are deleted, the associated flashback logs are removed

- When the startup initialization parameter `DB_RECOVERY_FILE_DEST_SIZE` is shrunk, the logs will be removed as needed

Several different steps can be used to resolve database hanging when it runs out of physical space in the FRA:

- Temporarily increase the size (`DB_RECOVERY_FILE_DEST_SIZE`).
- Relocate it to a different directory (`DB_RECOVERY_FILE_DEST`) with more room.
- Turn it off completely. Turning it off will require a database restart disconnecting all users.

We will return to investigate this feature. In the next section, flashback will be turned off in order to demonstrate finding data in undo segments. This is just meant to illustrate that the data is coming from the undo segments and not by any enabled Flashback technology. Several of the features have the word Flashback as part of their name but use undo data to perform the actual work.

Automatic Undo Management (AUM)

If you have installed an 11g database for this exercise, then AUM is the default method of Undo Management. With earlier versions of Oracle, Manual Undo Management was the only method available. DBAs needed to be good at the balancing act of managing rollback segments for different tasks in the database—batch jobs, data loads, smaller online transactions, and so on.

Identifying data in undo segments by flashing back to timestamp

There is a small trick in identifying data that may still exist in the undo segments. This won't work if the undo has already been overwritten, so it is best used when you are alerted to the mistake quickly. I have eliminated the possibility of flashback technology being involved by disabling it with the following commands (flashback is not required for this exercise):

```
SYS@NEWDB> SHUTDOWN IMMEDIATE;
SYS@NEWDB> STARTUP MOUNT;
SYS@NEWDB> ALTER DATABASE FLASHBACK OFF;
SYS@NEWDB> ALTER DATABASE OPEN;
SYS@NEWDB> show parameter recovery
```

1. Connect as a TTRACKER user, verify the existing data (you should get two rows—DAYTONA and Memphis), and update the tracks table but don't commit.

   ```
   TTRACKER@NEWDB> select * from ttracker.tracks;


   TTRACKER@NEWDB>  update tracks set trackname='Dallas' where
    trackname ='Memphis';
   ```

2. Any other session with the appropriate privileges can query the past, but only TTRACKER can see the changed (non-committed) data. Choose six minutes because internally Oracle stores the SCN value every five minutes, so rounding may occur if you use less than five minutes. The following queries will select data from the current time and six minutes ago. In this case study, there should be a difference in the data seen.

   ```
   TTRACKER@NEWDB> select * from ttracker.tracks;
   TTRACKER@NEWDB> select * from ttracker.tracks as of timestamp
   systimestamp - interval '6' minute ; --6 minutes ago
   ```

3. Now using a different window, connect as `sysdba` and `select` using timestamp query syntax. The output demonstrates read consistency again because `SYS` can only see the `DAYTONA` and `Memphis` entries. But you have already seen read consistency demonstrated from the first exercise in this chapter.

```
SYS@NEWDB>SELECT * FROM TTRACKER.TRACKS AS OF TIMESTAMP
SYSTIMESTAMP - INTERVAL '1' MINUTE; --1 minute ago
```

4. Switch back to the `TTRACKER` session and commit the transaction.

```
TTRACKER@NEWDB> COMMIT;
```

5. Now switch back to the `sysdba` session. Query the current data found in the tracks table (`DAYTONA` and `Dallas` should be returned) as well as the previous data. Six minutes ago the data would be `DAYTONA` and `Memphis`.

```
SYS@NEWDB> select * from ttracker.tracks;

SYS@NEWDB>SELECT * FROM TTRACKER.TRACKS AS OF TIMESTAMP
SYSTIMESTAMP - INTERVAL '6' MINUTE; --6 minutes ago
```

This method can also restore an object such as a package or procedure by querying the table `dba_source` in order to retrieve the version from an earlier time. Spool the output, edit as needed, and run as a SQL statement to restore. See the following example:

```
SYS@NEWDB> SELECT TEXT FROM DBA_SOURCE AS OF TIMESTAMP SYSTIMESTAMP
- INTERVAL '6 MINUTE WHERE NAME ='PACKAGENAME' ORDER BY LINE;
```

All queries done with the syntax (`SELECT AS OF`) are considered flashback queries, even though it is accomplished with the undo segments. Oracle has marketed everything with a step back in time as *Flashback*, but there are really several different major technologies involved, depending on the task. Here is a list of the flashback technologies and the underlying technology involved:

- Flashback Drop—Recycle Bin
- Flashback Database—Flashback Logs and RMAN
- Flashback Transaction Query—Flashback Logs
- Flashback Queries—Undo Segments
- Flashback Table—Rowid Changes and Undo Segments
- Flashback Transaction Backout—Log Miner and Flashback Logs

Flashback Query does not work through DDL operations that modify columns, or drop or truncate tables, and it will not work through a database restart.

We will take this a step further later on in the chapter and reverse more complex data sets that are linked by a single transaction ID (Xid); this requires flashback to be turned on. This is known as Flashback Transaction Query. You could extend this case study by dumping the actual undo block involved in the transaction to verify the data as you did in the first dump block exercise.

When to use Log Miner

Log Miner has both a GUI interface in OEM as well as the database package, DBMS_LOGMNR. When this utility is used by the DBA, its primary focus is to mine data from the online and archived redo logs. Internally Oracle uses the Log Miner technology for several other features, such as Flashback Transaction Backout, Streams, and Logical Standby Databases. This section is not on how to run Log Miner, but looks at the task of identifying the information to restore.

The Log Miner utility comes into play when you need to retrieve an older version of selected pieces of data without completely recovering the entire database. A complete recovery is usually a drastic measure that means downtime for all users and the possibility of lost transactions. Most often Log Miner is used for recovery purposes when the data consists of just a few tables or a single code change. Other purposes for Log Miner will be touched upon in the Tuning chapter.

Make sure supplemental logging is turned on (see the *Add Supplemental Logging* section). In this case, you discover that one or more of the following conditions apply when trying to recover a small amount of data that was recently changed:

- Flashback is not enabled
- Flashback logs that are needed are no longer available
- Data that is needed is not available in the online redo logs
- Data that is needed has been overwritten in the undo segments

Go to the last place available: archived redo logs. This requires the database to be in archivelog mode and for all archive logs that are needed to still be available or recoverable.

Identifying the data needed to restore

One of the hardest parts of restoring data is determining what to restore, the basic question being *when did the bad data become part of the collective?* Think the Borg from Star Trek! When you need to execute Log Miner to retrieve data from a production database, you will need to act fast. The older the transactions the longer it will take to recover and traverse with Log Miner. The newest (committed) transactions are processed first, proceeding backwards. The first question to ask is *when do you think the bad event happened?* Searching for data can be done in several different ways:

- SCN, timestamp, or log sequence number
- Pseudo column ORA_ROWSCN

SCN, timestamp, or log sequence number

f you are lucky, the application also writes a timestamp of when the data was last hanged. If that is the case, then you determine the archive log to mine by using the llowing queries. It is important to set the session NLS_DATE_FORMAT so that the me element is displayed along with the date, otherwise you will just get the fault date format of DD-MMM-RR. The data format comes from the database rtup parameters— the NLS_TERRITORY setting. Find the time when a log s archived and match that to the archive log needed.

```
SYS@NEWDB>SELECT * FROM V$LOG;
        1           1          88   52428800          1 YES INACTIVE
  3542532 24-NOV-2009 17:28:53

        2           1          89   52428800          1 YES INACTIVE
  3561977 24-NOV-2009 22:00:28

        3           1          90   52428800          1 NO  CURRENT
  3590213 25-NOV-2009 06:08:09

SYS@NEWDB>SELECT SEQUENCE#, FIRST_CHANGE#, FIRST_TIME FROM V$ARCHIVED_LOG;
  --shortened list

       87       3530746 24-NOV-2009 14:47:37
       88       3542532 24-NOV-2009 17:28:53
       89       3561977 24-NOV-2009 22:00:28
29 rows selected.

SYS@NEWDB> SELECT NAME FROM V$ARCHIVED_LOG WHERE SEQUENCE#=89;

/u01/app/oracle/product/11g/dbs/arch1_89_700654708.dbf
```

Pseudo column ORA_ROWSCN

While this method seems very elegant, it does not work perfectly, meaning it won't always return the correct answer. As it may not work every time or accurately, it is generally not recommended for Flashback Transaction Queries. It is definitely worth trying to narrow the window that you will have to search. It uses the SCN information that was stored for the associated transaction in the Interested Transaction List.

As with our first task in this chapter, you know that delayed block cleanout is involved. The pseudo column ORA_ROWSCN contains information for the approximate time this table was updated for each row. In the following example the table has three rows, with the last row being the one that was most recently updated. It gives me the time window to search the archive logs with Log Miner.

```
SYS@NEWDB> SELECT ORA_ROWSCN, SCN_TO_TIMESTAMP (ORA_ROWSCN) from ttracker.tracks
;

ORA_ROWSCN
----------
SCN_TO_TIMESTAMP(ORA_ROWSCN)
---------------------------------
   3100709
19-NOV-09 01.36.32.000000000 PM

   3100709
19-NOV-09 01.36.32.000000000 PM

   3099397
19-NOV-09 01.09.29.000000000 PM
```

Log Miner is the basic technology behind several of the database Maximum Availability Architecture capabilities—Logical Standby, Streams, and the following Flashback Transaction Backout exercise.

Flashback Transaction Query and Backout

Flashback technology was first introduced in Oracle9i Database. This feature allows you to view data at different points in time and with more recent timestamps (versions), and thus provides the capability to recover previous versions of data. In this chapter, we are dealing with **Flashback Transaction Query (FTQ)** and **Flashback Transaction Backout (FTB),** because they both deal with transaction IDs and integrate with the Log Miner utility. See the MOS document: *"What Do All 10g Flashback Features Rely on and what are their Limitations?" (Doc ID 435998.1).*

The other components in the Flashback suite will be explained in the next chapter as part of the Maximum Availability Architecture. Look for information on FTQ and FTB in the Advanced Application Developer's Guide documentation. It should give you a clue on how to use this feature at its best in your organization—as an advanced troubleshooting tool for complex transaction debugging in a non-production database by programming staff.

Flashback Transaction Query uses the transaction ID (Xid) that is stored with each row version in a Flashback Versions Query to display every transaction that changed the row. Currently, the only Flashback technology that can be used when the object(s) in question have been changed by DDL is Flashback Data Archive. There are other restrictions to using FTB with certain data types (VARRAYs, BFILES), which match the data type restrictions for Log Miner. This basically means if data types aren't supported, then you can't use Log Miner to find the undo and redo log entries.

When would you use FTQ or FTB instead of the previously described methods? The answer is when the data involves several tables with multiple constraints or extensive amounts of information. Similar to Log Miner, the database can be up and running while people are working online in other schemas of the database to accomplish this restore task.

An example of using FTB or FTQ would be to reverse a payroll batch job that was run with the wrong parameters. Most often a batch job is a compiled code (like C or Cobol) run against the database, with parameters built in by the application vendor. A wrong parameter could be the wrong payroll period, wrong set of employees, wrong tax calculations, or payroll deductions.

Enabling flashback logs

First off all flashback needs to be enabled in the database. Oracle Flashback is the database technology intended for a point-in-time recovery (PITR) by saving transactions in flashback logs. A flashback log is a temporary Oracle file and is required to be stored in the FRA, as it cannot be backed up to any other media. Extensive information on all of the ramifications of enabling flashback is found in the documentation labeled: Oracle Database Backup and Recovery User's Guide.

See the following section for an example of how to enable flashback:

```
SYS@NEWDB>ALTER SYSTEM SET DB_RECOVERY_FILE_DEST='/backup/flash_
recovery_area/NEWDB' SCOPE=BOTH;
SYS@NEWDB>ALTER SYSTEM SET DB_RECOVERY_FILE_DEST_SIZE=100M SCOPE=BOTH;
--this is sized for a small test database
SYS@NEWDB> SHUTDOWN IMMEDIATE;
SYS@NEWDB> STARTUP MOUNT EXCLUSIVE;
SYS@NEWDB> ALTER DATABASE FLASHBACK ON;
SYS@NEWDB> ALTER DATABASE OPEN;
SYS@NEWDB> SHOW PARAMETER RECOVERY;
```

The following query would then verify that FLASHBACK had been turned on:

```
SYS@NEWDB>SELECT FLASHBACK_ON FROM V$DATABASE;
```

Flashback Table

The Flashback Table command will restore a table before a designated event occurs (this is often referred to as logical corruption) by restore points, SCN, or timestamp. Restore points will be covered in a later chapter when discussing flashback with Physical Standby databases. There is another Oracle pseudo column associated with a table called a *rowid*, which is involved with the Flashback Table feature. This rowid consists of four components:

- The object number
- The data file the row exists in
- The data block of the data file
- The position of the row in the data block

The underlying mechanism moves the table back in time by changing the rowids. To allow a table to change rowids, the following statement must be run for each one involved in the flashback session:

```
SYS@NEWDB>ALTER TABLE TTRACKER.TRACKS ENABLE ROW MOVEMENT;
SYS@NEWDB>DELETE FROM TTRACKER.TRACKS; COMMIT;
```

Since flashback is enabled, there will be an entry in FLASHBACK_TRANSACTION_
QUERY for the above delete statement. Also notice it is identified by rowid. A
corresponding query and full output has been moved to the code directory for this
chapter (see flashback_tq.txt). The screenshot below is a small snippet of all the
rows returned:

```
SYS@NEWDB>SELECT * FROM FLASHBACK_TRANSACTION_QUERY WHERE TABLE_NAME ='TRACKS';
XID                START_SCN                COMMIT_SCN

08000900060B0000      3616561 25-NOV-09      3616637 25-NOV-09
TTRACKER                                           2 DELETE
TRACKS
TTRACKER                           AAAR1AAAIAAAACGAAA
insert into "TTRACKER"."TRACKS"("TRACKNO","TRACKNAME") values ('1','DALLAS');
```

Choosing the correct SCN in the above query, enables you to flashback the data to
being as it was before the delete statement.

```
SYS@NEWDB>SYS@NEWDB> FLASHBACK TABLE TTRACKER.TRACKS TO SCN 3616561;

SYS@NEWDB>SELECT * FROM TTRACKER.TRACKS;
```

After flashing back the table, the view DBA_FLASHBACK_TXN_STATE is populated.
This view will contain other completed flashback activity in this database, reflecting
the consistent state of the database when queried. This means other flashback events
may back out other dependent or compensating Xid(s), so they no longer appear in
this view.

```
SYS@NEWDB>SELECT * FROM DBA_FLASHBACK_TXN_STATE;
COMPENSATING_XID XID                  DEPENDENT_XID     BACKOUT_MODE
---------------- ------------------   ---------------   ------------
USERNAME
----------------------------------

05001C00C00A0000 08000900060B0000                       CASCADE
SYS
```

As an alternative, you could refer back in this chapter to the sections about Log Miner (*Identifying the data needed to restore* and *SCN, Timestamp, or Log Sequence Number*). This will identify the log needed for extracting the data using Log Miner. Finish the task below for Log Miner by identifying the UNDO statements that can be manually run in order to restore the deleted data.

```
SYS@NEWDB>begin
  dbms_logmnr.add_logfile
('/u01/app/oracle/product/11g/dbs/arch1_89_700654708.dbf',
  dbms_logmnr.new);
  end;
  /

SYS@NEWDB> execute dbms_logmnr.start_logmnr(options=>DBMS_LOGMNR.DICT_FROM_ONLIN
E_CATALOG);
SQL> select sql_undo from v$logmnr_contents where seg_name='TRACKS';
```

 For more information on decoding the rowid into a readable format visit http://www.experts-exchange.com/articles/Database/Oracle/Decoding-the-Oracle-ROWID-and-some-Base64-for-fun.html.

Flashback Transaction Query with pseudo columns

With Flashback Transaction Query, you can see all transactions that changed a row within a certain time period. It is based on the Xid providing not only the change, as seen in a Flashback Versions Query, but also who made the change.

The view FLASHBACK_TRANSACTION_QUERY actually provides SQL statements that you can use to undo the changes made by a particular transaction. In the example above, it contains the original delete statement that was actually executed plus the insert statements to *undo* the logical corruption.

Flashback Transaction Backout

Looking at the MOS document flashback transactions using dbms_flashback. transaction_backout procedure (Doc ID 737332.1), Log Miner is what actually extracts the information whereupon the package DBMS_FLASHBACK then rolls back the transactions. In 11gR2 the Flashback Transaction Backout process can track foreign key dependencies as compared to earlier versions of Oracle, but this requires resource-intensive foreign key supplemental logging.

Enabling flashback (using the command ALTER DATABASE FLASHBACK ON) records all of the critical pieces of information for recovery purposes into a flashback log for any particular row in the database. That information includes the physical rowid, Xid of a committed transaction, SCN, and timestamp. Once flashback is enabled for database use, the appropriate technology to extract the data is needed (Log Miner, Transaction Query, Transaction Backout) to resolve logical corruption issues.

There are exceptions and certain conditions that apply to using flashback and its associated technologies, as well as the limitations of creating additional flashback logs that use resources. As a DBA you will need to decide if the tradeoff in resource consumption is worth the benefit it provides. Oracle has reports from customers that the overhead may be from a low 2 percent increase (OLTP type) in the end user response time to over 30 percent (for a direct load Data Warehouse database). This overhead is partly due to the increased amount of redo being generated (an increased amount of information is captured), also there's more CPU and I/O to write the flashback logs to disk.

Using strings to remove binary components

An even easier way than dump block is to use the Unix strings command to find data in a binary file. This strings command can also strip the binary components from a spfile, which is helpful in situations when you don't have access to a working instance and want to see what is actually in the spfile.

In 11g you can create a pfile from an existing spfile even without a database instance. In the following example, a correctly formatted pfile would be created from $ORACLE_HOME/dbs/spfileNEWDB.ora (Unix example):

```
SYS@NEWDB>create pfile from spfile;
```

Using strings comes in handy for previous versions of Oracle databases, or if you don't have an installed $ORACLE_HOME to work with, just a standalone spfile. When using the strings command on an spfile, the 11g version will split long lines, so you will need to rejoin them with a text editor. The stripped spfile can be edited as needed and then copied to the appropriate directory (see OFA). It can also be renamed to be used as an init<ORACLE_SID>.ora file to start up a database. It is recommended to use the spfile for normal database startup. Using the pfile version is for testing or for circumstances that require its temporary use.

`Strings` can also pull out data from an export file, datapump, redo, or archive log. Several examples of using the strings command are as follows:

```
strings exportfile.dmp  > exportfile.txt
strings datafile.dbf  > datafile.txt
strings spfileNEWDB.ora   > spfileNEWDB.txt
```

As an example, I exported the table `TTRACKER.TRACKS` that contains a single row to show the data inside, and then used the strings command. Here is an excerpt from the export file after running the strings command:

```
CONNECT TTRACKER
TABLE "TRACKS"
CREATE TABLE "TRACKS" ("TRACKNO" NUMBER(1, 0), "TRACKNAME" VARCHAR2(7))  PCTFREE
 10 PCTUSED 40 INITRANS 1 MAXTRANS 255 STORAGE(INITIAL 65536 NEXT 1048576 MINEXT
ENTS 1 FREELISTS 1 FREELIST GROUPS 1 BUFFER_POOL DEFAULT) TABLESPACE "TRACK" LOG
GING NOCOMPRESS
INSERT INTO "TRACKS" ("TRACKNO", "TRACKNAME") VALUES (:1, :2)
DAYTONA
ANALSTATS TR "TRACKS"
BEGIN  DBMS_STATS.SET_TABLE_STATS(NULL,'"TRACKS"',NULL,NULL,NULL,1,5,11,6); END;
ANALSTATS TR "TRACKS" (more statistics)
```

Occasionally, you have to extract the data from a database for various reasons. Both of the utilities export and datapump allow you to do that effectively. They can also be used to recreate missing objects or even the entire database. Datapump is much more efficient for large amounts of data and gives more functionality than the older export utility, which will eventually become obsolete. Both import and export still exist in 11g for migrating databases from older versions of Oracle, and it was used for this demonstration for readability purposes.

Using strings on the actual data file reveals the data within, showing DAYTONA as the last committed entry from the first exercise in this chapter using dump block.

```
strings track_NEWDB.dbf  > track_NEWDB.txt

}|{z
NEWDB
TRACK
DAYTONA
```

Summary

In this chapter, we broke down an Oracle database into its smallest pieces—both logically and physically. We examined common threads on how to track transactions by Xid, SCN, and Timestamps. The physical components should be very clear to you as well—undo segments, redo logs, archived logs, and database files. And most important of all: how transactions travel through the physical parts of the database, from when the end user types in a change, to a row in a table identified by a rowid on a particular data block on a physical data file.

Several utilities were covered along with appropriate scenarios and suggested uses:

- Oracle's RDBMS SQL command `dump block`
- Oracle's RDBMS Log Miner utility
- Flashback Transaction Query and Backout
- Unix `strings` command

This chapter is a building block on which you keep adding as you continue through the book. The information in the next chapter (*Chapter 4, Achieving Maximum Uptime*) is based on the Maximum Availability Architecture standard created by Oracle: it starts at the big picture level, covering the enterprise as a whole. The enterprise IT structure is made up of many smaller components that can all fail at unexpected times. The information in this chapter is meant to help with some of the decisions and tradeoffs that occur when designing for 24/7 uptime.

 I would like to thank several people in the Oracle community for their research on Oracle Internals that were included in this chapter: Tanel Poder, Tom Kyte, Graham Thornton, Sandip Patel, Julian Dyke, and Uwe Hesse.

4

Achieving Maximum Uptime

The previous chapter was a view of the database at the most granular level. In this chapter, we will zoom out to the overall view of the database and its place within the enterprise. DBAs must know how the multiple components interact and be able to trace the data flow between the different nodes that comprise an application. It doesn't matter whether you or your organization aren't strictly governed by a formalized Service Level Agreement. Here you will be provided information on achieving high levels of service and data protection while eliminating single points of failure.

This chapter will be divided into four major sections, with each focusing on how to accomplish what everyone wants—maximum uptime:

- An overview of the Maximum Availability Architecture
- Optimizing Oracle Database Availability
- SQL*Net Hardening, Tuning, and Troubleshooting
- Grid Control High Availability and Disaster Recovery

You might think that a DBA should only concentrate on the administration of the database, but that is not true in the real world. Dinosaurs would only see what is in front of them, but it is time to shift thinking that you are at least partially responsible for the entire application. Data associated with any application travels across the network from the end user to an application server, which then talks to the database and back again. This complete trip is known as end-user response time. As a team player, you must test and test again, making sure that the components you are responsible for are functioning correctly and help out even when it is someone else's problem.

Maximum Availability Architecture (MAA)

The MAA methodology was designed by a dedicated team at Oracle with extensive input from the user community. It expounds the use of:

- Methods applicable to any-sized organization
- Inexpensive commodity hardware
- Multiple redundant components

The MAA recommendations include the following Oracle Products: Database, Application Server, Applications, and Grid Control. Be aware that there are additional licensed options for some features, such as the Advanced Security Option, that are part of the MAA recommendations.

Details about the different editions of Oracle and the licensed options can be found at: `http://download.oracle.com/docs/cd/ E11882_01/license.112/e10594/editions.htm#CJACGHEB`.

It is safe to assume that these recommendations from the MAA website will work in a general sense for most installations, but not without testing and verification. You will have to read each white paper published on the MAA website for your Oracle Database version to find the nuggets of wisdom contained within; keep checking back for updated material.

Find the MAA website here: `http://www.oracle.com/technology/ deploy/availability/htdocs/maa.htm`

The designers of MAA expound the use of smaller nodes in a scalable and redundant configuration. RAC (multiple instances that add memory and CPU), Multiple Middle Tiers, Load Balancers (SSL-enabled hardware version preferred), Failover Instances (Data Guard), and multiple data storage paths all provide redundancy and robustness to a large part of the plan. While failures can occur within any of the layers—hardware, software, network, or database—there can be multiple reasons for those failures, such as human error, corruption, natural disasters, or even the most common-planned outages.

Downtime—planned or unplanned

Oracle has surveyed customers with surprising results. 80% of downtime is planned most often for the following reasons (they are listed from the largest amount of time down to the smallest):

- Systems/hardware testing
- Routine systems maintenance/testing
- Database upgrade
- Application upgrade
- Systems/hardware migration
- Application migration
- Network upgrade

Planned downtime is still downtime, so don't get caught in the mental trap that you are implementing MAA for events that may never happen! MAA is intended for day-to-day standard operating procedures.

Newer features of 11g Oracle RDBMS should be researched for their applicability for your organization in minimizing planned downtime. Several of these require additional Oracle licenses, adequate testing facilities, and personnel comfortable with thinking outside the box:

- Rolling Upgrades (both ASM and database) for system changes—minimizes downtime to the smallest window possible, requiring large amounts of advance preparation, practice, and additional hardware
- Edition-based Redefinition—a method of migrating application code; it provides versioning as well as the ability to quickly back out changes
- Online Table Redefinition—allows DDL changes while the actual data is being used
- Online Reconfiguration—system changes while the database is online that include adding or removing CPUs, RAC nodes, or ASM disks.

High Availability with Oracle Database 11g Release 2 (white paper):
`http://www.oracle.com/technology/deploy/`
`availability/pdf/twp_databaseha_11gr2.pdf`

There are other architectural components that are often forgotten, easily neglected, and can be a show-stopping single point of failure for a critical application. These items aren't necessarily Oracle, but are often used as part of the architecture deployment. If the loss of an item in the following list would make a critical application unavailable, then it is time to re-architect to prevent future outages:

- Expiration or incorrect SSL certificates and intermediate certificates as part of the chain (Oracle products are not compatible with all cert types)
- Single load balancer instead of two
- Single key network router and/or switch
- Single network card or power supply in a node
- Undetected multiple drive failures in a standalone RAID configuration
- ChipSet failures or Cumulative Memory failures
- Battery-backed Write Back Cache failure
- Misconfigured multiple I/O paths
- No redundant LDAP or SSO server

As you probably surmised from the above list, most of these items are not usually considered to be under the direct responsibility of a DBA. Their inclusion in this book means that you are often asked to become well-versed in topics such as hardware, SSL certificates, and load balancers.

Most often the DBA is responsible for recommending hardware purchases and giving architectural deployment advice to the IT team at their organization. How can you give advice if you know nothing about them? You should at least be able to discuss the pros and cons of different hardware configurations for optimal MAA deployment. It is also time to gain some knowledge in diagnosing bottlenecks that may exist between the database and the end user, whether it is hardware, software, or network-based.

In order to achieve maximum availability, there are organizational practices and policies that need to be formalized within your IT organization as a commitment to high levels of service:

- Determine the cost of downtime for critical applications
- Define, test, and document Recovery Time Objective (RTO), and Recovery Point Objective (RPO) goals
- Service Level Agreements (SLA) documentation and maintenance
- Strict change control and security practices
- Test environment that mimics production as closely as possible

- Top-level monitoring software to auto-detect outages
- In-use crisis decision tree and practice scenarios
- Implementation of automatic failure detection and repairs

Once these policies have been formally outlined, then a migration to an MAA can be fleshed out with goals, personnel needs, and timelines. Consider this an ongoing project that is never finished, as most IT organizations can improve their uptime on critical applications.

While MAA is about deploying Oracle products in a grid-like fashion with reconfigurable components, it is not about improving performance with a quick fix. While performance may improve with some of the changes in the following list, these are not considered cure-alls for when end users complain that the database is slow:

- Adding another RAC node, disk spindle, more RAM, or CPU
- Converting a long-running query into parallel
- Upgrading to the latest Oracle version

MAA goals will always have a cost associated with them—hardware, software, network, personnel, or possibly even reduced performance from the database. MAA is within the reach of every customer, but it requires dedicated personnel to implement advanced features. Outsourcing is tempting for deploying advanced features when your personnel are stretched to the maximum with their daily job duties. But who do you call to fix things when that outsourced deployment breaks? The compromise seems to be outsourcing, but allow your personnel to work alongside the consultants learning as the deployment progresses.

MAA with commodity hardware: Case study

What would the MAA look like at a small site with a limited budget? Most universities have small IT budgets (compared to commercial organizations) and are used to having to do more with less. This type of situation tends to encourage creativity!

For example, at one institution, a remote disaster recovery site was implemented using commodity hardware and cooperatively-shared disaster sites within a state university system. Each site was co-located at a different university with appropriate firewall access using the Oracle Data Guard. This type of setup required trust from all the personnel and management involved. In this case, all of the participants worked under the same CSI number within MOS and were used to working with each other. This proof of concept project eventually evolved into a state-funded remote disaster site for all universities, each with their own dedicated network line.

While this remote site is excellent for protecting the data for extended outages or from a complete disaster for this institution, it isn't suitable for planned shorter outages due to the restricted bandwidth; it makes end user access slow and cumbersome. Shorter outages (the majority of which are planned) are generally only a few hours and fall under this institution's defined Recovery Time Objective (the longest amount of time you can take to recover) and Recovery Point Objective (how far back you can lose transactions). A local disaster site was designed and implemented for outages of less than 24 hours for planned database switchovers. See *Chapter 6, Extended RMAN* for more information about switchovers and how to extend the use of a disaster site for testing.

Creating this robust disaster site also required a complete hardware migration: from several databases on a single large node to the deployment of a single database on a smaller node. Having all of the databases on a single node was definitely the largest single point of failure in the existing architecture. A failover to the same node or server would only cover a database failure, not any hardware, software (both Oracle and OS), corruption, or human error for that server.

Going from a full rack node to a 2U footprint in terms of physical size, it was also decided to start migrating to a faster replacement cycle for the hardware in the future. Instead of extending the hardware and software proprietary licensing for up to a decade before replacement, it was decided to replace the hardware at the end of its normal warranty cycle, plus a one-year extension. This was coupled with the decision to use Linux (open source software) as the operating system, which is less expensive to license and maintain.

In the long run, using a larger number of smaller nodes distributed to three different physical sites running on commodity hardware and open source Linux Red Hat OS added up to large savings and resulted in a more robust disaster recovery plan. That is the heart and soul of the MAA: distributed grid computing, and it's scalable and robust along with the ability to redeploy or re-architect components when the business needs change.

Implementing a local disaster site for a database is certainly within the reach of most organizations, as it requires only a few components: the extra database node comparable in size to production, network access between the two sites, and a separate room (preferably a separate building, at least a different electrical system) for the node.

Data Guard controls the shipment of data from the primary site to the standby site in a controlled and efficient manner. The network must be protected at the alternate site due to the vulnerability of archive logs (as you learned in the previous chapter). There are licensing concerns when using Data Guard that only your Oracle sales account representative can address. Licensing costs can vary depending on your current Oracle licensing and how you utilize Data Guard (only for failover or extended testing).

This chapter will cover both Oracle Database and Grid Control as part of the MAA. It is out of the scope of this book to cover Oracle Application Server. While it is a key piece in the MAA infrastructure, your organization may use other web software (Tomcat, Apache, GlassFish, and so on) to deploy applications that use a backend Oracle database. Oracle has just released the 11g Fusion Middleware software, which requires WebCenter to be the application server dictating the future direction of the application server for Oracle applications or technologies that require an application server. The next section expands on details for optimizing the database for high availability.

Further information on MAA customer case studies can be found at the following URL: `http://www.oracle.com/technology/deploy/availability/htdocs/ha_casestudies.html`.

Optimizing Oracle Database High Availability

This section deals with the choices a DBA (as part of a team) must make to provide as much uptime as possible for an Oracle database. Consider this section to be essential in providing quality service and data protection for your customers. Each new version of Oracle provides an ever-deepening pool of features to maximize the availability of the database that comes as standard with the Enterprise License. These are the items that will be covered in the following section:

- Archivelog mode
- Database compatibility parameter and apfile, pfile management
- Storage—RAID, SAME, ASM, OMF
- Mirrored files—control files, redo logs
- Autoextending data files with MaxSize

- Auditing, log files, and Max Dump File Size
- Data Dictionary Healthcheck
- SQL*Net hardening, tuning, and troubleshooting

At this point, it is time to remind you about documenting changes to the database—start a formal logging procedure whether it is a spreadsheet, Wiki log, or Word document. Start a system where you can track changes, as they are applied in a non-production environment and their eventual migration to production; it will keep you from guessing when or how something was done.

Utilize a code management software such as the programming staff would use. You can copy and paste the commands that were run as part of the documentation procedure. There is a Unix program called `script` that can be used to capture all session activities executed at the command line. Executing RDAs during each major database change, while keeping them as a snapshot historical reference, would be very thorough and worth the time.

Other recommendations as part of the MAA will be covered in subsequent chapters. Data Guard plus Flashback Database is covered on its own in *Chapter 5*. We will be examining how the Data Recovery Advisor, Flash Recovery Area, and corruption detection and prevention relate to the Oracle RMAN utility in *Chapter 6*. Oracle Real Application Clusters (RAC) and Streams will not be covered in this book due to their complexity in design and implementation.

To archive or not to archive, you pick the mode

There have been cases of production databases operating in noarchivelog mode with no backups! If you are subscribed to an Oracle e-mail list or forum, this situation comes up regularly in the discussions or pleas for help.

Some database implementations require archivelog mode for functionality, such as Oracle Streams, Standby Databases, and Data Guard. Archivelog mode is also required for what is known as complete recovery, where all transactions up to a certain desired point are restored and recovered.

There are a few circumstances where a DBA might temporarily turn it off to speed up a particular process, such as using data pump to recreate the database, but these are exceptions to the rule. If this is a production instance and the data is considered irreplaceable or you can't recreate the transactions (usually, a data warehouse or reporting database), run it in archivelog mode. The previous chapter went through the actual process of turning on archivelog mode so that the redo logs are archived to disk.

While archivelog mode is the norm, making all of the processes involved work well takes testing and practice. Some of the most common issues encountered with archivelog mode are as follows:

- Running out of disk or backup tape space—hanging database or failed backups, alternate local archive destination on a different file system.
- Running out of Flash Recovery Area—no reclaimable space causes hanging due to unavailable archive destination.
- Archive destinations unavailable—SAN, NAS or other types of shared or network deployed storage become unavailable.
- Standby archiving destinations unavailable (see Chapter 5)—the degree of slowness or delay will be a combination of Data Guard Protection mode and the network bandwidth between the servers.

Some general rules apply to these situations, as each can be disastrous and cause database slowdowns or outages depending on what actually occurred. There are several features that Oracle introduced that complicate the archivelog methodology. Each of these features are complex enough (Data Guard is the best example) to have their own set of problems associated with deploying in a production database.

Multiple archive destinations

Even if you deploy standby archive destinations for failover reasons, it is critical that a locally defined archive destination (locally accessible storage device) be defined as well. There will be times a standby archive destination (if you use Data Guard) becomes unavailable due to network-related issues, and if a local destination is not defined, you will be left with no archive destination. Not having a valid archive destination with a database in archivelog mode means it will hang until you add one, which is done by altering startup initialization parameters—`log_archive_dest_n`.

At this point, I recommend a local archive destination outside the flash recovery area (FRA) until you are thoroughly comfortable with implementing both archivelog and FRA at the same time. It also takes some advanced knowledge and testing experience in using the RMAN database backup utility to maintain archivelogs in multiple destinations (see *Chapter 6, Extended RMAN*).

Moving the archive destination in an emergency

Be ready with an alternate destination if you need to move the archive destination. Occasionally, you may lose a local disk or other attached storage device. It can be done easily with the following command when the database has been started with an spfile. In this case, the third archive destination was chosen so as not to overwrite other destinations (for testing or troubleshooting reasons). You may choose a different destination number as needed:

```
SYS@NEWDB>ALTER SYSTEM set log_archive_dest_3='LOCATION=/new/path'
scope=both sid=*;
```

Archivelogs or their backups may end up in the $ORACLE_HOME/dbs file location, because that is the default backup location and is usually caused by misconfigured archive destinations or RMAN procedures. Check if the archive destinations are successful with the following command:

```
SYS@NEWDB>select dest_id,destination,status,target,
        schedule,process from v$archive_dest;
```

Using a different disk device or disk mount

Archivelogs saved to disk are typically not on the same physical disk device as data files. This may be due to performance differences in storage between the devices, as well as having a redundant device for recovery reasons. This is part of the OFA standard and can be implemented using Automatic Storage Management (ASM). Later in this chapter, ASM implementation will be mentioned, as it relates to high availability.

Monitoring all hard drive space and Archivelog space

It would be a mistake to assume someone else is keeping track of drive space usage on the database boxes. So run a script (DBMS_SCHEDULER with or without the use of the OEM console is a great tool for this) to check disk space to e-mail (or page) you when the disk device has reached percentage full threshold. This is also an excellent opportunity when automating an archivelog backup to free up disk space when the archive destination has reached a certain threshold. Once archivelogs are backed up, they can be removed from the disk to free up space.

If you are constantly fighting for hard drive space, then there may be something else wrong. Start looking for audit files (*.aud), trace files (*.trc), core dumps (directory labelled core_xxxx), large SQL*Net logs, and backups in the wrong location, as well as double checking your RMAN backup policies.

See the following list for suggestions to follow when disk space issues arise in reference to archivelogs:

- Merge incremental backups into fulls
- Compress or zip archivelogs, backup, data pump exports
- Run the archivelog maintenance routine as needed
- Monitor the Flash Recovery Area

All of the above items will be covered in more detail when we get to *Chapter 6, Extended RMAN*.

Database compatibility parameter with spfile, pfile management

Parts of this chapter are tips and suggestions for increasing uptime; some of these practices are directly related to preventing database outages, a primary concern for DBAs. The information is a combination of the MAA recommendations, personal experience, and knowledge gathered from a variety of sources, including My Oracle Support, Oracle-l, Oracle User Conferences as well as Oracle OpenWorld.

 `http://www.oracle.com/openworld`: Oracle Conference hosted by Oracle Corporation and held yearly in San Francisco, CA.

Attending conferences and reading books exposes you to new concepts and the next best thing in Oracle *stuff*. Don't come home and immediately turn that feature on! There is a lot of hard selling going on at those conferences and you aren't necessarily exposed to all of the details needed to implement that new feature.

How do you deploy features gradually? There might be quite a few features tied to the `init<ORACLE_SID>.ora` database startup initialization parameter (pfile) or the `spfile<ORACLE_SID>.ora` (spfile) parameter named `compatible`. We have already discussed that the spfile is a binary file that cannot be edited directly. The pfile is a text file that is edited manually, with changes that take effect the next time the database is started.

If you are migrating to 11g, it is recommended to keep `compatible` set at 10.0.0.0 until you have been live for at least a week. Then start advancing the appropriate parameter after a stabilization period. There is another critical reason to keep the older `compatible` parameter during a database migration; this will allow you to downgrade the database (without doing a complete restore and recovery) if an unforeseen snag or untested result occurs. The only exception to migrating to 11g and starting with the compatible set at 11.x would be if you had to have an 11g feature for the application to perform as tested.

It is important to learn to use an spfile instead of just a pfile for controlling database parameters. This allows you to adjust most parameters while the database is up, and write to the spfile at the same time, saving it for the next time the database recycles. To find out what type of parameter file is actually being used by a running database, use the show parameter command:

```
SYS@NEWDB> SHOW PARAMETER SPFILE;
```

This will show which spfile is in use. If that value is only the word **string**, then a pfile is in use. Take a look at all the non-default database parameters that are enabled from the startup (like the parameter spfile) at the `alert<ORACLE_SID>.log` or use the `adrci` command-line utility as shown in the following example:

```
adrci> SHOW ALERT -P "MESSAGE_TEXT LIKE '%=%'"

Choose the alert log from the following homes to view:

1: diag/tnslsnr/node/listener_one
2: diag/diagtool/user_oracle/host_3003607522_11
3: diag/rdbms/newdb/newdb
Q: to quit

Please select option: 3
Output the results to file: /tmp/alert_29495_4790_newdb_1.ado
2009-10-19 10:17:33.449000 -06:00
LICENSE_MAX_SESSION = 0
LICENSE_SESSIONS_WARNING = 0
IMODE=BR
ILAT =18
LICENSE_MAX_USERS = 0
  processes             = 150
  memory_target         = 316M
  control_files         = "/u01/oradata/newdb/control01.ctl"
  control_files         = "/u01/oradata/newdb/control02.ctl"
  control_files         = "/u01/oradata/newdb/control03.ctl"
  db_block_size         = 8192
```

The example above shows how to search by use of a specific string while using the `adrci` utility in Unix, in this case the equals (=) sign. Also, notice the various diagnostic directories that relate to Oracle software such as the `tnslsnr`, the Unix user account named `oracle`, and `rdbms`, which is the database diagnostic directory.

Notice that the above view of the alert log lists all the non-default database startup initialization parameter settings at every database startup. You can also use the following query:

```
SYS@NEWDB>SELECT  NAME, VALUE FROM  V$PARAMETER
    WHERE ISDEFAULT = 'FALSE';
```

In 11g, you can recreate a missing spfile or pfile from memory, but this requires the database compatible parameter to be set at 11.0.0.0 or above. The following example will recreate the pfile in the default location of $ORACLE_HOME/dbs, which can be edited as needed:

```
SYS@NEWDB> create pfile from memory;

File created.
SYS@NEWDB> !ls -altr $ORACLE_HOME/dbs
total 96
-rw-r--r--  1 oracle dba 12920 May   3  2001 initdw.ora
-rw-r--r--  1 oracle dba  2774 Sep 11  2007 init.ora
-rw-rw----  1 oracle dba  1544 Oct 19 10:17 hc_newdb.dat
-rw-r-----  1 oracle dba    24 Oct 19 10:18 lknewdb
drwxr-xr-x 73 oracle dba  4096 Oct 19 10:24 ..
-rw-r--r--  1 oracle dba   852 Oct 23 13:40 spfilenewdb.ora
-rw-r-----  1 oracle dba  1536 Nov 13 14:31 orapwnewdb
-rw-r--r--  1 oracle dba  4932 Dec 10 12:50 initnewdb.ora
   drwxr-xr-x  2 oracle dba  4096 Dec 10 12:51 .
```

In the previous chapter, the Unix `strings` command was used to demonstrate how to strip off the binary components to create a pfile from an spfile. Since non-default parameters are written to the alert log, you can also recreate a pfile from the lines that come after the words **System parameters with non-default values,** by copying and pasting with a text editor. That is basically what a pfile or spfile contains, everything that isn't default.

You will also see the character * (star) inside an `init<ORACLE_SID>.ora` file. This means that the parameter applies to all instances. If you see a ? mark in a pfile, it stands for `$ORACLE_HOME`, which is also a substitute command in SQL*Plus for `$ORACLE_HOME`.

Also, something else that many DBAs don't know about is how to reset a database parameter back to its default setting. This particular example would execute in memory and also write to the spfile for all instances (see the documentation on Real Application Clusters for more information on managing multiple instances of a database).

```
SYS@NEWDB> alter system reset optimizer_features_enable scope=both
sid=*;
```

Take a look at MOS documents: 166601.1 and 249664.1 for differences between spfile and pfiles, migrating between them, and lessons on using them correctly.

Dealing with storage—RAID, SAME, ASM, and OMF

Data storage implementations will be one of the most important decisions in achieving high availability, and most often take the form of one of the following hardware types:

- Storage Area Network (SAN)
- Network Attached Storage (NAS)
- iSCSI – directly attached SCSI across Network, which is usually Ethernet
- Directly attached disk drives – internal or Just Bunch of Disks (JBOD) external storage
- Emerging disk technologies – Solid State, High Capacity, High Performance

Each of the above hardware types come in a wide selection from many hardware vendors. How would you know which one to select? Most customers obtain test hardware from several different vendors and run a calibration tool (Oracle's own ORION tool will be introduced in *Chapter 8*) to create a proof-of-concept. You are trying to prove the vendor claims about their hardware performance and reliability with your data and personnel.

This would also be the time to let your system administrator(s) produce failures on that hardware for HA reasons. Failures can run the gamut of unplugging a live system, pulling a network cable, pulling hot-swappable hard drives (more than one), pulling out a power supply, pulling out the end of a fiber-attached external storage device, and misconfiguring storage device parameters – there is no limit to the atrocities that can be dreamed up. It wouldn't do much good to be destructive just to see what happens; it must be done with planning, with the proper testing tools in place, and careful documentation on what actually happens.

There are some general recommendations on how to slice and dice that storage, as it relates to database use. Different system administrators will have different philosophies or attitudes towards storage architecture and deployment practices. It is critical that you and your system administrators trust each other as you will work closely together on the storage details of your databases. The following are general recommendations and they may not fit with what your organization plans to do for any particular implementation. Often, it is the budget that decides how storage implementations play out.

RAID—Redundant Arrays of Inexpensive Disks

Implementing hardware RAID is very commonplace and considered the first step in preventing outages, whether there is a database or not. Disk drives have been around for over four decades, and because they contain moving parts, they are still vulnerable to mechanical, electric, magnetic, and even vendor-specific firmware problems. This makes them the number-one failing mechanical component in a computer even with huge advances in hard drive technology. It is not a question of if a hard drive will fail but when!

Software RAID is another option, but is generally considered harder to implement and prone to issues simply because it adds another layer of complexity that really isn't needed. Oracle has its own version of software RAID (ASM) that is more reliable and should be considered first, before any vendor-supplied software RAID.

There are different RAID levels with different combinations of mirroring, parity, and striping hard drive disks. See the next section for the recommended RAID level of 10 using the SAME methodology from Oracle.

See the following URL for a great discussion on different RAID levels: http://www.baarf.com (Battle Against Any Raid Five, also includes RAID level 3 and 4). There are also lists of valuable references to accompanying materials from the United Kingdom Oracle User Group.

SAME—Stripe and Mirror Everything

Oracle defined a best practice for RAID levels back in 2000 called SAME: it is an attempt to level out all of the differences between Oracle operation types (scan, lookup, load, insert, create index, join, LOB, sort, hash, backup, recovery, batch write) as well as operating system file types. Different file types associated with a database (data, log, temp, archive, undo, system, control, backup) perform differently at the I/O level with different storage configurations, depending on the actual operation. The exception to this may be the online redo logs that are written sequentially by the database, with any parallelism occurring at the operating system level.

Adding more disks requires a restripe of all RAID disks involved. This requires extensive planning and the ability to correctly forecast storage needs. As part of the SAME philosophy, it is recommended to stripe all files in a 1MB width across all of the disks and then mirror those disks for high availability (this combination of stripe and mirror is RAID 10).

The physical part of a disk drive where it's best to put the more frequently accessed data is the outside edge, which reduces the natural latency issues seen with disk drives. That being said, you will gain more performance improvements by dividing large tables using Oracle partition technology before trying to improve performance by placing them on specific disk drive locations or spindles.

A configuration using SAME is easily done when you know the total disk space and the I/O throughput, which determines the number of disks involved. This method is a balance of high availability with a mirrored copy, but efficient in striping the data across multiple disks or spindles. The hot-swappable features of hard drives, with automatic failure detection and notification, makes spreading data across multiple drives extremely resilient.

See the following URL for the complete Oracle White Paper on the SAME methodology: `http://www.oracle.com/technology/deploy/` `availability/pdf/oow2000_same.pdf`

ASM—Automatic Storage Management

ASM is gaining momentum across the industry, even with a database that won't be using RAC technology. Its basic function is to present the storage as a logical volume; this gives the ability to add storage as needed without completely reconfiguring all of the disk drives or moving data files to new storage, providing scalability without downtime.

In the earlier versions of ASM, implementations became complicated due to the third-party or vendor technologies required to integrate all of the needed file systems, clustering, volume managers, and hardware platforms. With the 11gR2 version of ASM, you can now use Oracle to manage other third-party file systems with Dynamic Volumes—ASM files + ASM volume type.

With 11gR2, extensive improvements to ASM were released:

- Extended administration commands (such as the `asmcmd` copy command)
- Increased performance with the fast mirror resync feature
- ASM Dynamic Volume Manager—with the asmvol attribute and its own striping and extent algorithm
- Rolling Upgrades of ASM Cluster File System now provide cluster-wide access to additional file types besides just data files and ASM spfiles:
  - File Oracle binaries application executables
  - Trace file alert logs
  - BFILEs, audio, video, and image file types

While ASM sounds like a great deal, it is an advanced feature that adds another layer of technology for the DBA to master. It is meant for larger databases, RAC, or one that is quickly growing, like a data warehouse. Some DBAs see ASM as a single point of failure—if the ASM instance goes down, the data files are unavailable.

It is a tool to add storage as needed and makes your job easier when large numbers of data files are involved. It is a technology that a novice DBA should gradually implement, starting with non-production instances to gain expertise.

That is one of the best arguments for a full complement of testing equipment (hardware, software, personnel)—it's comparable to production. Non-production instances can be just as important as production for this reason. You should be echoing the same implementation details for certain test databases—backups, archivelog mode, and SQL*Net tuning, so that problems encountered within these complex environments are tested as staff utilize these accessory databases.

Recommendations for implementing ASM

Oracle software binaries are installed in separate ORACLE_HOMES by version; ASM should be installed in its own home as well. An upper-level ASM home can service a down-level ORACLE_HOME, making a transition to the next version a gradual, controlled process (see *Chapter 7* for more detailed information).

Start with a Simple Disk and Disk Group Configuration—two ASM groups, one for data files and one for FRA. Use the redundancy of ASM plus hardware RAID. ASM redundancy is mirroring at the storage extent level, which is an advanced feature that can be added as your expertise and knowledge increase.

One of the keys to a successful ASM implementation is making sure the disk repair time is correct (this is adjustable) for your combination of disks and I/O throughput capacity. The disk repair timer attribute on your disk group is used to specify how long disks remain offline before being dropped. When a disk is dropped, extensive resources are consumed at the hardware level to migrate all of the ASM extents to new positions from the failed drive. You wouldn't want those resources to be used, as it would cause performance issues at the database level if the failure was a planned outage, simply temporary, or just transient.

Monitoring is important for disk failures at the hardware RAID level and allocation failures (disk group out of balance) at the ASM level. See the following URLs for more information on ASM deployment practices:

```
http://www.oracle.com/technology/products/database/asm/index.html
```

```
http://www.oracle.com/technology/products/database/asm/pdf/Extending%
20ASM%20to%20Manage%20All%20Data%20-%20Final%209-10-09_0.pdf
```

Oracle Managed Files (OMF) is a feature where the RDBMS takes over the control of the placement of data files while assigning a system-generated name.

These technologies such as OMF and ASM that simplify data file management are most often used with larger implementations with a disk storage device, such as a SAN. If your environment is using ASM, you are in fact already using OMF. The only difference in administration would be that you can now see your data files at the OS level with OMF.

Mirrored files—control files and online redo logs

There is always a chance of files becoming unusable when they are stored on a physical disk: they are vulnerable to human error or certain types of corruption. If data files are deleted, then a restore and recovery operation is usually in order to replace the missing data—if a temp file is deleted just recreate it. If a control file or online redo log is removed or unusable, then it is easier and faster to use the extra copy (or mirror) that you have on hand. It won't keep you from making a mistake, but keeps downtime to a minimum if an online redo log or control file is accidentally removed or becomes corrupt. This is especially important if you are using local file disks to store the data files among different mount points.

Online redo group—this contains one or more identical copies of an online redo log member with an identical log sequence number that are exactly the same size. The current log sequence number (refer to the last chapter) is written in the control file and header of each data file.

Two online redo groups—this is the minimum needed for normal operations; the optimal number depends on database activity. What do we mirror? Alternate members of each online redo group on different disks.

You will not be able to change a controlfile location while the database is up and open for use, as shown by the example below. After verifying on the operating system, level the correct location of a valid controlfile. You can then change the controlfile location and recycle the database for that change to take effect, as seen in the following example:

```
> mv control02.ctl control02.ctl.bad
oracle@nodename:/u01/oradata/newdb[newdb]
> sqlplus /nolog

SQL*Plus: Release 11.1.0.7.0 - Production on Sun Dec 13 07:32:21 2009

Copyright (c) 1982, 2008, Oracle.  All rights reserved.

@> connect / as sysdba
Connected.
SYS@NEWDB> select * from v$database;
select * from v$database
               *
ERROR at line 1:
ORA-00210: cannot open the specified control file
ORA-00202: control file: '/u01/oradata/NEWDB/control02.ctl'
ORA-27041: unable to open file
Linux-x86_64 Error: 2: No such file or directory
Additional information: 3

SYS@NEWDB> alter system set control_files='/u01/oradata/newdb/control01.ctl' scope=bo
th;
alter system set control_files='/u01/oradata/newdb/control01.ctl' scope=both
               *
ERROR at line 1:
ORA-02095: specified initialization parameter cannot be modified

SYS@NEWDB> alter system set control_files='/u01/oradata/newdb/control01.ctl'
  2  scope=spfile;;
```

Now shut down and start up the database and you are back in business.

If the database is down, you can manipulate the locations of a controlfile and also make an OS copy of a valid controlfile. ASM implementations would have a different procedure (see *Chapter 6, Extended RMAN*, for more information).

 See the following MOS document for more information related to moving redo log groups:

Maintenance of Online Redo Log Groups and Members [Doc ID 102995.1]

Autoextending data files

Allowing a data file to autoextend (grow in size by allowing the RDBMS to add more extents) is becoming the standard. There is a setting called UNLIMITED but that is a misnomer since there are obvious limits to objects that can exist in a database. The actual limit is equal to 4 million OS blocks, which depends on the database parameter DB_BLOCK_SIZE. If the database DB_BLOCK_SIZE is equal to 8KB, then the maximum file size for that database is 32GB.

 Database Limits [ID 336186.1]: This information comes from an important reference document found on MOS.

There is a tablespace feature called BIGFILE, which is intended to contain a single large data file. It is intended for VLDB in conjunction with ASM, Oracle-managed files (OMF), or other third-party volume managers. BIGFILE tablespaces can co-exist with the normal smallfile tablespaces, which makes it obvious that wisdom lies in grouping objects in the same tablespace that have similar life cycles and applications. BIGFILE(s) are only supported for locally managed tablespaces with ASSM.

A few years ago, it was standard practice to limit datafile sizes to 2GB because of certain operating system limits that prevented the use of anything larger. You can check with your system administrator or research on MOS if you are unsure. Now you can turn autoextend on and let it grow until the unlimited size for your OS is reached, but that is probably not a good thing. This will hang whatever process is trying to autoextend if the file space is exhausted. There are occasions when a process will spin out of control and create a huge datafile, tempfile, or undo segment unless there is some sort of limit imposed; this is where the MAXSIZE piece of storage attribute comes into play. Turning autoextend on is generally considered a way of allowing Oracle to manage extents as long as there is a maxsize limit.

What is also important about autoextending datafiles is what is called the NEXT size (the chunk of storage that the RDBMS allocates) and it depends on whether you are using OMF. With OMF, the default autoextend size is equal to the size of the datafile with a limit of 100MB. Without OMF, the default is 1 data block of the tablespace that the datafile belongs to. There is a new RDBMS background process called Space Management Coordinator (SMCO) in 11g, which gives some credence to the observation that the autoextension of datafiles is becoming more prevalent. In order for SMCO to autoextend a data file, the setting for AUTOEXTEND has to be ON, as is found in the following query:

```
SYS@NEWDB> SELECT TABLESPACE_NAME,FILE_NAME,AUTOEXTENSIBLE FROM DBA_
DATA_FILES;
```

SMCO coordinates and spawn slave processes are identifiable at the operating system with the following pattern (wnnn). An insert statement or loading a statement such as sql loader, import, or data pump needs another segment that doesn't have enough contiguous, sufficiently large, single chunk space in the tablespace. It will autoextend according to the NEXT storage parameter. The SCMO process performs the extension evenly across all the datafiles in that particular tablespace that haven't reached their maximum extension.

```
oracle@hostname:/u01/oradata/newdb[newdb]
> ps -ef | grep ora_w*
oracle      908     1  0 08:52 ?        00:00:00 ora_w000_newdb
oracle    2319 11541  0 09:02 pts/0     00:00:00 grep ora_w*
```

The above command-line query returns the active background process that starts with the pattern ora_w*. SCMO is also responsible for temporary segment space reclamation. That is the main reason you should only add tempfiles to a temporary tablespace (never permanent). The RDBMS is designed to release those temp segments automatically for other users in the database when queries no longer need those segments.

Auditing, log files, and max dump file size

There is nothing worse than a file system filling up unnecessarily, which can cause a database to crash or hang depending on which files are involved. Anything that can cause a database to hang or otherwise become unavailable is part of the MAA recommendations. This also includes protecting the data by standardizing database auditing procedures suitable for your organization. Several changes in the newer version of Oracle as well as standard logging and tracing utilities can cause the filesystem to fill up. This means that you, the DBA, have some ongoing maintenance to perform to monitor, rotate, and control the inherent logging with an Oracle database.

For example, there is a dramatic increase in auditing in 11g that will occur with a database that is created with the default settings. See the next section for the actual database privilege statements being audited. Notice that the default parameter settings write the files to the same location as previous versions of the RDBMS, as auditing output is not a part of the ADR. Most often the DBA manipulates the location and auditing levels depending on the security requirements of their organization.

```
SYS@NEWDB> show parameter audit

NAME                    TYPE        VALUE
----------------------- ----------- ------------------------------------
audit_file_dest         string      /u01/app/oracle/admin/newdb/adump
audit_sys_operations    boolean     FALSE
audit_syslog_level      string
audit_trail             string      DB
```

Using an OS command to view the current size of the audit logs for this small non-production database produced 2MB+ over a month.

```
oracle@nodename:/u01/app/oracle/admin/newdb/adump[newdb]
> du -h
2.2M      .
```

This is with no other major users or applications connecting other than sys, sysdba, dbsnmp, and the test cases for this book. Expect large amounts of files to be written with a full production instance, depending on the database parameter settings for `audit_trail`—DB, OS, DB, or DB EXTENDED. Extended captures the actual SQL involved.

Default settings for `audit_trail` insert entries in the base table `SYS.AUD$` (query the `DBA_AUDIT_TRAIL` view) as shown below:

```
SYS@NEWDB>SELECT USERNAME,ACTION,ACTION_NAME FROM DBA_AUDIT_TRAIL;
DBSNMP                              100 LOGON
DBSNMP                              101 LOGOFF
   115154 rows selected.
```

The majority of the entries for this test database are from the multiple logon/logoffs for the user DBSNMP, which is the Grid Control Management agent monitoring database user. Monitoring logons/logoffs is the easiest way to start auditing activity and will give you the most benefit for the amount of resources consumed. If a database is created using the Database Creation Assistant (DBCA), then the auditing of additional statements besides logon/logoff activity has already been enabled.

What is currently being audited?

Oracle provides several scripts on MOS. The following script lets you see what the current audit settings are as well as generate a script to turn them off and back on as well. It is just as important to know how to turn off these settings for emergency reasons as enabling them in the first place, and this is also an excellent way to document the current settings.

SCRIPT: *Generate AUDIT and NOAUDIT Statements for Current Audit Settings [Document ID 287436.1].* The script located in `$ORACLE_HOME/rdbms/admin/undoaud.sql` will reset the audit features back to 10gR2 defaults, which is NO auditing. This script is the one called when using the DBCA utility to remove auditing.

There are three database auditing types: objects, statements, and privileges. We will cover the privilege type, as it has to do with overall database activity and not specific objects that vary depending on the application and the organization's security policies. The default security settings when you use DBCA to create an 11g database enables the auditing of all of the following privilege statements:

```
ALTER ANY PROCEDURE
ALTER ANY TABLE
ALTER DATABASE
ALTER PROFILE
ALTER SYSTEM
ALTER USER
AUDIT SYSTEM
CREATE ANY JOB
CREATE ANY LIBRARY
CREATE ANY PROCEDURE
CREATE ANY TABLE
CREATE EXTERNAL JOB
CREATE PUBLIC DATABASE LINK
CREATE SESSION
CREATE USER
DROP ANY PROCEDURE
DROP ANY TABLE
DROP PROFILE
DROP USER
EXEMPT ACCESS POLICY
GRANT ANY OBJECT PRIVILEGE
GRANT ANY PRIVILEGE
GRANT ANY ROLE
ROLE
SYSTEM AUDIT
```

Why would this particular list of items be installed by default by Oracle? In an organization, there is often more than one person with advanced system privileges in a database. It would be helpful to know who was responsible when a particular event happened; it can also be looked at as a way of documenting what was done and by whom for external auditing purposes.

Auditing Session Activity

The very minimum a production database should audit when logons are unsuccessful will indicate patterns of abuse such as password cracking:

```
SYS@NEWDB>AUDIT ALL BY ACCESS WHENEVER NOT SUCCESSFUL;
```

Or the more broad statement of:

```
SYS@NEWDB>AUDIT SESSION;
```

Auditing statements are either:

BY SESSION: One audit record is inserted for one session, regardless of the number of times the statement is executed, this is default if not specified. The second statement above would audit all logon and logoffs and not just bad password attempts.

BY ACCESS: One audit record is inserted each time the statement is executed.

The query below shows all logon/logoffs for every user with `audit session` enabled. Note that the `comment$text` will contain the IP and port number of the client.

```
SYS@NEWDB>select timestamp#, userid, userhost, action#, returncode,
logoff$time, comment$text from aud$ where action# in (100,101);
```

A return code 1017 means ORA-1017 "invalid username/password; logon denied". It is easy to determine what the code means using the Oracle error utility called oerr on Unix, as seen in the following example:

```
oracle@nodename:/u01/app/oracle/patches[newdb]
> oerr ora 1017
01017, 00000, "invalid username/password; logon denied"
// *Cause:
// *Action:
```

Connections to the database by SYSDBA, SYSASM, or SYSOPER along with their actions (these include database startup/shutdown) are always logged. It doesn't matter: the `audit_trail` settings with the files showing up in the directory `$ORACLE_HOME/rdbms/audit` unless the `audit_file_dest` has been set to another directory location.

Before turning on any sort of auditing features, a DBA should design the accompanying archive/purge process of the SYS.AUD$ table (or OS directory depending on how auditing was enabled) to properly maintain historical records, making it a scheduled task.

The table SYS.AUD$ is stored in the system tablespace and allowing that to fill would cause the database to hang. It is generally recommended that you copy the entries from the original AUD$ table into a historical table, and export data to the operating system for long-term retention. The following lists other recommendations for an archive/purge process:

- Create a dedicated user for owning all of the custom archive/purge objects
- Create a dedicated tablespace
- Research the 11g compression features to save storage space
- Run a routine quarterly to exported archived data, truncate that table, and then load SYS.AUD$ table to the archived table and truncate SYS.AUD$
- Run a daily task to monitor the number of rows in SYS.AUD$ with alerts automated to notify DBA
- Write events to the alert log using `sys.dbms_system.ksdwrt` for every quarterly run of the audit procedure (see *Chapter 2, Maintaining Oracle Standards*, for the writing the DBID to the alert log example).

The new Oracle 11g option, called Audit Vault, automates the collection and purging of auditing data with a database package, but doing this would require an additional license. Here are some other important MOS documents for additional information on the archival of the auditing information:

- *How To Set the AUDIT_SYSLOG _LEVEL Parameter [Doc ID 553225.1]*
- *Moving AUD$ to Another Tablespace and Adding Triggers to AUD$ [Doc ID 72460.1]*

> Windows NT does not use the AUDIT_FILE_DEST parameter. Operating System auditing changes are recorded in the Security Event Viewer.

There is at least one other way of monitoring login activity without enabling auditing. For example, the following query finds the failed logins for any user since the last one that was successful. This wouldn't work for someone without a database account who might be trying to attempt a brute force type of attack.

```
SYS@NEWDB>select name, ltime, lcount from user$ where lcount > 1;
```

> Note that if you implement a separate ORACLE_HOME for ASM, there will be additional audit files (for SYSDBA and SYSASM access) produced that will need to be monitored and purged as needed.

Other logs to monitor

There is something that every DBA needs to be aware of: the location of logs and trace files produced with both normal and unusual database activity. You should also know how to rotate these logs while automating the process. Refer back to *Chapter 2* for the three major methods of scheduling: OS, DBMS_SCHEDULER, or OEM. The following list assumes you are using the default database initialization parameters for 11g:

- SQL*Net logs—located in ADR client location for any SQL*Net connection
- Listener log—located in the database ADR
- Audit logs—database parameter `audit_file_dest`
- Trace files—located in ADR unless redefined within a script or SQL*Plus session
- Install logs—located in the `orainventory` location
- Automatic Diagnostic Repository—holds the bulk of the database logging, incident packages, and workbench files
- Grid Control Management agent—`$ORACLE_HOME/sysman`
- MOS configuration manager—`$ORACLE_HOME/ccr`
- Other installation logs—`$ORACLE_HOME/cfgtoollogs/`
- RDA output—user-defined location
- Opatch—Oracle's one-off patching utility output, user-defined location

Out of the files above, the ones that could possibly cause the most problems will be the text versions of all the ADR logging located in the trace directories. There is an archiving and purging function component of the ADR, but that doesn't touch any of the files found in each of the trace directories. There are multiple trace directories within the ADR location that will be populated with data, depending on which Oracle components and features are implemented.

Don't forget the audit log location mentioned earlier. These will require a scripting mechanism (DBMS_SCHEDULER comes to mind) to rotate, remove the oldest versions on a regular basis, and keep a certain amount of history. The *xml versions of the logs mentioned above are automatically rotated along with the other ADR files, so growth is usually not something to worry about, along with the purge and archive functions. The Max Dump File Size database parameter has a default setting, as shown below. It is the only option used to limit the size of trace files that doesn't include the alert log:

```
max_dump_file_size                      string        unlimited
```

At this point in the book, you can probably recognize the need to change this as soon as possible. The only time it would need to be unlimited is when there is a known event occurring and you don't want to prevent the trace file from being produced if the setting is too small.

 For more information see: *What is the unit of measurement for OS block size? and the purpose of MAX_DUMP_FILE_SIZE initialization parameter? [Doc ID 886806.1]*

Data dictionary healthcheck

As a DBA, you should never insert, update, delete, or otherwise manipulate any of the SYS-owned objects, collectively known as the data dictionary. It also goes without saying that the SYS user is the exclusive owner of the data dictionary and that SYS should not be used as a schema to own application objects. What happens if you modify the underlying objects? It invalidates your support contract with Oracle, which means there's no help to get you out of the pickle you just put yourself into.

It is a worthwhile exercise, especially when you inherit databases from someone else to run a data dictionary health check just like running an RDA process as outlined in *Chapter 2*. It allows you to objectively judge the state of things. See the following documents for information on running a database health check and an interesting package that Oracle provides to help format the output called H* Helper scripts. Please use any new testing utility, packages, procedures, or scripts in a non-production database first.

"hcheck.sql" script to check for known problems in Oracle8i, Oracle9i, Oracle10g and Oracle 11g [Doc ID 136697.1]

Note:101468.1 *"hout.sql" script to install the "hOut" helper package*

Note:101466.1 *Introduction to the "H*" Helper Scripts*

122669.1 *Healthcheck*

250262.1 *Healthcheck/Validation Engine Guide*

SQL*Net hardening, tuning, and troubleshooting

Think of this section as the glue or string that ties all of the disparate components together; all applications travel on the network layer of the enterprise structure. You will become an expert at troubleshooting Oracle's network protocols over time. There will be plenty of opportunities, so to speak. Also, it is time to discuss some of the security implications of network traffic, as the default is clear text with only the logon password encrypted, unless the Advanced Security/Networking Option (AS/NO) is purchased and implemented. Browser-based, server-based application hosting, or VPN applications can utilize SSL technology for encryption, but the traffic between servers is definitely easily sniffed! Security tips as it relates to SQL*Net will be scattered throughout this section.

In a hardened environment where strict control is needed, SQL*Net is often configured with guidelines similar to the following:

- Give each database a different listener port.
- Don't use port 1521 for any listener; this keeps databases from autoregistering, which keeps the DBA in control.
- Disable database parameter *.dispatchers='(PROTOCOL=TCP) (SERVICE=sidXDB)'.
- Put the ORACLE_HOME of the database in the appropriate listener.ora entry if you're using the Listener in a different ORACLE_HOME.
- Define local_listener parameter in spfile.
- Database parameter _TRACE_FILES_PUBLIC=FALSE — limits access to trace files that can contain sensitive data.
- Create two Oracle TNS Listeners: one for the Oracle database and one for PL/SQL EXTPROC if the external procedure feature needs to be used.

One of the first questions for a novice DBA seems to be how to create multiple database entries in the listener.ora file, as the default file contains only a single one. Here is an example to follow that implements some of the hardening guidelines:

```
listener_NEWDB9 =
    (ADDRESS = (PROTOCOL = TCP)(HOST = SERVER)(PORT = 1522))
SID_LIST_listener_NEWDB9 =
    (SID_LIST =
    (SID_DESC =
    (SID_NAME = NEWDB9)
    (ORACLE_HOME = /u01/app/oracle/product/10204)
    )
```

```
        )
listener_NEWDB=
        (ADDRESS = (PROTOCOL = TCP)(HOST = SERVER)(PORT = 1523))
SID_LIST_listener_NEWDB =
        (SID_LIST =
        (SID_DESC =
        (SID_NAME = NEWDB)
        (ORACLE_HOME = /u01/app/oracle/product/11107)
        )
        )
ADMIN_RESTRICTIONS_listener_NEWDB=ON
LOG_FILE_listener_NEWDB=listener_newdb.log
INBOUND_CONNECT_TIMEOUT_listener_NEWDB = 120
ADMIN_RESTRICTIONS_listener_NEWDB9=ON
LOG_FILE_listener_NEWDB=listener_newdb9.log
INBOUND_CONNECT_TIMEOUT_listener_NEWDB9 = 120
```

Notice how each database is listening on its own port number and resides in different Oracle homes. In this case, listener_NEWDB9 is listening on port 1522 and listener_NEWDB is listening on port 1523. All of the entries line up correctly with no guessing on the number or location of ellipses. This `listener.ora` uses `SID_NAME` instead of `SERVICE_NAME`. For more information on the differences and how best to use them, consult the following MOS document: *SERVICE_NAME Parameter - Resolving The ORA-12514 Error [Doc ID 77640.1]*.

While you can service multiple databases with a single listener, there may be reasons that you want to control SQL*Net access by taking down the listener. Keeping separate listeners on separate ports allows you to independently control them on a single server.

There are additional parameters in the `listener.ora` related to securing the listener. See the preceding entries related to `ADMIN_RESTRICTIONS`, `LOG_FILE`, and `INBOUND_CONNECT`. Like the MOS document details above, you may have to set the database parameter `local_listener`. See the following example:

```
local_listener="(address=(protocol=tcp)(host=server.
domain)(port=1533))"
```

As of 11gR2, setting a listener password is deprecated (the capability will be removed in future releases) due to the default security mechanism of only allowing the OS user account who owns the files any access without a password.

Control is the name of the game when following the above suggestions; it allows multiple ORACLE_HOME(s) to use a single listener or even a listener from a different version. Just like ASM, a higher-versioned listener can be used for a lower-level database—there is a built-in compatibility (see Chapter 7 for a more detailed discussion). Keeping listeners off the default autoregister port 1521 allows you to turn off various listeners for various reasons; end users can be prevented from certain applications when there is a planned outage for example.

Manipulating SQL*Net parameters and resolutions is done most commonly with listener.ora, sqlnet.ora, and tnsnames.ora files. There are other files associated with different naming methods like LDAP or Advanced Networking or Security Options that won't be covered in this book.

The tnsnames.ora file is the one that is distributed to the applications that need to connect to the database. If you make a query from within one database to another database (called a database link), then the local host copy of tnsnames.ora for the database is the one used.

Data Guard implementations also use a local tnsnames.ora file to find the location of the standby databases in a configuration. Database entries in a tnsnames.ora files are simply an alias name (this can be anything you want) and should be used to disguise the real name of the database. This adds a layer of anonymity and security between the end users and the database.

The sqlnet.ora file is responsible for tuning and controlling SQL*Net behavior as well as the order of naming the resolution—tnsnames.ora file, Oracle Internet Directory (OID-LDAP), or using the Host Naming Adapter (DNS-resolution on the host). SQL*Net resolution order dictates that it first looks in the local tnsnames.ora, then Oracle Names servers, and then the Host Naming Adapter. The parameter that influences this lookup order is the NAMES.DIRECTORY_PATH parameter in the sqlnet.ora file. Research each of the following entries, setting them appropriately for your environment, as some can be set at several different connection points—database, application server, and/or client:

```
SQLNET.EXPIRE_TIME Dead Connection Detection (DCD) Explained [ID
151972.1]
DEFAULT_SDU_SIZE- Packet Sizing
NAMES.DIRECTORY_PATH
TCP.NODELAY - Flushes all data across network
RECV_BUF_SIZE - large data transfers
SEND_BUF_SIZE - accompanying buffer for large transfers
SQLNET.INBOUND_CONNECT_TIMEOUT - Time to receive authentication
TCP.VALIDNODE_CHECKING - Limits connections by node
TCP.INVITED_NODES
TCP.EXCLUDED_NODES
```

The only way to prove without a doubt that these parameters are set correctly is to produce a SQL*Net trace file as verification. This resulting verification trace file should be kept with other hard-copy documentation for your organization. Additional information on how to start tracing is included in the following section, called *What can go wrong?*

There is a Data Guard Redo Transport and Network Best Practices white paper on the MAA website, but it applies to Oracle version 10g and below. As of 11g, the RDBMS has been rewritten for data transfers of bulk operations such as the redo transport services, so reconfiguring the SEND or RECV_BUF_SIZE is no longer recommended for Data Guard implementations. There is also the MOS document *Oracle Net "Connect Time" Performance Tuning [Doc ID 214022.1]* for general guidelines in tuning different types of naming resolutions.

Troubleshooting

There are some common rules as to how SQL*Net acts, depending on where the application that uses SQL*Net is executed. There are lots of different types of applications that use SQL*Net, not just the utility SQL*Plus.

If the connection is made from a PC, the connect string (what SQL*Net uses to identify the database) is found as the entry in the locally defined `tnsnames.ora`. By the way, it would be easier to administer a network-available copy of `tnsnames.ora` by defining a TNS_ADMIN system variable on each PC that provides staff with a common read-only file. This keeps you from having to troubleshoot staff desktop issues. As stated earlier, if a connection is done by a database link to another database, this resolution will be done by the local SQL*Net files on the database node.

Here is the TNS_ADMIN resolution list, as to which SQL*Net files are queried first and then in what order. It's great for troubleshooting complex issues:

- `TNS_ADMIN` defined as a locally global environment variable
- `TNS_ADMIN` set within the session or within a script
- SQL*Net files in `/var/opt/oracle` or `/etc` depending on Unix OS
- SQL*Net files in `$ORACLE_HOME/network/admin`

What can go wrong?

If the database was started with a different TNS_ADMIN set, then that is currently in effect, no matter how hard you try to reset it. The following `ps` command will show what variables are in effect for a process. It is a great troubleshooting tool! Some of the output was shortened for brevity.

```
oracle@nodename:/etc[newdb]
> ps -ef | grep smon
oracle   12700 11541   0 10:29 pts/0    00:00:00 grep smon
oracle   29111     1   0 Dec10 ?        00:00:37 ora_smon_newdb
oracle@nodename:/etc[newdb]
> ps eauwww  29111

TNS_ADMIN=/u01/app/oracle/product/11g/network/admin USER=oracle _AST_FEATURES=UNIVERS
E - ucb
```

Tracing is the primary method of troubleshooting a SQL*Net connection. You will need some practice to get the resulting trace files in the location desired: *MOS Note 219968.1: SQL*Net, Net8, Oracle Net Services - Tracing and Logging at a Glance.*

A recommendation is to keep a copy of appropriately-edited `sqlnet.ora` files for tracing, handy, to put into service when a connectivity issue comes up. And, as a side note, you must always be wary turning on full tracing for any type of troubleshooting in production: it may completely fill up the hard drive space! Use at first with caution until you are familiar with normal behaviour and then ramp up the tracing level as needed. Most DBAs would direct tracing to a filesystem not used for the database, such as `/tmp`. Another method on Unix systems is to use an operating system utility (`strace` in Linux, `struss` in BSD UNIX types) that can attach to a specific process being investigated. This is an advanced troubleshooting tool that can be used for any type of connection to the database that has a specific process ID that can be found by the following query:

```
SYS@NEWDB> select SPID from v$process where ADDR in
(select PADDR from v$session where username='<username of client>');
```

Then you can run the command with that specific server process ID; there are both `strace` and `struss` examples depending on your operating system.

```
struss -r all -w all -aefd -o <output filename> -p <server process id>
strace -p <server process id> -o <output filename>
```

For a free, highly recommended, open source utility called TNSMANAGER that resolves SQL*Net connections by LDAP protocols visit `http://www.shutdownabort.com/tnsmanager/`

Grid Control High Availability and Disaster Recovery

The Grid Control (GC) version of OEM is free, but its functionality is limited without the additional purchase of the Management Packs. It also includes two licenses not ordinarily included in the Enterprise Version of the database—Partitioning and RAC. Note that you are only allowed to use these free optional components on a repository (which is an Oracle database) dedicated to EM use. If you have a single database to administer, it is most likely you will use the Database Control Utility instead of the fully-fledged GC application; there is a difference in the features and functionality between the two versions. This section will deal with GC only. When GC 10.2.0.5 is mentioned in this chapter, it is referring to the OEM Server version and not a database version.

The Management Packs and Enhancements in GC 10.2.0.5 are:

- 11gR1+ Database Features—real-time SQL monitoring, Partition Advisor, Automatic SQL Tuning, Database Replay, and ADDM for RAC
- Diagnostics and Tuning Packs—highly recommended
- Data Masking Pack—condition-based, compound (multiple columns) masking, masking during cloning
- Provisioning Pack
- Database Change Pack—data dictionary synchronization
- Configuration Pack—new console, auditing features
- New- HA Console, MAA Config Advisor, Streams, and Oracle Backup
- Oracle Application Server—configuration, diagnostics, provisioning
- Host—configuration, audit, provisioning, system plugin
- Unbreakable Linux RPM management, bare-metal provisioning
- Virtualization Management Console – both physical and virtual
- Forms and Service Level Monitoring

The features and full functionality of GC is overwhelming to a novice DBA. It is assumed that the size of the organization and the number of servers you have to administer dictates the need for an enterprise-wide monitoring tool. GC doesn't install and run by itself and has a history of being difficult to install and administer.

Migrations to a different operating system and even standard GC upgrades have been nightmarish, causing a few of us very experienced DBAs to throw up our hands and trash an existing install and start completely over losing the valuable historical data. By the end of this section, you will see that the newest version of GC (10.2.0.5 at this writing) is finally able to be made highly available. This section contains quite a bit of advanced material that you may want to come back to later when you are actually involved with a GC install or migration project.

Recommended installation for GC 10.2.0.5+

With the release of GC 10.2.0.5, there are several more tools, utilities, and command-line options available for installing, migrating, or upgrading the repository. It is highly recommended to use the processes in the GC Advanced Configuration documentation called:

- *Enterprise Manager 10g Grid Control Install Using an Existing Database*

- *Silent Install Scenario — Installing Software Only and Configuring Later*

Both of these methods can be used for any 10.2.0.4+ version of Oracle Management Server. GC consists of three components—an Oracle database repository (repository), Oracle Management Server (OMS), and Oracle Management agents (agents). The repository contains all of the information that each of the individual agents upload by way of the OMS server processes.

The procedure recommended above has the repository and OMS install separated, not the default, if you run the GUI install for GC. The recommended installation is considered to be a complete custom installation.

A custom installation includes the different components installed in a particular order: install an Oracle Database configured with the prerequisities for a GC repository, install OMS server, and finally, the agents on any servers you want to monitor with GC.

Why should I install a separate database?

Because you tend to get caught (a painful migration) when a major change is required—such as the required time zone updates, CPUs, database and/or OMS patch sets, migrations to different nodes or operating systems, and so on. "If your Enterprise Manager Grid Control Release is 10.1.0.2, you cannot move your Repository (from the native 9.0.1.5 to) a 10.1.0.3 database." is a direct quote from the document on how to uncouple the native database installation: *How to Move a Grid Control Repository to a 10.1.0.3 Database [Note: 285087.1].*

Separating the installation allows the database install to be at 64-bit (64-bit OS) and keep the OMS install on 32-bit on a different node (32-bit OS). It also allows the use of 10.2.0.3+ for the database version. If you prefer, start with 11g, which will allow you to perform the install during Daylight Savings Time (patch set contains the required DST fixes); the caveat is that this method can't be used to migrate any OMS installation less than 10.2.0.4.

 The silent install of the Linux 32-bit GC 10.2.0.1 lets you install the 32-bit version onto a 64-bit OS (not good!). The 10.2.0.5 patch set halts the installation in this situation.

Install the Enterprise Edition database 10.1.0.4+ (see MOS Document ID 412431.1 for compatibility). I would recommend using, at the least, Oracle RDBMS version 10.2.0.3+. See *How to Pre-configure a 10g Database to Become the EM 10g Management Repository [Note: 285209.1]* for more information.

If you're using the GUI installation, specify full installation type (doesn't matter what version because you are upgrading to GC 10.2.0.4 or 10.2.0.5 immediately), using an Existing Database Option (note that if database spfile parameters are not at the recommended minimums, this install will fail).

Cookbook for silent install and configuring later

Before starting the install of the Base 10.2.0.1 or 10.2.0.2 OMS, the repository has already been created (see the MOS note in the preceding paragraph for exact details). Unzip the installation directories and create the response files (`em_using_existing_db.rsp` and `patchset_oms.rsp`, `patchset_agent.rsp`) in advance by using the documentation and MOS notes as a guide.

Double check the variables in the response files as shown in the following example, because there is no feedback on its success or failure until you run the configure script. Make a copy of the response files before starting. You will need two different sets of a response files for patching both the OMS and agent. The following is an example install on Unix using this method with notes scattered within.

```
./runInstaller -noconfig -silent -responseFile <exact_path>/em_using_existing_db.rsp
-force
$OMS_HOME/oraInstRoot.sh (as root, if no previous oracle products installed)
$OMS_HOME/allroot.sh (as root)
$OMS_HOME/opmn/bin/opmnctl stopall
Immediately install the 10.2.0.5 patchset (release notes explicitly tell you not to s
tart an unpatched OMS server)
./runInstaller -noconfig -silent -responseFile <exact_path>/patchset_oms.rsp -force
$OMS_HOME/root.sh (as root)
Now patch the agent (the reponse files are different)
./runInstaller -noconfig -silent -responseFile <exact_path>/patchset_agent.rsp -force
$AGENT_HOME/root.sh (as root)
export PERL5LIB=$OMS_HOME/perl/lib/5.6.1
$OMS_HOME/perl/bin/perl $OMS_HOME/sysman/install/ConfigureGC.pl <GC Base Dir>
There is a bug..in the following file you will see the error message below.
 $OMS_HOME/oms10g/sysman/log/emca_repos_drop<serial #>.log file
Could not connect to connect string ORA-01017: Invalid username/passsword: logon deni
ed (DBD ERROR: OCISessionBegin)
ALTER user SYS identified by "default"; (repository database)
$OMS_HOME/perl/bin/perl $OMS_HOME/sysman/install/ConfigureGC.pl <GC Base Dir> (run ag
ain it will fail again)
ALTER user SYS identified by "realpassword"; (repository database)
$OMS_HOME/perl/bin/perl $OMS_HOME/sysman/install/ConfigureGC.pl <GC Base Dir> (run ag
ain it should work this time to completion)
```

Note.763314.1: *How to Install Enterprise Manager Grid Control 10.2.0.5.0 Using a New Database with the Software Only Method*

Note.763347.1: *How to Install Enterprise Manager Grid Control 10.2.0.5.0 Using an Existing Database with the Software Only Method*

Note.793870.1: *How to Install Grid Control 10.2.0.5.0 on Enterprise Linux 4 Using the Existing Database (11g) Option*

Note.784963.1: *How to Install Grid Control 10.2.0.5.0 on Enterprise Linux 5 Using the Existing Database (11g) Option*

As a couple of side notes, there is an MAA advisor in the GC console and depending on the Oracle Database version as to whether it is a checklist or actual links. There also seems to be a concerted effort by Oracle to get you to install the Oracle Configuration Manager utility (as discussed in *Chapter 2, Maintaining Oracle Standards*). The Oracle Universal Installer (OUI), as part of the GC 10.2.0.5 install, hints that you are a *bad DBA* for staying uninformed about critical security issues! Do not buy into this, you are in control here. Say no until you are ready because information will be uploaded to MOS that can't be removed. The first screenshot shows part of the OUI for GC 10.2.0.5 where OCM is part of the install, you can always install this later.

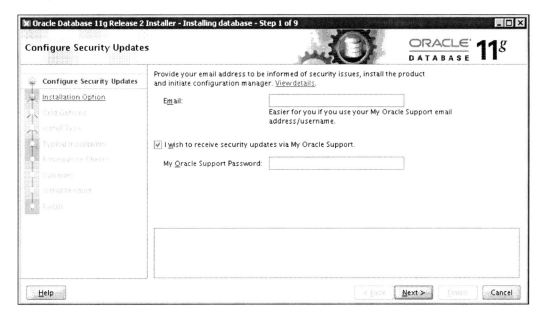

The second smaller screenshot happens if you don't choose to install OCM during this install with a smaller reminder.

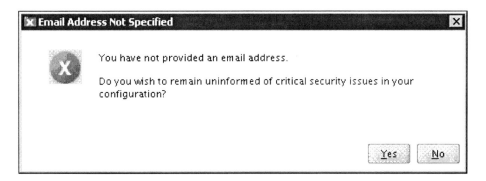

Migrating GC repositories

Grid Control (GC) Repository Database migrations such as moving to a new node, changing operating systems, character sets, or bit size are more daunting than working with the typical database.

For example, when moving an Oracle Management System (OMS) database repository version from 10.2.0.4 to 11.1.0.6 and changing the database character set to UTF8, there is no migration path. At the time of this migration: OMS 10.2.0.4 was only available as a patch set and not available as a full download. This was coupled with the fact that the OMS 10.2.0.1 base install didn't work with an existing 11.1.0.6 database, and also that the character set change prohibited a migration utilizing transportable tablespaces (see *Chapter 6, Extended RMAN* for more information on transportable tablespaces).

As you can probably tell, I was personally affected by this tragic series of events. This was the main impetus behind the research for this section. It wasn't going to get the best of me! Oracle has since provided a migration path for those clients wanting to install a 11g database for GC repository using the following instructions: *How to Install Grid Control 10.2.0.5.0 on OEL/RHEL5/SLES10 Using the Existing Database (11g) Option [ID 784963.1] or GC 10.2.0.4.0 [ID 467677.1]*.

Here are a few additional MOS documents and articles related to migrations:

- *Article-ID: Note 388090.1; Circulation: UNDER_EDIT (LIMITED); Title: Cross Platform EM Grid Control Repository/OMS Migration*

  ```
  http://kr.forums.oracle.com/forums/thread.jspa?threadID=
  517164&tstart=-6
  ```

- *The Grid Control Repository upgrade fails when upgrading the Grid Control [Note: 457877.1]*

- *Installation Checklist for EM 10g Grid Control 10.2.0.x to 10.2.0.3 OMS and Repository Upgrades [Note: 422061.1]*

- *Invalid Sysman Objects After Upgrading The Db Via Export/Import Note: 604129.1*

Transportable tablespace migrations

Transportable tablespaces (TT) are the recommended method for migrating GC repositories across platforms and they can even be utilized for upgrading the database version. We will be looking at the coolest tool a DBA has in their arsenal of weapons for migrating databases and TT in *Chapter 6, Extended RMAN*.

Limitations and requirements for using TT for GC:

- The source and target database must use the same character set
- If the source and target database are NOT on 10g—only Export/Import can be used for cross-platform migration
- If source and target database are on 10g—transportable tablespaces migration, data pump, or Export/Import can be used for cross-platform repository migration
- GC tablespace(s) cannot already exist
- Both databases must have compatibility set to at least 10.0
- Query the V$TRANSPORTABLE_PLATFORM to determine their platform IDs and their endian format (byte ordering) compatibility
- Source and destination host should both have an EM agent running and configured to the database that is to be migrated
- If target database has EM repository installed, it should be first dropped using the GC utility `RepManager` before the target database-related steps are carried out

There is another way to migrate across platforms or versions for both the OMS and repository components. It is quick, but you will lose historical information as follows: default purging policies—7 days raw data, 31 days of the one-hour aggregated metric data, 365 days of the one-day aggregated metric data, custom UDM, custom reports, and custom jobs. See the following list for the generalized steps:

1. Install the grid control/repository on the new server(s), then fully patch.
2. Configure host agents to talk to new OMS server-stop agent, edit `emoms.properties` for correct URL. Restart the agent.
3. Configure OMS manually to point to the new repository—this is done by stopping all services, editing `targets.xml` and `emoms.properties`, and restarting.
4. Will have to redefine all custom items: jobs/reports, preferred credentials, notifications, and pack access agreement.
5. Can fallback to previous version or even use them concurrently with different agents communicating between the two OMS servers.

Keeping the repository highly available

Just as with any other Oracle database, there are several recommended practices to keep it highly available: RAC, archivelog mode, RMAN backups full + incremental, the flashback database, block change tracking, and/or the use of physical standbys.

For advanced users, there is an Enterprise Manager Diagnostics Kit available from Metalink with an example: *EMDiagkit – How to Use the Repository Diagnostics [Note: 421563.1]*

```
./repvfy -usr SYSMAN -pwd password -tns nodename:port:SID
```

 See "Maintaining and Troubleshooting the Management Repository" at:
http://download.oracle.com/docs/cd/B16240_01/doc/
em.102/e10954/repository.htm

Repository backups, restores, or imports

When you use RMAN database backup and recovery, there may be issues that are specific to GC, depending on the type of recovery used.

- Full recovery same host—no issues except for blackout targets during restore
- Partial or point-in-time—agent will resynch correct information—emctl resync repos
- Target nodes need to be in Blackout because agents keep collecting data and may overrun certain disk thresholds set in <AGENT10G_HOME>/sysman/config/emd.properties

From the following URL, there are steps that are important to run following a migration or restore using the import method:

http://download.oracle.com/docs/cd/B16240_01/doc/em.102/e10954/
repository.htm

Post-repository import EM steps:

1. Recompile invalid objects.
2. Create missing public synonyms.
3. Create other users needed for GC functionality.
4. Enable VPD.
5. Re-pin certain sysman packages.
6. Recreate partitions—this improves performance and free license with GC.
7. DBMS_JOBS reset to remove invalid entries.
8. emoms.properties needs to be adjusted for the correct entries.

OMS patch sets have no de-installation: this means you need to fully restore the OMS home, repository, and inventory with a backup copy.

Note 733848.1: *How to backup and restore Grid Control*

Enterprise Manager 10gR2/R3 Backup, Recovery and Disaster Recovery Considerations

`http://www.oracle.com/technology/deploy/availability/`
`pdf/EM10gR2_BR_WP.pdf`

Doc ID 733530.1: *How to Move Grid Control Repository Using DBCA*

Doc ID 602955.1: *How To Move the Grid Control Repository Using an Inconsistent (Hot) Database Backup*

MAA—repository on a physical standby database

How do you duplicate a GC repository for failing over when there is an outage on the primary database? This is where Data Guard comes into play, where you will be installing a physical standby (see the next chapter on Data Guard) with special steps taken in order to provide a useable GC repository when outages occur. These are the general steps for providing a GC repository standby that can be failed over if the primary is down:

1. Create a physical standby repository.

2. Install and configure additional standby OMS linked to primary database.

3. Edit standby OMS `emoms.properties` to point to the standby database repository.

4. Replicate data upload directory on standby OMS node to limit transaction loss. This is an optional step.

5. Configure Fast Start Failover for the standby repository if desired.

6. Use custom-written triggers to start OMS at standby.

7. Configure standby Load Balancer at a remote site for multiple OMS if installed, for complete redundancy.

This simplified method is quick, works well, and is much easier to implement than the Active/Active or Active/Passive methods that Oracle invented. Investigate all of the methods yourself to decide which is best for your environment.

Oracle's Method – *Active/Active or Active/Passive - How To Configure Grid Control Components for High Availability [ID 330072.1]*

OMS and agents' high availability

While the standard database procedures are used to keep the repository highly available, there are other tactics for the Agent and OMS components of GC. Scaling GC upward is mostly done by adding OMS servers, architecturally speaking in a horizontal fashion. Multiple OMS servers, each installed on their own server, are all configured to communicate with a single repository database. Agents can be configured to talk to different OMS servers for load balancing in a large environment.

Keeping the Agents highly available is best achieved with multiple installed OMS with a Hardware Load Balancer front end. That would mean the agent would only communicate the uploaded data to a single SSL-enabled URL, with multiple OMS installed behind the load balancer in a pool. In theory, this would result in no downtime for monitoring activities for any active agent and also provides a pool of OMS boxes that can be taken offline for outages without affecting normal GC functionality.

If you can't afford all of the hardware to replicate the repository, at the very least you should install a redundant OMS, as it is the easiest task to accomplish. The additional OMS can reside on a small node and take over if the primary OMS becomes unavailable. You can configure agents to talk to multiple OMS (called an upload pool), which will provide a poor-man's load balancing, but the agents would have to be reconfigured if one of the OMS servers is not available.

Cloning Management agents

Finally, Oracle has done something truly useful for installing agents. They tried over the years with push and pull technologies that didn't always work, required too much effort or required additional utilities.

See the following URL for the documentation on cloning an agent:
`http://download.oracle.com/docs/cd/B16240_01/doc/`
`install.102/e10953/cloning_agent.htm#CIHFGEEE`

In the following example, `$AGENT_HOME` is the directory where the agent is installed, and making it unique from any other Oracle install requires an `ORACLE_HOME_NAME`. This name is a short description of your choosing, it doesn't have to match the previously installed `ORACLE_HOME_NAME`.

Now it is so simple! First install a 10.2.0.5 Management agent on the appropriate OS that you want to clone, then:

1. Zip and transfer the entire previously installed agent directory $AGENT_HOME.

2. If upgrading, put in the same location as before (not in instructions). Otherwise pick an appropriate directory that is part of the OFA standards.

   - `$AGENT_HOME/oui/bin/runInstaller -clone -forceClone ORACLE_HOME= ORACLE_HOME_NAME= -noconfig -silent`
   - `$AGENT_HOME/bin/agentca -f`
   - `$AGENT_HOME/root.sh (as root)`

Since you cloned an existing install, it automatically configures the same settings (OMS and upload port) to configure the agent for this node.

> This is a list of ports and associated configuration files for agents:
>
> Secure Upload Port — 1159 — httpd_em.conf, emoms.properties, portlist.ini
>
> Agent Registration Port — 4889 — httpd_em.conf, emoms.properties, portlist.ini
>
> Secure Console Port — 4444 — ssl.conf (See MOS Note: 353736.1)

GC at a very large site

There are certain recommendations from the MAA website if your GC is larger than most, but there seems to be conflicting information on what actually defines a large site. Oracle defines one as having more than 100 targets (database, application servers, listeners, or applications) to monitor. If your site is smaller than that, then the following list is probably overkill.

- Multiple OMS servers
- Hardware load balancer
- Dual repositories in an active/passive configuration (see MAA website)
- Upload pools for multiple OMS
- Large repository — true in emoms.properties

A couple of parting tips for this section:

One of the best ideas for GC is to create groups of target databases and configure backup jobs on the entire group. Using GC to backup databases is a personal choice and some DBAs choose to control each one carefully using their own tools (see *Chapter 6, Extended RMAN*). It depends on the database size and complexity of the architecture within your enterprise.

How to obtain the Job details – Parameters / Scripts from the Grid Control Repository [Note: 601554.1], which outlines a simple method for extracting the actual scripts, runs as part of the reporting feature within the GC console.

Taking more time in the beginning with the Grid Control install will allow for fewer interruptions in service when the next migration, upgrade, patch, or patch set is required. Don't do the default install of all components on the same box. If GC is to be your enterprise-wide monitoring tool, then a certain amount of time and effort will be required to keep it robust and available when it is needed most.

Summary

This is an advanced chapter that you will need to refer back to when major changes happen within your enterprise, such as when any piece of hardware is due for replacement. There may be a way of using the older hardware (if the budget is tight) to redeploy for redundancy reasons or it may be a great way of getting your hands on a DBA-only test box.

Maximum Availability Architecture is a methodology, best practiced for maximizing the amount of uptime for your critical applications. Committing to maximizing uptime not only takes physical components but several key organizational practices to be in place. This is where the managers in your IT department need to become involved. If the organizational practices are not present in your organization, maybe it is time to speak up about their validity and importance in today's IT-centric organizations. As an Oracle DBA, you will have some pull in matters such as these. So you can take a stand for improving your situation.

This chapter covered some of the topics on the MAA website with some additional information researched when the documentation was found lacking. It wasn't a rehash of the MAA website, but an integration of real-world implementations and practices as they apply to the following components of HA organizations:

- Overview of Maximum Availability Architecture
- Optimizing Oracle Database Availability
- SQL*Net hardening, tuning and troubleshooting
- Grid Control High Availability and Disaster Recovery

MAA is all about redundancy, and that includes you the DBA. You will be responsible most often for your own redundancy in a smaller IT organization, which means documenting what you do carefully with both an electronic and hard paper copy for your backup to be able to carry on if you are unavailable. Sorry, there is nothing like a physical standby for a person, yet. What a great lead in for the next chapter!

5
Data Guard and Flashback

There are three types of standby database available in the Enterprise edition of 11g Oracle: Logical, Snapshot, and Physical. This chapter will cover the differences between the standby types, implementation details, and testing/recovery scenarios using both Data Guard and Flashback technologies in tandem for stress testing, hot fixes, and data recovery. Oracle has made further improvements to Data Guard to facilitate the use of standbys for testing purposes—one of these is called Database States. It is a simplified method of turning off the data flow from one standby to another, giving the DBA total control over the process.

 Oracle Standard Edition, which doesn't include the automatically managed recovery capabilities found in Data Guard, can be used for some of the steps outlined in this chapter. The basic concepts are the same, all commands will be carried out with SQL*Plus and shell scripting to transport the archivelogs used for recovery. See the following MOS document for more details: *Alternative for standby/dataguard in standard edition [ID 333749.1]*

A Data Guard configuration consists of all databases that are involved: the primary that contains the original data and any copy of that data in separate databases (on different servers) that are kept in synch with the primary. In 11gR2, a configuration can consist of up to 30 databases—any combination of RAC, non-RAC, physical, logical, or snapshot.

In this chapter, we will describe different scenarios for utilizing the standby database technology in Oracle for something other than just failover for the primary database or a copy of production data for reporting purposes. Look for interesting features and implementation details as they apply in the different situations, providing answers to the long-standing problem: How do you reduce downtime? You learned in the last chapter that 80% of downtime was most often caused by known, planned outages, making this chapter a logical extension to the last chapter about Maximum Availability Architecture.

Transitions from one database role to another are called switchovers (planned events) or failovers (unplanned events), where Data Guard can actually execute all of the tasks of the transition with just a few commands. All of the specialized tasks in this chapter in the scenario section are being illustrated with SQL*Plus, allowing the reader to see all the operations that are being executed versus using the GUI Enterprise Manager console or the dgmgrl command-line utility.

To fully address all issues related to using Data Guard for disaster recovery, your organization must first define time limits to keep from overusing the physical standby for tasks outlined in this chapter that are other than a full switchover or failover from the primary. Balancing the primary objective of being able to switchover with the least amount of downtime with the ability to more fully utilize the failover hardware in a testing configuration should be in measurable limits. These limits can be simply defined in the following terms: Recovery Point Objective (how far back you can lose transactions) and Recovery Time Objective (the longest amount of time you can take to recover) will be the basis to gauge the point of no return.

The combination of Flashback and Data Guard for recovery scenarios and hot fix patching (installing a patch on a database while it is open) on a physical standby are possible because it is making the standby read/write temporarily. This can reduce or eliminate downtime for the primary database for certain types of recovery situations and may reduce or eliminate the need for duplication of hardware for testing purposes.

These are the database connection descriptors and ORACLE_SID designations for the remainder of this chapter as well as the book:

```
PRIMARY>
STANDBY>
LOGICAL>
ORACLE_SID
ORCL (primary),STANDBY (physical standby),LOGL (logical standby)
```

In *Chapter 3, Tracking the Bits and Bytes*, you learned that redo logs are vulnerable to anyone with the Oracle standard utility LogMiner. Now in 11g, the standby redo stream is encrypted by an SSL Authenticated Redo Session between the databases in a configuration.

Physical, snapshot, and logical standbys

A **physical** standby is a block-for-block copy of the primary using Redo Apply with different levels of protection against data loss, depending on desired performance and resource restrictions. A **snapshot** standby is almost identical to a standard physical standby except that it is a snapshot of the data at a point in time. This type of database was designed for performing various testing scenarios without affecting the production database.

A **logical** standby is a read-only copy of the primary (production database) where redo data from the primary is applied while the database is open, via a process called SQL Apply. Additional read/write schemas can be added to the logical standby while still protecting the primary information in read-only mode. Certain data types are not supported and some DDL is skipped during the SQL Apply process. Logical standbys can also be used for Rolling Upgrades, which is purported to be the smallest amount of downtime achievable. That topic will be further discussed in *Chapter 7*.

As a DBA, there are usually more than one ways to administer an Oracle product. In this case, you have a choice between the High Availability Console of Grid Control to administer standbys, Data Guard's command-line utility called `dgmgrl`, or even just SQL commands within SQL*Plus for configuring and administering all of the components.

This chapter utilizes several of Oracle's advanced features, which may require your organization to purchase additional licenses. Your IT staff will need to consult with your Oracle Sales Representative to determine the extent of testing that can occur before violating any licensing agreements. In a general sense, Oracle trusts their customers because the software is free to download and beta test, provided that none of your production data is involved with the testing environment.

There are plenty of examples on the Internet for creating huge amounts of fake data for testing new features or versions of Oracle:

Large data examples on *Ask Tom*: `http://asktom.oracle.com`.

OTN forum post also has some examples for creating large amounts of data:

`http://forums.oracle.com/forums/thread.jspa?threadID=964611`.

Physical standby database

This is the beginning point for creating any type of standby; it is most easily accomplished using Oracle's RMAN utility (see *Chapter 6, Extended RMAN* for more details). A physical standby is primarily meant as a failover (or switchover) in case there is a production down issue on the primary database. A physical standby is sitting idly waiting for something disastrous to happen in production. Why not use this same hardware for testing?

Here are some areas that are the same or similar for failover and testing:

- Similar hardware as production, in most cases an exact duplicate
- Same Oracle products, same version as production as part of standby requirement
- Same data as production

It is easy to see that all of the work the DBA has done to get the standby ready for failover can also be used towards creating a valid testing environment. Oracle has several optional products (Active Data Guard, Real Application Testing, and SQL Performance Analyzer) that are meant for testing in a Data Guard standby environment. These options are not required for utilizing the framework of the Data Guard for your own testing; the basic Oracle license required for standbys is the Enterprise Edition. The difference is that your organization will have to come up with your own testing suite of tools (see Oracle's free Orion tool in *Chapter 8*).

Snapshot standby database

There is the introduction of a third version of a standby database in 11g called a snapshot database. A snapshot database is converted from a physical standby with a snapshot, designating that all data has been frozen at a certain point of time. Redo from the primary is received and archived, but it is not applied.

This makes using a physical standby for the scenarios in the previous sections easier, as the steps are now combined into a single feature known as snapshot standby, receiving redo while functioning as a reporting database (read-only) or a testing environment (read/write). Enhancements in 11g also reduce the number of steps (SQL commands) executed.

Logs can still be shipped from the primary while running the scenarios. This reduces the standby recovery time after testing is finished. Flashback database must be enabled with a flash recovery area on the standby. It takes a guaranteed restore point and opens it up in read/write mode while still receiving redo with a single command (actually more because you may have to cancel any managed recovery in progress, shut down after conversion, and bring it back up).

```
STANDBY> ALTER DATABASE CONVERT TO SNAPSHOT STANDBY;
```

Then a single command returns it back to a physical standby, flashing it back to the guaranteed restore point (after shutting it down and mounting).

```
STANDBY> ALTER DATABASE CONVERT TO PHYSICAL STANDBY;
```

The database will have to be shut down and mounted again, with managed recovery restarted, before it will resume its full functionality of a physical standby database.

Logical standby database

In 11g, there are two options when creating a logical standby database. The first option allows a read-only copy of the primary in addition to any read/write schemas that might be created. This would be very useful for a reporting database that not only keeps all of the primary read-only data but also the addition of indexes, materialized views, and other database objects typically only found in a data warehouse environment—the best of both worlds in one database.

The command to use the logical standby for reporting only (run during creation steps) and never use it for failing over from a primary database is:

```
LOGICAL> ALTER DATABASE RECOVER TO LOGICAL STANDBY db_name;
```

The second option is to use the logical standby for disaster recovery (for failover and be able to switch back and forth with primary) as well as reporting needs, so the following command is issued instead:

```
LOGICAL> ALTER DATABASE RECOVER TO LOGICAL STANDBY KEEP IDENTITY;
```

This keeps the same DBID and DB_NAME identical as the primary. The main reason for the new KEEP IDENTITY clause option is that a physical standby database can be temporarily converted into a logical standby database for what Oracle calls a rolling upgrade. This temporary conversion step allows for very short outages during an Oracle upgrade or patch set application. It is used to convert this database back into a primary and physical standby when the upgrade is over. More information on using a logical standby for rolling upgrades will be covered in *Chapter 7, Migrating to 11g: Step-Ordered Approach*.

A logical standby is not a guaranteed copy and there may be any combination of missing data (due to incompatible data types), additional R/W schemas, materialized views, and/or indexes in the logical standby. That is why there are two different commands available, as shown above in the code lines in this section. If your logical standby database doesn't contain any unsupported data types, then you can use it for both purposes: failover and reporting.

A logical standby can guard all objects in the reporting instance from being modified or only those objects that have the transactions being transferred from the primary database (standby). This behavior is regulated by the following commands and is run during the creation steps:

```
LOGICAL>alter database guard standby;
LOGICAL>alter database guard all;
```

Commodity hardware and mixed environments

Our organization utilizes inexpensive commodity hardware, where the trade-off for less durability is compensated by running more standbys. This reduces our costs overall while ensuring a more robust testing and disaster recovery environment.

Certain Data Guard configurations can also run in a mixed Oracle binary environment—64-bit and 32-bit, while part of the same operating system family (Linux, Solaris, AIX, among others), making physical standbys adaptable to more environments. You can mix hardware from different manufacturers; the number of CPU's, RAM, storage differences, processor, operating systems versions, and distributions will provide even more flexibility in designing the architecture (see *MOS Note: 413484.1* for exact details). While this sounds good, it will have tradeoffs, which may include reduced performance due to the differences in capacity as well as increased complexity that may interfere with a smooth transition from primary to the standby site.

There are some major issues with working in a mixed environment—lack of good documentation, reverting to older technology for backups and restores (not RMAN) and the possibility of more errors or problems during switchover and/or failovers.

 Data Guard cannot be used, only the SQL*Plus command-line for mixed environments in 10gR2; this limitation is removed as of 11g. Also, note that in a mixture of 32- and 64-bit environments that an extra step has to be done before switching over (see *MOS Note: 62290.1 Changing between 32-bit and 64-bit Word Sizes*).

An example of an issue found in a heterogeneous environment with a mixture of 32-bit Linux and Windows 11.1.0.7 Physical Standbys is as follows: `ORA-16191: Primary log shipping client not logged on standby`. The password file was interpreted with a different case than what it was created with. This was fixed by turning off the case-sensitivity option by changing the spfile parameter `SEC_CASE_SENSITIVE_LOGON=FALSE`, creating the password files on both servers using the same password, and passing `ignorecase=Y` to the `orapwd` utility.

What is Data Guard broker?

Data Guard broker is itself a background Oracle monitor process (DMON) that provides a complex set of role management services governing all of the databases in a configuration; it can be executed at the command line (either SQL*Plus or `dgmgrl`) or with the GUI GC High Availability console. This broker controls the redo transport services component of Data Guard and is accountable for transmitting defect-free archive logs from any possible archive location, thereby automatically resolving any gaps due to network failures or database unavailability. The Log Apply Services within Data Guard are responsible for maintaining the synchronization of transactions between the primary and standbys.

What controls the Data Guard broker?

The Data Guard broker process can be configured in two different ways. One is at the database level with a parameter. The default setting is shown below and if you run a query from the operating system a new background process has been started:

```
SYS@PRMY>   show parameter broker
SYS@PRMY>   dg_broker_start          boolean      FALSE

SYS@PRMY>   alter system set dg_broker_start =true scope=both;
System altered.

oracle@nodename:/u01/app/oracle/bk[PRMY]
>ps -ef | grep dmon
oracle   25601    1   0 09:31 ?        00:00:00 ora_dmon_newdb
```

The other way is that the Data Guard broker is controlled by configuration files located at the operating system level for access by the `dgmgrl` utility. The location is defined by the database parameters, as seen in the example below. These files are binary and not directly edited.

```
SYS@PRMY> show parameter broker_config
NAME                            TYPE          VALUE
------------------------------  ------------  ------------------------------
dg_broker_config_file1          string        /u01/app/oracle/product/11g/dbs/dr1PRMY.da
t
dg_broker_config_file2          string        /u01/app/oracle/product/11g/dbs/dr2PRMY.da
t
```

There are occasions when the properties of the Data Guard broker viewed and edited using the command-line utility `dgmgrl` are not in sync with what the database parameters are. These situations usually occur during the initial standby creation steps or after a manual adjustment using SQL*Plus. Use of the GC HA console automatically checks for synchronization issues, asks you which one to use and makes the correct adjustments as needed.

In a testing environment, you may want to remove all traces of a configuration. I would recommend removing the `dr*.dat` files found in `$ORACLE_HOME/dbs`, but doing so only after the Data Guard broker process has been stopped on all databases and the configuration has been removed. A configuration can be removed using either the `dgmgrl` or the GC HA console. For additional troubleshooting, log monitoring as well as rotation tasks, also check the Data Guard log located in the ADR home trace directory with a pattern of `drc<ORACLE_SID>.log`.

Which tool is best?

There are DBAs who want more control over all of the configuration details for physical standbys without the use of the Data Guard broker. That would dictate using only the SQL*Plus commands and may be fully scripted with extensive testing. More commands are required but you maintain strict control over every step during creation, any transition, and monitoring processes.

If you want to monitor and change the configuration using the GC HA console, then the Data Guard broker is required to be running. It is up to you to decide on how best to implement the different details of standby databases accomplished, by testing different scenarios on the hardware available in your situation.

Even in 11gR2 you will not be able to accomplish everything using only one method or utility, so familiarity with all of the available methods is a good idea. Reliance on one might leave your site vulnerable to outages if the utility you tested isn't available in a disaster situation. The foolproof method would be the reason for SQL*Plus changing the database parameters.

Over the years in using the standby technology (since version 8i), there were times I used all three methods of access with standbys. SQL*Plus is the one that is fundamental and universal for changing a Data Guard configuration. Some of the reasoning is included as follows:

SQL*Plus (both interactively and through shell scripting):

- Initial standby database creation along with RMAN
- `LOG_ARCHIVE_DEST_n` initialization parameter—initial redo transport setup
- Troubleshooting and adjusting database parameter settings
- Implementing advanced features not available through the console
- Monitoring when the GC console is not available

You can find SQL*Plus instructions in the Oracle documentation titled *Data Guard Concepts and Administration*.

DGMGRL (interactive on the primary database):

- Initial setup of the configuration with existing databases
- Failover and switchover commands
- Changing the protection mode
- Viewing diagnostic information
- Checking SQL Apply and Redo Apply rates

Information on the command-line tool `dgmgrl` is found in the document labeled *Data Guard Broker*.

GC High Availability (HA) console:

- Adding existing standby databases
- Changing protection mode (except for Maximum Protection)
- Monitoring the diagnostic and redo rates
- Creating standby redo logs

I would recommend the use of the GC HA console for becoming familiar with the entire process and the initial testing with smaller amounts of data. The console is most useful for learning the correct formatting of the database parameters (`log_archive_dest_state_x`) that can become quite long and convoluted when using standby databases in a complicated multisite configuration. These long strings are seen in the next section.

To use the GC HA console requires a working network connection between the servers with a properly configured `/etc/hosts` file that has entries for all the hosts involved. To use GC, Intelligent Agent is also required to be up and running on all of the same hosts. If there are connection issues with GC HA, try logging out of all databases and the console itself and try again.

It may also require a restart of the listeners on several of the nodes to recognize certain changes that have occurred — the least disruptive way to accomplish this is with a reload command in a production environment. It rereads the `listener.ora` and `sqlnet.ora` keeping currently connected sessions while any new sessions can connect with the updated configuration.

```
ORACLE@PRIMARYNODE[ORCL]
>$ORACLE_HOME/bin
> lsnrctl

LSNRCTL for Linux: Version 11.1.0.7.0 - Production on 04-JAN-2010 14:34:50

Copyright (c) 1991, 2008, Oracle.  All rights reserved.

Welcome to LSNRCTL, type "help" for information.

LSNRCTL>set current_listener listener_orcl
LSNRCTL>reload
```

Start with the default configuration—maximum performance

To begin using physical standbys, I would recommend starting off with the simplest of features and ramping up as your experience and expertise improves. The minimum database parameters will be listed in this section. These are the implementation details for a single primary and physical standby configuration.

These are the default settings for a single database parameter archive destination when creating a standby using an HA console in GC:

```
log_archive_dest_2  string  service="(DESCRIPTION=(ADDRESS
                            =(PROTOCOL=tcp)(HOST=servername)(PORT=numb
er))(CONNECT_DATA                              =(SERVICE_
NAME=ORCL1)(SERVER=DEDICATED)))",
LGWR
ASYNC
NOAFFIRM
delay=0
optional
compression=disable
max_failure=0
max_connections=1
reopen=300 ----try again every 300 seconds
db_unique_name="ORCL1"
net_timeout=30,
valid_for=(all_logfiles,primary_role)
```

Put all of these parameters into a SQL file, which can be edited and run within SQL*Plus instead of trying to type this long database parameter! Worth noting is that Oracle reserves the `log_archive_dest_1` for your local archive destination. This is where I state (you will hear this again in the *Chapter 6*) that you need a local operating system location in addition to a flash recovery area and/or a standby archive destination for your archived redo logs.

The GC console is lacking when it comes to adjusting or fine tuning Data Guard specific initialization parameters. Tweaking some of these parameters can only be done by SQL*Plus by editing the database initialization parameters or `dgmgrl`.

View the same default configuration created by GC using the `dgmgrl` utility:

```
oracle@nodename:/u01/app/oracle[orcl]
> dgmgrl
DGMGRL for Linux: Version 11.2.0.1.0 - 64bit Production

Copyright (c) 2000, 2009, Oracle. All rights reserved.

Welcome to DGMGRL, type "help" for information.
DGMGRL> connect sys/password
Connected.
DGMGRL> show configuration

Configuration - ORCL

  Protection Mode: MaxPerformance
  Databases:
    ORCL  - Primary database
    ORCL1 - Physical standby database

Fast-Start Failover: DISABLED

Configuration Status:
SUCCESS
```

Utilizing multiple standby sites

Our IT organization has two standby sites. One is located in a different building within the same city block, and is labeled as a Local Disaster Recovery Site. The other is located 80 miles away in a datacenter facility and is known as the Remote Disaster Recovery Site. All of the stress testing, hot fixing, and flashback occurs on the remote site that has a larger Recovery Time Objective window than the local site. That allows me up to 24 hours to use the Remote Standby Database for testing until the Recovery Time Objective is exhausted.

In our production environment, the time it took to switchover for a planned outage on the primary instance was less than two minutes, but failing all clients beforehand lengthened the actual process to 15. To ensure that no data loss would occur, we decided to shut down all clients/sessions before switching over as stated in the *Switchover and Failover Best Practices: Oracle Data Guard 10g Release 2*. This white paper is available at the MAA website. Further reduction in time can be gained by scripting the event to run concurrently on the various server applications involved in automating the shutdown of clients, switching over, and then bringing the client applications backup.

 For Maximum Availability Architecture go to http://www.oracle.com/technology/deploy/availability/ htdocs/maa.htm.

Making a failover or switchover to the standbys transparent to the end users is a worthwhile objective but hard to achieve. In our case, the major desktop ERP application utilizes Oracle Forms, which cannot survive this transition without a disconnect to the client. Failover transparency is easier to achieve with web-based and/or read-only client connections.

There are several factors that determine whether the client has to completely restart the application or just log on again with the presentation of a dialog box for the username and password:

- How long the connection is down
- A read-only versus a read-write application
- Network and router configuration—timeout or automatic disconnect settings
- SQL*Net settings (such as Dead Connection Detection)

Protection modes and real-time apply

Performance and data protection for a standby database are tied to what is called the protection mode, each of which is implemented with slightly different processes and procedures. Each of these modes are tied to a combination of database parameters and the data dictionary, as seen in the v$database view.

```
SYS@PRIMARY>select protection_mode from v$database;
```

You will see a maximum performance setting on all databases even if they aren't involved in a Data Guard configuration, as it is the default setting. In 11g, there is also another setting related to standbys that is called a database state. Look for that discussion further down in this chapter.

Maximum performance (default)

This data protection mode has the least performance impact on a primary database and has to wait only for the local transaction to be written to the database's online redo logs. ASYNC means asynchronous or that each is an independent action because the writes to the standby are done after the commit. The other settings are as follows:

- Redo Archival Process: LGWR or ARCH
- Network Transmission mode: ASYNC when using LGWR only
- Disk Write Option: NOAFFIRM
- Standby Redo Logs: Not required

As long as the LNS process is able to empty this buffer faster than the LGWR can fill it, the LGWR will never stall. If the LNS cannot keep up, then the buffer will become full and the LGWR will stall until either sufficient buffer space is freed up by a successful network transmission or a timeout occurs. For further information on the buffer, see the *Data Guard Concepts and Administration* guide regarding `LOG_ARCHIVE_DEST_N` and the `SYNC/ASYNC` attributes.

When remotely archiving using the ARCH attribute, redo logs are transmitted to the destination during an archival operation. The archiver processes (ARCH) serve as the redo log transport service. Using ARCH to remotely archive does not impact the primary database throughput as long as enough sufficiently sized redo log groups exist, so that the most recently used group can be archived before that group is reopened.

Maximum performance recommendations

There is a good reason why this protection mode is the default—it keeps performance degradation on the primary to a minimum. The wait event (where the database is waiting on a particular resource) most often encountered is `LNS wait on SENDREQ` by the LGWR process and is defined as follows:

This wait event monitors the amount of time spent by all LNS processes to write the received redo to disk as well as open and close the remote archived redo logs.

There is a tunable buffer in 512 byte blocks in the ASYNC attribute. In the example below, an ASYNC buffer size of 2048 * 512 byte = 1MB:

```
log_archive_dest_2   string  service="(DESCRIPTION=(ADDRESS
                              =(PROTOCOL=tcp)(HOST=servername)(PORT=numb
er))(CONNECT_DATA                                  =(SERVICE_
NAME=ORCL1)(SERVER=DEDICATED)))",
LGWR
ASYNC=2048
NOAFFIRM
delay=0
optional
compression=disable
max_failure=0
max_connections=1
reopen=300
db_unique_name="ORCL1"
net_timeout=30,
valid_for=(all_logfiles,primary_role)
```

If the LNS process can keep this buffer empty, LGWR will have no problem keeping up, but if there is a network outage that is longer than the reopen setting then the waits will occur as described above.

Fast Start Failover for maximum performance mode: As of 11g, there is more control and more configurable options to determine specific conditions for the more transient or temporary outages before the automatic failover occurs. Look in the Data Guard broker documentation for the DBMS_DG PL/SQL package details.

These are the health conditions that can be automatically detected for Automatic Fast Start Failover: Datafile Offline, Corrupted Dictionary, Corrupted Controlfile, Inaccessible Logfile, or Stuck Archiver. This is an essential list for a DBA of some of the most common problems encountered on a primary database that would cause downtime. We have already covered the prevention of several of these items in the last chapter, and we will cover how to resolve the remaining items when you don't have a standby to fail over in *Chapter 6*. Several of these can be fixed quickly if you have the proper procedure in place to detect and notify you when the alert log records these errors, but you must have practiced the fix in a non-production database and documented the exact procedure.

Maximum availability

Transactions on the primary do not commit until written to both the primary's online redo log and to at least one standby redo log, but falls back to maximum performance mode if the remote redo task fails a second time:

- Redo Archival Process: LGWR
- Network Transmission mode: SYNC
- Disk Write Option: AFFIRM
- Standby Redo Logs: Yes

Maximum availability recommendations

With this protection mode, there will be a database wait for transactions that are considered writes (basically anything that is not a select statement). While having more than one physical standby will ensure the likelihood that at least one of them will always be written to, there are no guarantees that a network event won't take all standbys offline. Even transient network events (depending on other parameters associated with the archive destinations) can be disruptive to the standby processes.

This protection mode translates into the need for more horsepower (faster CPU, more memory, faster I/O bandwidth) for this database to keep those waits as short as possible. There is no hard-and-fast formula for calculating how well a database will perform under these circumstances. As a DBA, you will have to run through full production tests with a valid measuring tool. This is what a physical standby would be best used for—testing a full production load. Stay tuned for more of these details later in this chapter.

There are other features that are usually recommended to be implemented at the same time if you decide on this mode, such as using the fast-start failover procedure to fail over all clients automatically when the primary database is no longer available. This requires the use of the Data Guard broker process and a separate server install of an Observer process.

The Observer monitors all members of a Data Guard configuration (via a heartbeat ping), updating all of the Data Guard process(es) as to everyone's status. It is the DG broker that will implement that automatic failover process, so this type of protection mode requires the use of the DG broker and is most often implemented using the dgmgrl utility.

Maximum protection and recommendations

This mode is difficult to implement and should only be tested for the first time with small databases of just a few GBs. The protection mode is meant to preserve all transactions by ensuring that the redo information is written to the primary online redo log and to at least one standby redo log. If both writes are not successfully communicated back to the primary database, then the primary database just shuts down to prevent any further possible data loss:

- Redo Archival Process: LGWR
- Network Transmission mode: SYNC (Synchronous — dependent commit)
- Disk Write Option: AFFIRM
- Standby Redo Logs Required: Yes

If you have a Data Guard configuration running either in maximum availability or maximum protection mode and need to remove your Data Guard environment for any reason, there are certain steps to follow. Start by removing the standby database, delete all configuration files (`$ORACLE_HOME/dbs/*dr.dat`) and unset all of the `LOG_ARCHIVE_DEST_x` parameters. If you want to restart the primary database, the startup may fail in mount state with one or more errors: *ORA-16072: a minimum of one standby database destination is required* and/or *ORA-03113: End-of-file on Communication Channel.*

The problem is that the protection mode is actually part of the data dictionary and not set with database parameters. This is one of the times you must start up the database in mount state (this state opens the control file but not the database) and set the protection mode back to the default `Maximum Performance`:

```
PRIMARY> ALTER DATABASE SET STANDBY DATABASE TO MAXIMIZE PERFORMANCE;
```

Shut down the primary database and restart it to complete the changeover.

Database states

11g version of Oracle Database gives us different states that are tied to a database's role in a Data Guard configuration that control the log transport services. This is basically a switch that governs whether data is being transferred from one database to another and/or being applied depending on the database role of primary, physical, or logical.

States of log services are as follows:

Primary	TRANSPORT-ON	TRANSPORT-OFF
Physical standby (REDO APPLY)	APPLY-ON	APPLY-OFF
Snapshot standby (REDO APPLY)		APPLY-OFF
Logical standby (SQL APPLY)	APPLY-ON	APPLY-OFF

There is no APPLY-ON available for snapshot because it would no longer be a snapshot of the data at a point in time. This ability to turn off the transport and/or the application of redo logs gives you the flexibility in using the standbys for multiple tasks temporarily and then changing the state back on.

Manual failover with physical standby

To help you visualize the difference between a primary and physical standby, the following steps have been detailed for a manual failover of a primary to a physical standby. All of the specialized tasks in this first section are done via SQL*Plus to see all operations that are executed, and then we will repeat these steps with `dgmgrl`.

The following figure shows the starting role for each **Server** and the direction of **Redo Apply** before any transition event occurs. This is the interaction between a primary and a physical standby database, with the arrow showing the direction of data transfer:

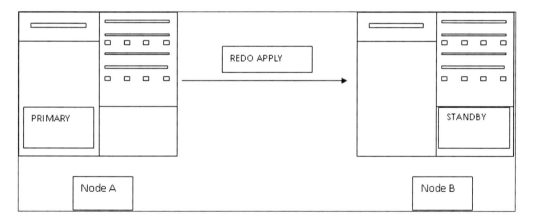

A failover transition event means that the database on **Node A** is unavailable for some reason. There may be data loss depending on the Data Guard protection mode and whether you have implemented the real-time apply option, which is highly recommended. The following figure shows the actual steps and which server they are executed on:

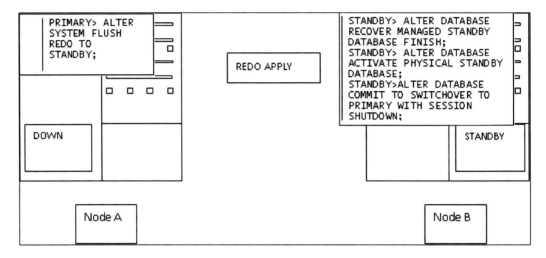

At this point (see the following figure) **Node B** has the **PRIMARY** role as the production database, with the original database and the server still out of commission:

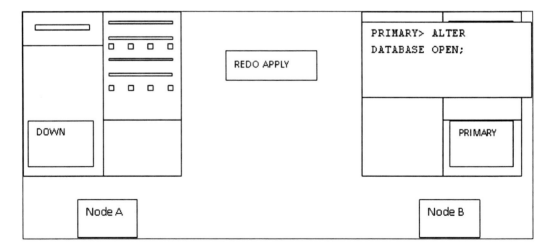

Manual failover with DGMGRL

If you were to do a manual failover on the Data Guard Management Utility on the standby server, then it would go something like this:

```
DGMGRL>connect sys/password;
DGMGRL> FAILOVER TO STANDBY IMMEDIATE;
```

The use of the keyword `IMMEDIATE` means no remaining outstanding redo would be applied; the database would be made active at that point, taking over the primary database role.

Flashback and guaranteed restore points

Flashback technology allows you to roll back or undo queries, changed data in tables, dropped tables, or even the entire database. A Flashback database can be used to revert logical corruption, patch, or a hot fix, but it rolls back all transactions that can be disruptive in a production instance, depending on when and how the original transactions were created.

This reversion of all the transactions is the same behavior as when you would perform a complete restore of the entire database from a backup. It is easier and less disruptive to use Flashback on a physical standby rolling it back to a time before the issue occurred. Use SQL*Plus, export, or data pump to move the missing or changed data back into production. The production instance is still up and running during all of this time, with minimal disruption to the few affected users.

To enable Flashback on a physical standby, the database should already be mounted but not open (normal operation for a physical standby during Redo Apply). Note that all `SQL>` designations indicate which database they are executed on, the `STANDBY>`, `PRIMARY>`, `LOGICAL>`, or `SNAPSHOT>`:

```
STANDBY> ALTER DATABASE RECOVER MANAGED STANDBY DATABASE CANCEL;
STANDBY> ALTER DATABASE Flashback ON;
STANDBY> ALTER SYSTEM SET DB_RECOVERY_FILE_DEST_SIZE=50G; # 2X
Database size
STANDBY> ALTER SYSTEM SET DB_RECOVERY_FILE_DEST='/YOURFILEDEST/';
STANDBY> ALTER SYSTEM SET DB_Flashback_RETENTION_TARGET=1440; # 1440
minutes
STANDBY> ALTER DATABASE RECOVER MANAGED STANDBY DATABASE USING CURRENT
LOGFILE DISCONNECT; # using current logfile starts real-time apply
```

To fully utilize the Flashback technology for stress testing, implementing hot fixes, or patching Oracle, I would recommend saving a Guaranteed Restore Point before opening the standby for read/write. This makes it easy to convert the physical standby back to its original state after testing is over, returning it to the correct SCN to resume its role as a physical standby.

 Flashback web resources:
`http://www.oracle.com/technology/deploy/availability/`
`htdocs/Flashback_Overview.htm`

Possible testing/recovery scenarios for Flashback and Data Guard

The following is a list of different reasons to use a physical standby, other than just to failover when the primary database is not available:

- Preventing or fixing physical corruption
- Fixing logical corruption
- Reversing an application vendor upgrade
- Batch job reversal
- Untested hot fix
- Untested Oracle patch
- Stress testing
- Testing Oracle upgrades
- Testing ASM, OMF, SAME, or OFA changes
- Testing hardware updates or changes
- Testing OS upgrades, patches, or changes
- Testing Network or SQL*Net parameter changes
- Real application testing
- SQL performance analyzing

Physical corruption on a primary database can't be transmitted to the standby if the data files exist on a separate file system and the members in a configuration don't participate in hardware-level mirroring. With `db_block_checking` and `db_block_checksum` enabled on the primary and `db_block_checksum` on the physical standby, it can detect any physical corruption before applying redo.

There is always a warning when enabling `db_block_checking` and/or `db_block_checksum`, as it may overload an already CPU-intensive environment. Be careful to monitor before putting these settings into a production environment. If the physical corruption is extensive enough to prevent the primary database from being open, then failing over to the physical standby would be the best option.

To use a physical standby to fix logical corruption, the corruption needs to be widespread enough to warrant the time and trouble it takes to extract the data from the physical standby and import it back into production—multiple tables, multiple schemas, and so on. Any application vendor upgrade or batch job (such as an incorrect payroll run) could be dealt with using the physical standby to manually reverse SQL changes to data. This is also an excellent time to use the Flashback Transaction process discussed in *Chapter 3*, easily done on a snapshot standby frozen at the point just before the bad event occurred.

Any kind of testing could be done using the physical standby with the latest copy of production data that may not be available in the testing environment. Testing an Oracle upgrade and/or change in something as simple as database initialization parameters using a physical standby would give you the least amount of downtime. There is always a certain amount of unpredictability with hardware and operating system changes, or when migrating to an RAC or ASM instance. You should make the change to the physical standby first, open it in read/write mode, test for functionality, and revert to the physical standby using Flashback before attempting the same changes on the primary instance.

Lost-write detection using a physical standby database

Lost-write database corruption happens when the I/O subsystem has acknowledged the completion of a block write but in actuality the write did not make it to disk. This type of corruption is detected by Data Guard comparing SCNs of blocks in the redo stream on the primary to the SCNs of blocks on the physical standby.

If the block SCN on primary is lower than standby—ORA-752—the lost-write happens on the primary. If the SCN on the primary is higher than the standby—ORA-600 [3020], then it is a lost-write on the standby. If the lost-write is on the standby it is unusable and the standby database will have to be removed and recreated.

Detection of a lost-write on the primary halts the managed recovery process on the standby and recovers to the consistent SCN. At that point it is recommended to failover because the physical standby is currently the most consistent as compared to the primary database. Any further transactions that happened on the primary after the SCN are assumed to be lost or in other words unrecoverable. Refer to the documentation for *Steps to Failover to a Physical Standby After Lost-Writes Are Detected on the Primary.*

This capability is controlled by the database parameter DB_LOST_WRITE_PROTECT and has different settings with FULL, NONE, or TYPICAL. The default is NONE.

The TYPICAL setting logs the buffer cache block reads in the redo stream for only the read/write tablespaces. It is this redo stream that is transmitted to the Data Guard database. You can expect a performance hit of at least 5% on both the primary and standbys because there is additional work being done and this setting needs to be done in both locations.

The FULL also records the same as TYPICAL and adds in the read-only tablespaces. TYPICAL settings will most often fulfill the most environments, because DBAs are used to having to recreate a read-only tablespace with other methods such as export/import or data pump.

The most important thing to know at this point is that if corruption happens on the primary, it can no longer be used in its present state for anything! All data files must be removed and a new database should be created because this type of corruption is permanent. At this point, you are safe to assume that the standby you failed over to has no corruption because it is located on a different server on a different hardware (most often the reason for this type of corruption will be hardware-based).

There are other methods for fixing corruption at several different levels (block, tablespace, data file), as a physical standby is an exact block-for-block copy of the primary. Several methods are covered in *Chapter 6.*

Corruption, patch reversal, upgrades, or testing scenarios

The only disturbance to the primary during this scenario would be the lack of protection against data loss on the primary during the testing. This limitation is removed with 11g (see Snapshot Standby in a later section). With the physical standby being actively used for testing, it would have to be flashed back to the restore point. A delay might occur depending on the amount of archivelogs produced on the primary during testing.

A delay in shipping might occur if you temporarily disable the Data Guard broker unless there is an additional `log_archive_dest` on this same node to receive the logs. See *MOS Note: 434164.1 Data Guard Redo Log Repository Example* to create what is known as an archivelog repository.

Since 11g, there is a new feature for standbys known as the database state (see the previous section). This is where changing the state comes into play—turning the transport off or on depending on the current need, the logs are still being transported to the physical standby, but they just aren't being applied. Once your testing is finished and you restart the APPLY process, it applies to all of the outstanding archived logs.

Start the process by canceling Redo Apply on the physical standby and taking a guaranteed restore point:

```
STANDBY> ALTER DATABASE RECOVER MANAGED STANDBY DATABASE CANCEL;
STANDBY> CREATE RESTORE POINT HOTFIX1 GUARANTEE Flashback DATABASE;
```

The above command sends all current data from the production instance and then stops the Redo Apply process temporarily to the physical standby where testing will occur. All redo shipping to other archive destinations from the primary in the same configuration is not affected by this interruption. Oracle Support recommends turning off the Data Guard when using SQL commands to make changes to the configuration, otherwise it will enable the archive destination automatically.

```
PRIMARY> ALTER SYSTEM ARCHIVE LOG CURRENT;
PRIMARY> ALTER SYSTEM SET DG_BROKER_START=FALSE;
PRIMARY> ALTER SYSTEM SET LOG_ARCHIVE_DEST_STATE_2=DEFER;
```

There is an option of changing the database state instead of deferring the archive destination and turning off the broker, but this can only be done with `dgmgrl`.

```
oracle@primaryservername:/u01/app/oracle[PRMY]
DGMGRL>connect sys/password;
DGMGRL> EDIT DATABASE 'PRMY' SET STATE='TRANSPORT-OFF';
```

Also, at this point, I would recommend changing the database state for the standby:

```
oracle@standbyservername:/u01/app/oracle[STBY]
DGMGRL>connect sys/password;
DGMGRL> EDIT DATABASE 'STBY' SET STATE='APPLY-OFF';
```

Activating the physical standby into read/write mode allows us to run the testing on an actual working copy of the primary database where we can change data, run batch jobs, and change `init.ora` parameters.

```
STANDBY> ALTER DATABASE ACTIVATE STANDBY DATABASE;
```

At this point, the database thinks it is now the PRIMARY. Be sure to defer any cascading archive destinations (or change database states as needed) that receive transactions from this database, so that the testing DML is not propagated to other standbys or back to the primary:

```
STANDBY> select * from v$database;
DATABASE_ROLE  DB_UNIQUE OPEN_MODE   PROTECTION_MODE SWITCHOVER_STATUS
-----------------------------------------------------------------------
PRIMARY             STANDBY     MOUNTED     UNPROTECTED     SESSIONS ACTIVE

STANDBY> ALTER SYSTEM SET LOG_ARCHIVE_DEST_STATE_2=DEFER;
STANDBY> ALTER DATABASE SET STANDBY DATABASE TO MAXIMIZE PERFORMANCE;
STANDBY> ALTER DATABASE OPEN;
```

From this point on the physical standby, execute any testing DML, export the wanted data from the standby to import into production, and apply hot fix, patch, or stress testing on the physical standby. There isn't any current protection against data loss on the primary database at this point, unless you have a second physical standby. In case a switchover is required or failover occurs, you need to flash back the standby to the initial restore point (HOTFIX1). Then convert it back to a physical standby and recover any logs that were generated during the testing. Drop the restore point when you are sure it is no longer needed. These steps are outlined below:

```
STANDBY> STARTUP MOUNT FORCE;
STANDBY> Flashback DATABASE TO RESTORE POINT HOTFIX1;
STANDBY> ALTER DATABASE CONVERT TO PHYSICAL STANDBY;
STANDBY> STARTUP MOUNT FORCE;
STANDBY> ALTER DATABASE RECOVER MANAGED STANDBY DATABASE USING CURRENT LOGFILE DISCON
NECT;
STANDBY> select * from v$database;
DATABASE_ROLE     DB_UNIQUE   OPEN_MODE   PROTECTION_MODE  SWITCHOVER_STATUS
-----------------------------------------------------------------------
PHYSICAL STANDBY     STANDBY     MOUNTED  MAXIMUM_PERFORMANCE  SESSIONS ACTIVE

STANDBY> DROP RESTORE POINT HOTFIX1;
```

Enable the LOG_ARCHIVE_DEST_STATE_2 on the primary database (or whichever is appropriate to restart the Redo Apply on the standby):

```
PRIMARY> ALTER SYSTEM SET DG_BROKER_START=TRUE;
PRIMARY> ALTER SYSTEM SET LOG_ARCHIVE_DEST_STATE_2=ENABLE;
```

Reinstate failed primary scenario

Anytime the primary instance has been switched over to a standby database, it is easiest to reinstate the failed database back into the primary role by making it a physical standby, until all of the logs that were generated while it was unavailable have been applied. In the previous versions, you would have to restore/recover the entire database before being able to switch back to the original primary instance. With this scenario, you only have to apply changes (archivelogs) that have occurred after the transition event.

On the new primary instance (which used to be the standby) query, find the correct SCN:

```
ORIG_PRIMARY> SELECT TO_CHAR(STANDY_BECAME_PRIMARY_SCN) FROM
V$DATABASE;
```

This scenario assumes that the data files on the original primary are recoverable. These are the steps to run to convert the old primary into a new physical standby. This allows all redo since the failover for eventual transition of this standby to be applied back into the production instance.

```
ORIG_STANDBY>SHUTDOWN IMMEDIATE;
ORIG_STANDBY>STARTUP MOUNT;
ORIG_STANDBY>Flashback DATABASE TO SCN <STANDBY_BECAME_PRIMARY_SCN>;

ORIG_STANDBY>ALTER DATABASE CONVERT TO PHYSICAL STANDBY;
ORIG_STANDBY>SHUTDOWN IMMEDIATE;
ORIG_STANDBY>STARTUP MOUNT;
ORIG_STANDBY>ALTER DATABASE RECOVER MANAGED STANDBY DATABASE USING
CURRENT CONTROLFILE DISCONNECT;
```

Once you have determined that all outstanding redo has been applied, switch back to the original primary. This would be considered a **switchover**, which is a planned event with no data loss as the desired result. First, stop all job processing and client sessions. You can make sure there is no gap in the amount of redo applied from the NEW_primary database to the NEW_standby by issuing the following statement on both databases:

```
SQL> SELECT THREAD#, MAX(SEQUENCE#)
FROM V$LOG_HISTORY GROUP BY THREAD#;
```

The following statement executed on the standby database indicates the number of redo blocks applied for a specific log sequence (see **block#**). Run it several times to show the progress:

```
STANDBY> SELECT PROCESS, SEQUENCE#, THREAD#, BLOCK#, BLOCKS, TO_CHAR(SYSDATE, 'DD-MON
-YYYY HH:MI:SS') TIME
from V$MANAGED_STANDBY WHERE PROCESS='MRP0';
PROCESS       SEQUENCE#     THREAD#    BLOCK#    BLOCKS    TIME
MRP0               2125     1          278912    307200    30-MAY-2007 09:54:54
PROCESS       SEQUENCE#     THREAD#    BLOCK#    BLOCKS    TIME
MRP0               2126     1          1         307200    30-MAY-2007 09:55:49
```

Start the switchover process by issuing the following statement, waiting until it completes to continue on to the next step:

```
PRIMARY> ALTER DATABASE COMMIT TO SWITCHOVER TO STANDBY WITH SESSION
SHUTDOWN;
```

Redo Apply is currently not running.

```
STANDBY> ALTER DATABASE COMMIT TO SWITCHOVER TO PRIMARY;
PRIMARY> ALTER DATABASE OPEN;
```

At this point the situation is where we first started. Redo Apply is now traveling the other direction, with the original primary back as the primary database and the standby in its original role as well.

All testing outlined above was done on several versions—10.2.0.4 and 11.1.0.7 Enterprise Edition of Oracle Database with a single primary, single physical standby, and single logical standby in the Data Guard configuration in maximum performance mode using real-time apply.

The section above was very detailed, helping to illustrate the steps involved with a Data Guard transition. While it is great that the 11g version of Oracle has condensed most of these steps into just a few Data Guard commands, it is important for the DBA to understand what is happening behind the scenes.

Troubleshooting the logical standby

The major issue with a logical standby is that certain events will cause the SQL Apply process to halt, requiring manual intervention to resolve the issue. Most of the monitoring is done on the logical standby database to make sure that the transactions are in sync with the primary.

It would be best to have a script that executes every few minutes, scanning the alert log of the logical standby for any errors that occur, and notifying you when the apply process is halted. You can also configure a job using GC to notify the DBA when the standbys are no longer synchronized with the primary.

Monitoring the logical apply process to see if all changes have been applied is a task that should be run multiple times a day, as there may be something that doesn't stop the process but causes the process to hang. The following SQL command will let you know the status between the primary and logical database, which is executed on the logical:

```
LOGICAL> SELECT APPLIED_SCN, APPLIED_TIME, READ_SCN, READ_TIME,  NEWEST_SCN, NEWEST_T
IME   FROM DBA_LOGSTDBY_PROGRESS;

APPLIED_SCN APPLIED_T    READ_SCN READ_TIME NEWEST_SCN NEWEST_TI
----------- --------- ----------- --------- ---------- ---------
 1429876462 29-DEC-09 1429826257 29-DEC-09 1429876462 29-DEC-09
```

What you are looking for is the **APPLIED_SCN** and **NEWEST_SCN** to match. The **READ_SCN** is the next log that has not been archived on the primary yet. So according to the above output the two databases are in sync.

The following SQL statement executed on the logical standby lets you know if the SQL APPLY process is running; it was shortened for brevity. If it has no rows returned, then the SQL Apply process has been halted. Notice that there are multiple processes working to apply any outstanding transactions for normal apply activity. The message **no work available** can be ignored if the SCNs match in the query above.

```
LOGICAL>SELECT PID, TYPE, STATUS, HIGH_SCN  FROM V$LOGSTDBY;
............. 2863          APPLIER
ORA-16116: no work available
1429885451

2865          APPLIER
ORA-16116: no work available
1429885453

2867          APPLIER
ORA-16116: no work available
1429885441

2869          APPLIER
ORA-16116: no work available
1429885443
```

The next step, if you receive the `no rows returned` from the above query, is to run the following to see what the problem is:

```
LOGICAL> select xidusn, xidslt, xidsqn, status, status_code from dba_logstdby_events
where event_time= (select max(event_time) from dba_logstdby_events);

        41          47          74
ORA-16226: DDL skipped due to lack of support
      16226

        29          16         704
ORA-16226: DDL skipped due to lack of support
      16226
```

The above output shows normal apply activity for unsupported data types that have been skipped, and depend on the Oracle version.

Options for resolving errors that stop the SQL Apply process

You should know in advance that having a logical standby database will require dedication and several months of close attention in a production environment before you can declare it production ready. That means you will need to run it in production with your site-specific data changes before allowing anyone to use it for reporting reasons. That is because there may be something specific about the data or processes that run regularly in your environment that may cause excessive downtime on the logical standby.

Before the 10.2.0.4 version of Oracle RDBMS, logical standbys were a day-to-day battle keeping it current with production. Outages would be normal, as large transactions hung the SQL Apply process. The SQL Apply process actually strips out the SQL statements that it executes one at a time (serialized) on the logical standby. This pulling of the SQL statements is actually done by the Log Miner process that you investigated earlier in this book.

Even with tuning suggestions, it was almost a monthly task to rebuild the entire logical standby database with a new backup from the primary. It was faster to rebuild this logical standby than entering a service request for Oracle to resolve the issue, as they didn't consider the loss of a logical standby to not be a production down issue since it wasn't the primary!

Since 10.2.0.4 and higher Oracle database versions, the logical standby is rebuilt only when a major change like an Oracle upgrade is scheduled. Now that I have scared you into not using it, what the logical standby was designed to do is offload reporting from the primary to another server. Moving end users to their own separate reporting database will help solve some of the common performance problems a DBA encounters for a heavily used OLTP primary database.

How to skip a single transaction

Research on what the original problem statement was that the SQL Apply process was halted as shown in the above section. Statements executed on the primary that are typically not an issue might include dropping a non-existent database object like a synonym.

The following SQL query will show what transactions were being executed when the SQL Apply process stopped:

```
LOGICAL>select to_char(event_time, 'MM/DD HH24:MI:SS') time,
        commit_scn, current_scn, event, status
    from dba_logstdby_events
    order by event_time, commit_scn, current_scn;
```

After researching a problem SQL statement and determining that a single transaction is not critical, use the following query to skip that transaction. The second line contains an actual transaction number, identified by its unique combination of transaction identifiers — XIDUSN, XIDSLT and XIDSQN. Your transaction numbers will be different:

```
LOGICAL>SELECT 'EXECUTE DBMS_LOGSTDBY.SKIP_TRANSACTION ('||XIDUSN||','||XIDSLT||','
||XIDSQN||');'
FROM DBA_LOGSTDBY_EVENTS
WHERE EVENT_TIME = (SELECT MAX(EVENT_TIME) FROM DBA_LOGSTDBY_EVENTS);
LOGICAL>EXECUTE DBMS_LOGSTDBY.SKIP_TRANSACTION (17,23,10769);
```

Both Oracle and I recommend skipping certain types of transactions that cause problems if they aren't needed for reporting reasons and if you aren't using this logical standby for failover purposes. To accomplish this, the logical standby process needs to be stopped:

```
LOGICAL>alter database stop logical standby apply;
```

Skip certain users who have the ability to create their own objects in the primary database, such as programmers or what DBAs often call power users for both DDL and DML SQL statements. See the following example:

```
exec dbms_logstdby.skip('SCHEMA_DDL','SCHEMAOWNERORPROGRAMMER','%');
exec dbms_logstdby.skip('DML','SCHEMAOWNERORPROGRAMMER','%');
```

These are the commands used to start the logical standby database to change some of the default settings, which are related to improving performance. The actual settings used are for our environment and may not be applicable in your situation. One note about `preserve_commit_order`: if this is turned to `false`, then the transactions are applied on the logical database in a different order than on the primary. While this would speed up the slower serialized process of SQL Apply, reporting applications will experience errors related to transaction inconsistency on the logical standby:

```
LOGICAL>alter database stop logical standby apply;
alter system set parallel_max_servers =28 scope=both;
exec DBMS_LOGSTDBY.APPLY_SET('PRESERVE_COMMIT_ORDER','TRUE');
execute dbms_logstdby.apply_set('MAX_SERVERS',28);
execute dbms_logstdby.apply_set('MAX_SGA',2045);
exec dbms_logstdby.apply_set('APPLY_SERVERS',7);
alter database guard standby;
alter database start logical standby apply immediate;
```

Skip those tables that have certain data types not supported and aren't needed for any type of reporting, because they often cause the SQL Apply process to halt.

> See the following documents for more information on how to accomplish the skipping of bulk transactions as well as other tuning and troubleshooting tips: *How To Skip A Complete Schema From Application on Logical Standby Database [MOS Document ID 741325.1]* and *Troubleshooting Logical Standby [MOS Document ID 215020.1]*.
>
> `http://www.oracle.com/technology/deploy/availability/pdf/proactively_optimize_sqlapply.pdf` Oracle White Paper "Developer and DBA Tips for Pro-Actively Optimizing SQL Apply Performance", this is still applicable to 10gR2 as well as 11g logical standby databases.

Active Data Guard and RMAN

Now you can have your cake and eat it too! Active Data Guard, an optional license, is a physical standby that is open for reporting and current with the primary database; this functionality was not available until 11g. To enable Active Data Guard, entail opening the database for read/write operations before starting the managed recovery, which also keeps it in sync with the primary. If you try to update data in a physical standby in managed recovery mode, in previous Oracle versions you would get ORA-16000: database open for read-only access.

This is a completely different reporting standby database type than a logical standby database, as you cannot add additional objects such as materialized views, additional schemas, or other read-only tablespaces. The Active Data Guard option will only contain the data and transactions, as they originate from the primary database.

In 10gR2, there were several issues associated with using RMAN in a Data Guard environment due to the DBID being identical on the primary and any physical standbys. In the previous versions, it was recommended to label backups with a tag command appending the node name, because RMAN couldn't distinguish between the different databases.

Backing up a physical standby is useful for offloading the performance hit on the primary instance during backup operations. RMAN tracks all filenames within the RMAN repository catalog. This allows you to backup a tablespace, data file, archivelog, or controlfile on a physical standby and restore to a primary or vice versa with every file or backup labeled with a DB_UNIQUE_NAME in 11g. It also provides faster incremental backups on the physical standby with Block Change Tracking enabled (licensed option). In 10gR2, there were also performance problems, depending on the apply mode when using the physical standby to offload RMAN backups.

See *Chapter 11, Using RMAN to Back Up and Restore Files* of the *Data Guard Concepts and Administration Manual*.

Check out MOS *Note: 331924.1 RMAN backups in Max Performance/Max Availability Data Guard Environment* for the init.ora parameter _log_ deletion_policy='ALL' (recommended for 10g)

Other Data Guard notes and features

All of this failing or switching over needs to be taken seriously, even though the Data Guard broker makes it a very easy task. It is my personal opinion that this can be very dangerous when something is too easy to do, because it makes mistakes just as easy to accomplish!

A database is automatically disabled by Data Guard after a transition event (failover or switchover), because it is assumed there was a good reason you committed to that change. These discarded databases have to be either reinstated (an actual command) or recreated, depending on the circumstances that led to their demise.

Data Guard will let you know the current status of a database and whether it can be easily reinstated with either `dgmgrl` or GC HA console. Reinstatement is most often done after being used for a testing scenario, as listed earlier in this chapter. Note that reinstatement capability requires the use of Flashback to be able to restore to the SCN at the time of role transition.

```
ORA-16661: the standby database needs to be reinstated
ORA-16795: the standby database needs to be re-created
```

11g has made it easier to recreate a physical standby. This assumes that the data files on the server are still available and free from corruption.

Real Application Testing, an optional license, consists of two major components: Database Replay and SQL Performance Analyzer (SPA). Using these utilities in a Data Guard implementation makes sense because there is a requirement when using Database Replay that the database must be restored to the correct SCN. There are other methods such as point-in-time recovery, flashback, and/or import/export utilities, but it is easier to accomplish using the snapshot database feature.

Summary

As a DBA that has been investigating time and effort in the standby technology since Oracle Database version 8i, it has been interesting to see the improvements along the way. Physical standbys have proven standard from the very first version, but the older implementation required the DBA to create their own script to manually transfer the archived redo logs from the primary database to the standby. Since 10gR2, all standby technology has improved dramatically from the early versions. Redo Apply is now fully automated, resilient, and SSL-encrypted. SQL Apply has matured enough that a logical standby can be depended on if a DBA takes the time to follow the Oracle-recommended tuning steps.

In 10gR2, most of the scenarios that were previously highly detailed manual steps have been shortened to a single command using the Data Guard command-line utility in 11g. Oracle has extended the functionality of using Data Guard for other reasons than just disaster recovery with several optional licensed components— Active Data Guard and Real Application Testing. You can take advantage of the added extensions to Data Guard features (in the Enterprise Edition of Oracle Database) without having to use the licensed options by carefully manipulating the Database States and database parameters as needed.

Using Flashback on the entire database was hard to justify on the primary production database, making this feature mostly unusable, except for the direst of circumstances. Using this on a physical standby is easily done with little to no impact on production. Several scenarios were outlined as creative solutions to some of the most often encountered technical obstacles for testing: large databases, small downtime windows, or limited testing hardware.

Even in 11g, SQL*Plus is still the definitive utility for all of the implementation steps from creation, deployment, configuration, and ongoing maintenance. Both the HA Console of OEM and the `dgmgrl` utility are able to make transitions (switchover or failover) faster with fewer typed commands than SQL*Plus. There are still certain issues that can only be resolved with SQL*Plus.

The new Data Recovery Adviser, in conjunction with RMAN, now uses Data Guard as a viable repair option for a primary database that cannot be repaired in a timely manner. This is my segue for the next chapter — *Extended RMAN.*

These scripts are invaluable for troubleshooting an issue with a standby — check with the latest version on MOS to keep current:

Script to Collect Data Guard Logical Standby Diagnostic Information [MOS Document ID 241512.1]

Script to Collect Data Guard Primary Site Diagnostic Information [MOS Document ID 241374.1]

Script to Collect Data Guard Logical Standby Table Information [MOS Document ID 269954.1]

6
Extended RMAN

The acronym **RMAN** stands for Oracle's **Recovery Manager**, with an emphasis on the word **Recovery**. Backups are worthless if you can't use them to restore lost data! RMAN is Oracle's recommended standard for database backups for any sized organization. There are other storage-based technologies that are also available for database backup—each one is vendor-specific. If your environment is still using the old-fashioned hot or cold backups (also known as user-managed), it is time to come out of the dinosaur age. The RMAN utility is easy to automate by scripting with the command-line version, which the provided example code for this chapter utilizes.

RMAN is used for many different tasks as part of the DBA to-do list presented back in *Chapter 1* of this book. That importance deserves its own section in the book. This chapter will touch only briefly on some of the basics, with the understanding that you have gained some knowledge from previous chapters in this book, have read through the Oracle Concepts Manual, and are becoming familiar with the RMAN User's Guide. All of the following items will be touched upon in this chapter with scripts, comments, tips, and techniques scattered throughout:

- Recovery goals determine backup configuration
- Backup types and the default configuration
- Oracle's recommended backup strategy
- Catalog versus control file RMAN recordkeeping and retention policies
- Corruption detection and the Data Recovery Adviser
- What does RMAN backup, restore, and recover?
- What doesn't RMAN backup, restore, and recover?
- What do I do before starting a restore and recovery?
- RMAN cloning and standbys—physical, snapshot, or logical

The RMAN utility is an executable file found in all Oracle Database Installation types. To prevent problems due to version mismatches, feature, and compatibility issues, the best one to use is the local RMAN utility that is installed as part of the database's own $ORACLE_HOME.

We won't be covering the technical details related to the following items, as each is unique to the hardware and security implementation details of your organization: Virtual Private Catalogs, Tape Settings, Removable Media (CD or DVD), Media Management Settings, and Oracle Secure Backup. Due to length constraints, data pump as a logical backup will only be touched upon briefly.

> See the *RMAN Restore Performance [ID 740911.1]* document for extensive information on allocating channels, especially tape types known as SBT.

It is assumed for this entire chapter that all RMAN backups are done with SYSDBA privileges, as that is a prerequisite. It should also be noted that backups should *never* be delegated to someone who is not a DBA. Implementation details in this chapter assume you are not using OMF or ASM to start with, because it complicates certain types of backup and recovery scenarios. As a beginner, start with normal disk copies and migrate to ASM or OMF as you gain experience.

It would be worth your while to read through the *RMAN Concepts* section of the *Recovery Managers User's Guide* for additional background information for this topic. This chapter will start with the default configuration for the Enterprise Edition of the 11.2.0.1 version of Oracle RDBMS.

> Oracle Documentation for 11gR2 Database contains the term Fast Recovery Area, which is the same as an earlier term known as Flashback Recovery Area. Oracle recommends the overall use of this area for any type of backup and recovery and not just for Flashback.

Recovery goals determine backup configuration

A successful RMAN implementation will include the formal definition of both backup and recovery goals. You could refer back to Chapter 5 for RTO and RPO as a starting point. **Mean Time to Recover (MTTR)** is another objective that will be touched on in this chapter.

MTTR (also known as fast-start checkpointing) is not enabled in 11g by default. It allows the database to recover (apply committed transactions, rollback uncommitted), which automatically occurs while bringing up a database after a crash or during an actual restore and recovery session. To enable this feature, the following database parameter is set to a non-zero number.

```
fast_start_mttr_target              integer    0
```

At the same time, reset the following database parameters back to zero:

```
LOG_CHECKPOINT_INTERVAL
LOG_CHECKPOINT_TIMEOUT
FAST_START_IO_TARGET
```

You should know from the previous chapters that faster checkpoints (synchronizing all the datafile headers, flushes data written to disk) provide a faster recovery time. MTTR affects several different components and can have a large impact on performance, either good or bad. The MTTR is also tied with what is known as OPTIMAL_LOGFILE_SIZE (online redo log size), which comes from the view V$INSTANCE_RECOVERY. This view is graphically represented as the MTTR Advisor in OEM.

Higher MTTR goals can be accomplished by using the Oracle recommended backup—Incrementally Updated Full. These are image copies, which are an exact bit-for-bit duplicate of the original datafile. Oracle also recommends saving these to the **Flash Recovery Area** (**FRA**), which is often implemented as cheaper (most often slower) disk storage. The fastest way to restore using the Incrementally Updated Method would be to use the restore command—SWITCH DATABASE TO COPY—which switches the datafiles to the copy in the FRA.

The larger the database, the less time is needed to recover versus other methods of recovery, as *no* restore (which is the process of copying backups to the restore location) is actually done. Less than 24 hours of archivelogs would need to be applied during the recovery process if the incremental backup and archivelog was done on a daily basis.

It is the recovery goals that will define the method, mode, location, and frequency of your backups. Once the recovery goals are formally outlined for each application, you can start designing a backup strategy for the database:

- How often do we backup? (Daily, weekly).
- Which backup type? (Incremental and/or full backup sets or image copies).
- Where do we backup? (FRA, disk, and/or tape).
- Should we skip any part of the database during backups? (Read-only).

- Should we use compression? (Recovery slower, more CPU, backups faster and less space).

- Do we have a retention strategy for tablespaces, image copies, and archived redo logs?

Backup types and the default configuration

This section lists a few definitions that will need to be referred to for understanding the recommended backup strategy:

- **Backup sets**: Default type of RMAN backup that contains what you want backed up, which can be datafiles, controlfiles, archived redo logs, or spfiles. Each backup set consists of pieces, which can be subsets (a backup of a large datafile cut up into small chunks) of the item you want backed up. You cannot cut up a large datafile across different backup sets or mix different types of files into the same backup set, but you can multiplex several database files into a single backup piece.

- **Image copy**: Type of backup that is a bit-for-bit copy of the original — the same as creating a copy at the OS level (with Unix `cp` or `dd` commands), but is known to the RMAN utility. Making it known to RMAN means that the location and header file information has been recorded in either the control file or, optionally, the RMAN catalog. Archived redo logs that are copied by the archiver process to the operating system are also considered image copies. An image copy will be larger in actual file size than an RMAN backup set because an RMAN backup will have the content of only the used extents for locally managed tablespaces.

Backup incremental levels

There are two incremental levels as part of a recommended backup strategy and it is important to understand the differences:

- Level 0 incremental: Backs up all data blocks; equal to full backup as part of incremental backup strategy.

- Level 1 incremental: Only backs up changed blocks; can be differential (different since last 0 or 1) or cumulative (updates since last 0).

There are quite a few combinations of the different incremental, cumulative, and differential levels. Unless you have disk or tape storage concerns, start with the simplest combination—full weekly plus a daily cumulative (either normal backup or merged incremental). Both of these types of backups will result in a shorter length of recovery time. An incremental backup strategy can be started with a simple command as follows:

```
RMAN> backup incremental level 1 cumulative with tag 'LEVEL1_INC'
database;
```

If there is no existing full backup with this tag, then a full level 0 (required as part of an incremental backup strategy) will be created automatically by RMAN. The difference between a normal incremental and the merge method is the recover command that comes before the backup and the `for recover of` keywords in the backup command:

```
RMAN>recover copy of database with tag 'ORA$OEM_LEVEL_0';
RMAN>backup incremental level 1 cumulative  copies=1 for recover of
copy with tag 'ORA$OEM_LEVEL_0' database;
```

Incremental backups usually take less time than a full backup, but not always. This is due to the fact that every block SCN number is being checked during the process. This comparison SCN checking may make the read slower, but writing to disk will be faster due to having fewer used blocks. Block Change Tracking (extra license cost of Active Data Guard if used on a physical standby) can improve the performance because it reduces the number of scans needed for SCN comparing; it keeps a running count of previously scanned blocks. A different feature known as **Unused block compression in backups** (default with the Enterprise Edition of 10gR2+) is where RMAN excludes blocks that have never been used. There are several other RMAN compression enhancements, but they won't be covered in this book.

Incremental backups will only be used for recovery; restoring datafiles will come from the last full backup or Level 0 backup. Comparison SCN checking as part of Block Change Tracking is why the incremental merge backup and restore method saves both backup and recovery time.

Full backup

All database blocks that contain used extents in locally managed tablespaces will result in a smaller-sized backup as compared to an image copy. If tablespaces are not locally managed, RMAN reads and backs up all blocks. This fact is important enough to mention because it is a common misconception.

Logical backup

A logical backup contains both the metadata of database objects as well as the actual data. It is important to briefly mention logical backups because they are part of the complete backup strategy used in conjunction with RMAN. There are two different utilities used to extract or input data in this format—*Export/Import and Data Pump*. Data Pump is the more recent utility and should be the one you generally use. Export/Import is used for backwards compatibility with older versions of Oracle.

These types of backups were mentioned in an earlier chapter, as the output files need protection from unauthorized access. I recommend doing both a logical backup and a physical backup on a regular basis for a database, most often daily. A full logical backup can be your last method of restoring the complete database if other recovery methods are unsuccessful. A logical backup is also an easy method to recover structures, such as table or index creation statements, as well as transfer a smaller subset of data from one database to another.

Oracle's suggested backup: What is missing?

Listed below is the default recommended backup script from Oracle when using OEM. It is minimal at first glance, but contains the recommended method called an **incremental merge backup**. The critical part of this is that the configure commands are run separately and only need to be run once to control the behavior of what happens during the backup. You don't know the contents of the configuration by looking at just the following script:

```
run {
allocate channel oem_disk_backup device type disk;
recover copy of database with tag 'ORA$OEM_LEVEL_0';
backup incremental level 1 cumulative  copies=1 for recover of copy
with tag 'ORA$OEM_LEVEL_0' database;
}
```

All of the backup types (database, archivelog, spfile) are different commands. This single line will only backup the datafiles—backup database. The spfile and controlfile may or may not be backed up together according to the persistent (stored) configure command—CONFIGURE CONTROLFILE AUTOBACKUP. See the following section for what happens between two different commands; the first one is the spfile:

```
RMAN> backup spfile; --backs up both of them but in different locations

Starting backup at 11-JAN-10
using channel ORA_DISK_1
channel ORA_DISK_1: starting full data file backup set
channel ORA_DISK_1: specifying data file(s) in backup set
including current SPFILE in backup set
channel ORA_DISK_1: starting piece 1 at 11-JAN-10
channel ORA_DISK_1: finished piece 1 at 11-JAN-10
piece handle=/backup/flash_recovery_area/ORCL/backupset/2010_01_11/o1_mf_nnsnf_TAG201
00111T142808_5nq5z8or_.bkp tag=TAG20100111T142808 comment=NONE
channel ORA_DISK_1: backup set complete, elapsed time: 00:00:01
Finished backup at 11-JAN-10

Starting Control File and SPFILE Autobackup at 11-JAN-10
piece handle=/u01/app/oracle/product/11.2.0/dbhome_1/dbs/c-1234670555-20100111-01 com
ment=NONE
Finished Control File and SPFILE Autobackup at 11-JAN-10
```

Notice in the following command the word current, meaning what is currently
in use by the database. RMAN can manipulate previous copies or backups of
the controlfile, which is important for different types of recovery scenarios.
Remember from earlier chapters that the controlfile tracks all of the datafile
headers, synchronizing them with the database SCN for consistency and
transaction integrity.

```
RMAN> backup current controlfile; --only backs up the controlfile but puts it into th
e location defined by configure command

Starting backup at 14-JAN-10
using channel ORA_DISK_1
using channel ORA_DISK_2
channel ORA_DISK_1: starting compressed full data file backupset
channel ORA_DISK_1: specifying data file(s) in backupset
including current control file in backupset
channel ORA_DISK_1: starting piece 1 at 14-JAN-10
channel ORA_DISK_1: finished piece 1 at 14-JAN-10
piece handle=/backup/ora_df708273458_s125_s1 tag=TAG20100114T143738 comment=NONE
channel ORA_DISK_1: backup set complete, elapsed time: 00:00:01
Finished backup at 14-JAN-10

Starting Control File Autobackup at 14-JAN-10
piece handle=/backup/rman/c-3416182518-20100114-06_rman comment=NONE
Finished Control File Autobackup at 14-JAN-10
```

The following will show all available backups. In order to get the full date timestamp, a Unix environmental variable is set and should be included in all of your RMAN scripts. Notice the **Ckp SCN (Checkpoint System Change Number)**.

```
export NLS_DATE_FORMAT='YYYY-MM-DD:HH24:MI:SS';
RMAN>list backup;

BS Key  Type LV Size    Device Type Elapsed Time Completion Time
------- ---- -- ------  ----------- ------------ ----------------
2166848 Full    9.45M   DISK        00:00:00     2010-01-15:10:00:40
BP Key: 2166850 Status: AVAILABLE  Compressed: NO Tag: TAG20100115T100040
        Piece Name: /backup/rman/c-3416182518-20100115-01_rman
Control File Included: Ckp SCN: 1458840057 Ckp time: 2010-01-15:10:00:40
SYS@ORCL> select * from V$BACKUP_CONTROLFILE_DETAILS;

BACKUPSET           78         55         55     708342408  708343240
        133 13-JAN-10        1458526142 13-JAN-10      1458840057 15-JAN-10
    9879552                   1
      9.42M
```

A simple backup can be done using the following command, with the configuration set as the defaults and a flash recovery area defined for this database. This is only the start of database backup and recovery strategy, but this is not enough to keep you protected against data loss. This backup is missing the controlfile, spfile, and any archived logs, which will all be required for a complete recovery.

```
RMAN> backup database;

Starting backup at 11-JAN-10
using channel ORA_DISK_1
channel ORA_DISK_1: starting full data file backup set
channel ORA_DISK_1: specifying data file(s) in backup set
input data file file number=00001 name=/u01/oradata/orcl/orcl/system01.dbf
input data file file number=00002 name=/u01/oradata/orcl/orcl/sysaux01.dbf
input data file file number=00003 name=/u01/oradata/orcl/orcl/undotbs01.dbf
input data file file number=00005 name=/u01/oradata/orcl/orcl/syst02.dbf
input data file file number=00004 name=/u01/oradata/orcl/orcl/users01.dbf
channel ORA_DISK_1: starting piece 1 at 11-JAN-10
channel ORA_DISK_1: finished piece 1 at 11-JAN-10
piece handle=/backup/flash_recovery_area/ORCL/backupset/2010_01_11/o1_mf_nnndf_TAG201
00111T134703_5nq317o9_.bkp tag=TAG20100111T134703 comment=NONE
channel ORA_DISK_1: backup set complete, elapsed time: 00:00:15
Finished backup at 11-JAN-10
```

All backups are recorded in the control file, which can be seen in the data dictionary view v$controlfile_record_section. See the following code for some of the different types as they relate to backups:

```
SQL> select TYPE, RECORDS_TOTAL, RECORDS_USED
  from v$controlfile_record_section
  where type like '%BACKUP%';
BACKUP SET                      409         2
BACKUP PIECE                    200         2
BACKUP DATA FILE                245         2
BACKUP REDOLOG                  215         0
BACKUP CORRUPTION               371         0
BACKUP SPFILE                   131         0
```

Controlfiles—an important part of backup and recovery

Another important database parameter is the following, as it relates to how long the controlfile keeps records before overwriting them to save space. Make this number larger than your recovery window that is mentioned in the following paragraph:

```
control_file_record_keep_time        integer      7
```

This setting would need to relate to your recovery strategy, which really should be a 6-to-13 or 20-day window. Why 6, 13, or 20? A 7-day window would include three full backups (or Level 0), assuming you do a weekly full backup. If you take a 6-day window, it would be all inclusive—two fulls (or Level 0) plus all of the differential or cumulative backups for that week, a simple way of compartmentalizing a robust backup and recovery strategy. Thirteen days would cover two weeks and 20 days, would cover a 3-week strategy.

When CONFIGURE CONTROLFILE AUTOBACKUP is ON, then RMAN will backup the controlfile and spfile. In the following situations, the BACKUP or COPY command is issued at the RMAN prompt:

- BACKUP or COPY is followed by a command that is neither BACKUP nor COPY
- The last command of a run block was BACKUP or COPY
- Adding a new tablespace
- Altering a tablespace or datafile
- Adding a new online redo log or redo thread
- Renaming a file

How often should backups occur?

I recommend backing up everything (controlfile, spfile, archived logs, datafiles, and files that are backed up at the OS level) at least once daily for production databases. Files that are backed up using OS backup software include Oracle binaries, diagnostic destination, trace files, logical backups, and any custom files for your implementation. An OS backup can also be used to backup any disk-based backups that RMAN produces.

The type of backup (full, incremental, cumulative, and/or logical) will depend on a combination of your backup and recovery strategy (how much time to restore and recover) and the amount of resources (I/O, CPU, disk, and/or tape) available.

The default backup script assumes that you have enabled a `flash_recovery_area` as a database parameter, so all backups are automatically written in that location. If you don't have an FRA, then look for the backups to show up in `$ORACLE_HOME/dbs`, which has the unintended result of filling up disk space for your Oracle binaries.

RMAN has more than one way to accomplish the same task, as you can define the location for the datafile backups with the configure command or within the actual backup command, as shown in these two different examples:

```
RMAN> CONFIGURE CHANNEL DEVICE TYPE DISK FORMAT '/backup/rm_%d_0_%t_
%U.df';

RMAN> BACKUP FORMAT '/backup/rm_%d_0_%t_%U.df' DATABASE;
```

Look for a later section where a more complete backup and recovery strategy is implemented using some of the more advanced commands.

Default configuration details

The actual configuration can be determined by looking at an OEM page, but that doesn't produce the concise output from simply running the show all command within RMAN. This connection was done without a catalog connection, so I am using the RMAN utility to query what backup information the database controlfile contains. A catalog is an Oracle database repository used for multiple databases as well as multiple DBAs. It can retain backup and recovery information longer than the controlfile and is a requirement when using advanced database features such as Data Guard.

The following code shows the RMAN utility version, the database `ORACLE_SID`, and `DBID`, along with the default configuration settings. The target is the database that I am connecting to perform RMAN commands against, in this case querying the configure settings.

```
RMAN> connect target /

connected to target database: ORCL (DBID=1234670555)

RMAN> show all;

using target database control file instead of recovery catalog
RMAN configuration parameters for database with db_unique_name ORCL are:
CONFIGURE RETENTION POLICY TO REDUNDANCY 1; # default
CONFIGURE BACKUP OPTIMIZATION OFF; # default
CONFIGURE DEFAULT DEVICE TYPE TO DISK; # default
CONFIGURE CONTROLFILE AUTOBACKUP OFF; # default
CONFIGURE CONTROLFILE AUTOBACKUP FORMAT FOR DEVICE TYPE DISK TO '%F'; # default
CONFIGURE DEVICE TYPE DISK PARALLELISM 1 BACKUP TYPE TO BACKUPSET; # default
CONFIGURE DATA FILE BACKUP COPIES FOR DEVICE TYPE DISK TO 1; # default
CONFIGURE ARCHIVELOG BACKUP COPIES FOR DEVICE TYPE DISK TO 1; # default
CONFIGURE MAXSETSIZE TO UNLIMITED; # default
CONFIGURE ENCRYPTION FOR DATABASE OFF; # default
CONFIGURE ENCRYPTION ALGORITHM 'AES128'; # default
CONFIGURE COMPRESSION ALGORITHM 'BASIC' AS OF RELEASE 'DEFAULT' OPTIMIZE FOR LOAD TRU
E ; # default
CONFIGURE ARCHIVELOG DELETION POLICY TO NONE; # default
CONFIGURE SNAPSHOT CONTROLFILE NAME TO '/u01/app/oracle/product/11.2.0/dbhome_1/dbs/s
napcf orcl.f'; # default
```

You can also find the non-default parameters with SQL*Plus. That isn't of much help in this situation (a newly created database) because none of them has been changed. That leaves you with `no rows returned` when querying `v$rman_configuration`:

```
SYS@ORCL>  select * from v$rman_configuration;
```

Once you attach to this target database using RMAN and run the `configure` commands (it doesn't matter if you don't change the actual setting), it populates the `v$rman_configuration` view, making these settings persistent. Persistent configuration settings will control what happens during all subsequent backups until the `configure` command is run again. In the following code listing from the database view, I indicated the three that were actually changed:

```
SYS@ORCL> select * from v$rman_configuration;
     1 RETENTION POLICY TO REDUNDANCY 3 # changed
     2 BACKUP OPTIMIZATION OFF
     3 DEFAULT DEVICE TYPE TO DISK
     4 CONTROLFILE AUTOBACKUP ON   # changed
     5 CONTROLFILE AUTOBACKUP FORMAT FOR DEVICE TYPE DISK TO '%F'
     6 DEVICE TYPE DISK PARALLELISM 1 BACKUP TYPE TO BACKUPSET
     7 DATA FILE BACKUP COPIES FOR DEVICE TYPE DISK TO 1
     8 ARCHIVELOG BACKUP COPIES FOR DEVICE TYPE DISK TO 1
     9 MAXSETSIZE TO UNLIMITED
    10 ENCRYPTION FOR DATABASE OFF
    11 ENCRYPTION ALGORITHM 'AES128'
    12 COMPRESSION ALGORITHM 'BASIC' AS OF RELEASE 'DEFAULT' OPTIMIZE FOR LOAD TR
UE
    13 ARCHIVELOG DELETION POLICY TO NONE
    14 SNAPSHOT CONTROLFILE NAME
TO '/backup/flash recovery area/ORCL/snap orcl.dbf'# changed
```

Most of the default settings will work for smaller databases configured with a Flash Recovery Area and a Redundancy setting of 1. This makes all incremental backups obsolete as soon as they are applied to the original full copy. See the RMAN `OBSOLETE` and `EXPIRED` section for more details on these maintenance tasks.

The default setting that most DBAs have an issue with is:

```
RMAN> CONFIGURE CONTROLFILE AUTOBACKUP OFF; # default
```

Personal experience has taught me that this setting should be turned on and left **ON** (persistent). By default the controlfile autobackup will go to the $ORACLE_HOME/dbs directory in case of Unix and the $ORACLE_HOME/database directory for Windows, unless you specify a location with the configure command CONTROLFILE AUTOBACKUP FORMAT FOR DEVICE TYPE DISK TO '%F'. That behaviour is demonstrated in the following code section. If a Flash Recovery Area is in use, then the controlfile autobackup will go to the FRA, unless you specify an alternate location using the configure command.

```
Starting Control File Autobackup at 11-JAN-10
piece handle=/u01/app/oracle/product/11.2.0/dbhome_1/dbs/c-1234670555-20100111-00 com
ment=NONE
Finished Control File Autobackup at 11-JAN-10
```

Notice from the following listing how the spfile is also backed up with the controlfile. This is because the persistent setting autobackup is on. The file labelled snapcf_orcl.f is mentioned later in the chapter. As the spfileorcl.ora has a specific name, it will be overwritten unless you use an FRA, because FRA writes each daily backups in dated directories.

```
-rw-r-----  1 oracle dba 9814016 Jan 11 13:12 snapcf_orcl.f
-rw-r-----  1 oracle dba 9863168 Jan 11 13:47 c-1234670555-20100111-00
-rw-r-----  1 oracle dba    2560 Jan 11 14:23 spfileorcl.ora
-rw-r-----  1 oracle dba 9895936 Jan 11 14:28 c-1234670555-20100111-01
   drwxr-xr-x 2 oracle dba    4096 Jan 11 14:30 .
```

The following backup commands are more complicated, but contain most if not all of what is recommended for a robust backup and recovery strategy. Note how you can integrate Unix environmental variables identified by ${} within a backup script. You shouldn't implement all of these steps without extensive testing from several weeks to months before you can understand what the commands actually accomplish. Comments are scattered throughout the code in the following command window:

```
set echo on; --restates the command run, highly recommended, required outside the run
 command.
run {
allocate channel d1 type disk;

recover copy of database with tag 'FULL_$SERVERNAME' until time  "SYSDATE-7"; --Allow
s restores beyond incrementally updated full
backup
    incremental level 1 cumulative -all changes since last backup
    check logical database -check for corruption
    copies=1
    for recovery of copy with tag 'FULL_${SERVERNAME}'  --merge
    format '${BACKUPDIR}/rm_%d_${BACKUPLEV}_%t_%U.df''
    (database filesperset=1)  --one datafile per backup set
    plus archivelog
    tag '$DAT_ARCHIVE' filesperset 8  --8 logs per backupset
       format '${BACKUPDIR}/%d_${BACKUPLEV}_%t_%U.df'';

backup current controlfile for standby tag=' FULL_${SERVERNAME}'; --backs up a copy o
f the controlfile type needed for standbys

backup current controlfile tag=' FULL_${SERVERNAME}';

backup spfile; -- this is included with controlfile autobackup, this is redundant sin
ce the controlfile autobackup is on, can be done as a separate command.

backup archivelog all not backed up 3 times format
"${LOGDIR}/rm_%d_%U_%p.log" delete input; --backs up all archivelogs for at least 3 t
imes before removing from this particular location
```

There are specific recommendations that allow you to have dependable backups, which you can rely on to be there when doing a restore. Tagging backups with the intended purpose, backing up items multiple times over several days, and user-defined locations are all points of control for you as the DBA. This is not a script for everyone's taste or environment, only you can decide what works for you by testing and comparing the results. As you can see there is a little more to it than just backup database.

Do not specify delete all input when backing up archivelogs.

It is important to draw attention to this small change (delete all input) because it is very important and this command is found again and again in Oracle's documentation. If you use the delete all input as part of the command, any backups done from one destination will delete all copies of the archivelog in all the locations you have defined as an archive destination database parameter.

I recommend simply using delete input so that backups from one location will only delete what has been backed up from that single archive destination. As you learned from *Chapter 4*, you should have more than one archivelog destination; what good would that additional location be if your RMAN backups deleted them unexpectedly?

Included in the code section for this chapter of the book is a folder called `Windows_rman`, which contains a complete set of backup scripts utilizing RMAN on Windows. It will work with versions as far back as 8i, but requires changes needed to define the location of your backups: `ORACLE_HOME` and `ORACLE_SID`. Consider installing the open source software called `blat`, which will e-mail files on a Windows box, excellent for sending backup logs to the DBA.

Oracle's recommended backup strategy

A rolling updated full backup strategy has its place in a production environment. Here is a short list of the best reasons and features:

- It reduces the number of repeated full backups
- It can reduce the restore time if `switch to copy` is used
- It reduces network bandwidth to transport backups offsite and incremental(s) take up less space
- Improved Tape bandwidth due to less reads
- Option for restoring objects changed with NOLOGGING option because changed data blocks are captured
- It synchronizes the physical standby with incremental merge changes
- There is no need to modify `CONTROL_FILE_RECORD_KEEP_TIME`
- It's useful for merging monthly datawarehouse backups with transportable tablespaces

Issues with incremental merge backups

Just as there are positives to Oracle's recommended method of backups and recovery, there are also some downsides that need to be covered:

- The amount of disk storage needed is higher for the image copy backup versus a single full RMAN backup. That would be the current size of the database plus incremental backups plus archivelogs.
- It limits point in time recovery, all previously applied incrementals become obsolete.
- It requires RMAN catalog for Point-In-Time Restores.
- Issues with retention policies other than redundancy=1, [Refer *Note:351455.1*].
- Performance issues may require a block change tracking feature.
- OMF-style format for datafiles may not be used to merge backups or for the use of transportable tablespaces from one database to another.

A note on the point about **OMF (Oracle Managed Files)**: several of the implementation details will change if you use OMF and/or ASM. There just isn't room in this chapter to cover all of those changes. I suggest starting to use RMAN with normal datafiles that aren't OMF or ASM-based. Once you have gained expertise, add the OMF or ASM features for further testing. Issues will appear when trying to use RMAN to implement the more advanced features, such as standbys and transportable tablespaces, or restoring files between different databases when one has ASM and/or OMF and the other doesn't.

Restore and recovery comparison

Here is a simplified restore and recovery, comparing the method to an Incremental Merge restore.

Traditional Backup Restore:

1. **Restore database**: Restore the last full or level 0 incremental backup.
2. **Recover database**: Apply all incremental backups since last full.
3. **Media recovery**: Apply all archivelogs since incremental backup.

Incremental Merge Restore:

1. **Restore database**: Eliminated if switch database to copy.
2. **Recover database**: Also eliminated database is switched to copy.
3. **Media recovery**: Apply all archivelogs since incremental backup.

As you can see an Incremental Merge is the fastest recovery method for recovering, but it would only be helpful in certain situations. This is the same for any recovery session, only certain methods or procedures will work in one particular situation. It depends on what happened, how much you have left to work with, and which backup is needed. This fast recovery wouldn't help when the server is no longer available (won't boot) or the hard drives that contain important files other than just the database files or backups are lost.

Recommendations for Incremental Merge backup

Think of the daily update of an Incremental Merge as being like a database—it is a changing entity (more so for OLTP than a data warehouse) and there are only certain situations where you want to reverse or go back much farther than the most recent backups.

In situations where you want to recover a database farther back than just the most recent backup, there is a variation of the default RMAN command to use for your backups. To implement the retention policy based on recovery window for the incremental merge, do not use the CONFIGURE command. Instead use the UNTIL CLAUSE in the RECOVER COMMAND.

```
RMAN>RECOVER COPY OF DATABASE WITH TAG <tagname> UNTIL TIME "SYSDATE-
7";
```

The until time syntax changes the backup as follows:

- First time executed image copy backup with tag
- Two to seven times executed a level 1 differential backup with tag
- Executed more than eight times, the level 1 are applied to the image copy made 7 days ago, and a new level 1 backup is produced

This would keep the copy of the database to satisfy a retention strategy of six days. Notice the with tag clause of the above command. That is a recommended method of marking a particular backup with an easily identified purpose.

Calculating the FRA disk space needed

If you choose to use Oracle's Incremental Merged Backups, then determining the amount of disk space is necessary before implementing that strategy in conjunction with FRA; if you run out of disk space during a backup that leaves you very vulnerable. Most DBAs plan on using a lower-cost storage for FRA as a backup area. Recovering the database by switching to the copy in the FRA may hinder database performance. A compromise would be to keep the database performance items like the incrementally updated backups on faster, higher cost storage, with others less dependent on disk performance in the FRA.

The following formula is Oracle's recommended backup strategy — Incrementally Merged backups with everything located in the FRA:

> Disk space needed in FRA = copy of database + incremental backup + (n+1) days of archived redo logs + controlfile + online redo log member * number of log groups + flashback logs (DB_FLASHBACK_RETENTION_TARGET)

You can simply calculate the space required using the du -h command. You can use this command for any amount of backups you would want to keep on disk for any type of file backed up by RMAN. Don't forget to provide more disk space for growth, with at least 10 to 20% additional space in addition to what has been allocated for the FRA.

You can have a look at the following:

Note. 262853.1 RMAN Fast Incremental Backups

Note. 303861.1 Incrementally Updated Backup In 10G

Catalog versus controlfile RMAN recordkeeping and retention policies

There aren't any licensing concerns, as Oracle doesn't charge extra for maintaining a separate database for hosting the catalogs for all your licensed databases. This same database is also a good candidate for the Grid Control Repository because they are both similar in functionality and for exclusive DBA use. You may want to connect directly to the controlfile to obtain information, complete backups as well as restore and recovery sessions to begin with. Add in the RMAN repository catalog when you expand your backup and recovery across multiple databases or start using Data Guard technology. It is now time to flesh out reasons to use a catalog as part of a complete backup and recovery strategy.

The RMAN catalog repository is most often used for an MAA with multiple standby databases. It is a requirement for several of the RMAN-related Data Guard features—creating standbys with RMAN, live network duplication as well as backing up and restoring files between the primary and standbys. Think of the catalog as a way of keeping all the information about multiple Oracle database backups in a single location. The RMAN repository can keep all backup information or only the bare minimum (a few weeks worth), depending on your business needs. Some IT departments have a security or auditing requirement to keep backups and even test restore capability for a certain amount of time before destroying backups.

RMAN stored script and substitution variables

What the RMAN catalog does best is help you to manage the complex task of administering many different types of databases. One of its best features is the ability to store scripts, but in the past DBAs shied away from this practice because the scripts were not flexible or changeable when executed on different servers or database types.

Use the RMAN command REPLACE SCRIPT to create a backup script that includes substitution variables that are adjustable depending on the input values. RMAN will prompt you for the inputs when it is run to store the script in the catalog repository.

```
RMAN> REPLACE SCRIPT
2> backup_inc { BACKUP DATA FILE &1 TAG &2.1 FORMAT '/backup/&1_%U'; }
Enter value for 1: 1
Enter value for 2: incremental_backup
Enter value for 3: inc
starting full resync of recovery catalog
full resync complete
created script backup_inc
EXECUTE SCRIPT
```

At runtime, you can use the backup_inc script with the inputs specific to that backup—in this case input &1 = 1, &2 = dailybackup. This allows you to use a single script for multiple databases in a centralized repository, another way of automating your world.

```
RMAN> RUN { EXECUTE SCRIPT backup_inc USING 1 dailybackup inc1; }
```

The actual script that is run after the appropriate substitutions is:

```
RMAN> BACKUP DATA FILE 1 TAG dailybackup.1 FORMAT '/backup/1_%U';
```

The *RMAN: How to Query the RMAN Recovery Catalog [ID 98342.1]* MOS document will help you understand the actual tables behind the RMAN respository catalog, and is invaluable for diagnosing, tuning, and advanced troubleshooting issues.

Both the current controlfile (or previous incarnations of a controlfile) and the catalog have mechanisms to maintain the length of time for which circular records are kept in the controlfile. Recreating the controlfile will remove all existing records for backups, which is another reason to create an RMAN repository. The following database parameter controls how long to keep reusable records such as the RMAN backups (and archivelog records) before overwriting to save space (this is the default setting):

```
control_file_record_keep_time          integer       7
```

Oracle recommends the following formula for calculating this database parameter: CONTROL_FILE_RECORD_KEEP_TIME = retention period + level 0 backup interval + 1. This means that, for a level 0 (full) backup each week with a retention policy of 6 days, this parameter would calculate to be 14 = 6+7+1. When setting CONTROL_FILE_RECORD_KEEP_TIME, keep in mind that level 0 backups can go beyond the recovery window period, which is why I recommend it.

If you use the Oracle-recommended backup strategy of an updated (incrementally) full backup, then the `control_file_record_keep_time` setting doesn't play as big a role. Each time the datafile copy is updated, the older datafile records automatically age out. The records containing the backups won't be removed (or age out) until they are deleted from the FRA.

Since Oracle 10.2, all sections of the controlfile are auto extended for MAXLOGFILE, MAXLOGMEMBERS, MAXLOGHISTORY, MAXDATAFILES, and MAXINSTANCES parameters. This is important, as they used to be hard set limits that required a controlfile recreation to go above the current settings; this step would require a database restart. There are other records in the controlfile, datafile, tablespace, and redo thread records, which are never reused unless the corresponding object is dropped from the appropriate tablespace.

> Please don't set `CONTROL_FILE_RECORD_KEEP_TIME = 0`, as that would actually keep the controlfile from expanding temporarily, in order to delete obsolete records when using RMAN.

Retention policies: Recovery window or redundancy?

A retention policy describes which backups will be kept and for how long. This policy can be changed by running the `CONFIGURE RETENTION POLICY` command, whether you are using a catalog or connecting directly to the current controlfile.

```
RMAN>CONFIGURE RETENTION POLICY TO RECOVERY WINDOW OF x DAYS;
```

While a recovery window policy is generally considered the better method, the number of backups can and will vary according to the backup schedule. The number of backups is calculated using the time from now and going back by X many days. Now you may think that a reasonable recovery window should be based on seven days, but that may not be optimal, depending on your resources and recovery strategies.

```
RMAN>CONFIGURE RETENTION POLICY TO REDUNDANCY x;
```

Redundancy is the number of backups kept on disk for the datafile in question.

```
RMAN>CONFIGURE RETENTION POLICY TO NONE;
```

If the retention policy is configured to NONE, then REPORT OBSOLETE and DELETE OBSOLETE will no longer work to remove older backups no longer needed for recovery.

The following configure command works in conjunction with a window retention period to minimize disk usage.

```
RMAN>configure optimize backup on;
```

Not needed (OBSOLETE) versus not found (EXPIRED)

The term "obsolete" does not mean the same as an "expired" backup. A backup is obsolete when REPORT OBSOLETE or DELETE OBSOLETE is run and is based on the user-defined retention policy to determine which backups are no longer needed for recovery. A backup is considered "expired" only when RMAN performs a crosscheck and cannot find the file.

From the perspective of a retention policy, a datafile backup is a full or level 0 backup of an individual file. It does not matter whether the backup is an image copy or part of a backup set. For file backups that are part of a backup set, RMAN will not remove the backup set until all of the individual backups within the backup set are obsolete.

RMAN considers as obsolete all archived logs and incremental level 1 backups that are not needed to recover the oldest datafile or controlfile backup. KEEP UNTIL TIME LOGS command specifies to keep all logs required to recover that database backup. If you specify NOLOGS, the logs required to recover the backup are not kept. This is only used for consistent, closed backups. There is an UNTIL clause for a certain time to mark a backup as obsolete or the FOREVER command to never remove it.

Use the crosscheck command within RMAN to search for any backups that it may know about. This verifies their current existence on the actual device (tape, disk, CD), and the original location they were backed up to.

The following are examples of crosscheck commands:

```
CROSSCHECK BACKUP; # checks backup sets and image copies
CROSSCHECK COPY OF DATABASE;
CROSSCHECK BACKUPSET 1338, 1339, 1340;
CROSSCHECK BACKUPPIECE TAG 'nightly_fullbackup';
CROSSCHECK BACKUP OF ARCHIVELOG ALL SPFILE;
CROSSCHECK BACKUP OF DATA FILE "?/oradata/orcl/system01.dbf"
COMPLETED AFTER 'SYSDATE-14';
CROSSCHECK CONTROLFILECOPY '/tmp/control01.ctl';
CROSSCHECK DATA FILECOPY 113, 114, 115;
```

Once a crosscheck command is run against a backup, copy, archivelog, and so on, and it doesn't exist on disk, then RMAN marks that file as expired. The following section will check for the existence of known backups and delete the ones it doesn't find. The `noprompt` command allows you to run it as a script. Otherwise it will wait for you to answer yes or no to the question: Do you really, really want to do this?

```
crosscheck backup of database;
crosscheck backup of controlfile;
crosscheck backup of archivelog all;
crosscheck backup of archivelog all spfile;
delete noprompt expired backup of database;
delete noprompt expired backup of archivelog all;
delete noprompt expired backup of controlfile;
report need backup;
report obsolete orphan;
delete noprompt obsolete;
```

However, beware that if you are backing up to tape using SBT commands, you will have problems if you remove backups from the catalog or controlfile and need to restore in the future. Carefully review all crosscheck and delete obsolete commands before implementing them in your environment. You will have problems retrieving backups that reside on tape and are marked expired or obsolete. I recommend entering an Oracle Service Request, as there are undocumented commands that can retrieve these types of backups.

 Refer to a recent blog post on undocumented commands for cataloging tape backups: http://erpondb.blogspot.com/2008/09/catalog-rman-backuppieces.html.

Why would you want to expire backups? This is for manually controlling all of the backups and archivelog destinations in a location outside the FRA. It is also done to reduce the number of entries in the repository catalog, keeping RMAN running at peak performance. At the OS level, you can remove these files based on a date/time stamp. Then, use the `crosscheck` and `delete expired` commands so that RMAN can remove them from the disk as well as the repository catalog when they are no longer needed for recovery.

It may be the case that backups are on disk, but are showing up as obsolete or expired when doing the `list backup` RMAN command. More than likely the information about these backups have been overwritten or removed from the controlfile. Make sure the `control_file_record_keep_time` parameter value is set to a value higher than the retention policy of the recovery window or consider using a repository for the RMAN catalog.

What if I want to keep certain backups?

The backup command changes slightly for archival type of backups at any point of retention you want. These are most often done at weekly, monthly, and/or yearly intervals. The purpose of the keep command is to exempt a backup from the retention policy. I didn't include all of the other backup commands demonstrated earlier just for brevity. It would be easier to maintain backups without changing scripts by using the syntax in the second command listed below. In this case the date is not hard coded, but it is recalculated at every run:

```
Rman > BACKUP DATABASE KEEP UNTIL TIME "TO_DATE('31-DEC-2009' 'dd-mon-
yyyy')" NOLOGS;
Rman > BACKUP DATABASE KEEP UNTIL TIME 'sysdate +365' NOLOGS;
```

Corruption detection

There are several types of database corruptions that can cause extensive data loss if due diligence is not taken to prevent it from happening in the first place:

- Datafile block corruption—physical or logical
- Table/index inconsistency
- Extents inconsistencies
- Data dictionary inconsistencies

Physical corruption

Physical corruption is most often caused by defective memory boards, power disruption, I/O controller problems, or broken sectors on a hard disk drive. A defective physical component prevents the complete write to the data block, which also includes the accompanying update to the header block. You may have block corruption, but the database will appear to operate normally because reads usually don't have an issue but writes will report the corruption error as something similar to the following:

```
ORA-01578:
ORACLE data block corrupted (file # string, block # string)
```

Don't always expect issues such as corruption to show up in an obvious way. While doing testing for this chapter, a corrupted datafile first showed an error that could have been caused by something other than corruption. After intentionally corrupting a specific datafile created for this purpose, I attempted to create a new table and this was the resulting error:

```
ORA-01658: unable to create INITIAL extent for segment in tablespace
```

This error usually means some sort of storage problem—there are not enough segments with manual segment management or the datafile is unable to extend to accommodate the new table segment. If I didn't know better, corruption would be the last thing I would have thought of. So what is the important thing to take away from this? Check the alert logs first, even on minor errors, in order to double check. See the following listing for the corresponding entry in the alert log while I was trying to create a new table segment in a corrupt datafile:

```
Fri Jan 22 16:04:19 2010
Corrupt Block Found
        TSN = 6, TSNAME = TESTING
        RFN = 6, BLK = 3, RDBA = 25165827
        OBJN = 1, OBJD = -1, OBJECT = , SUBOBJECT =
        SEGMENT OWNER = , SEGMENT TYPE =
Fri Jan 22 16:04:24 2010
Sweep [inc][17010]: completed
Sweep [inc][17009]: completed
Sweep [inc2][17009]: completed
Hex dump of (file 6, block 1) in trace file /u01/app/oracle/diag/rdbms/orcl/orcl/inci
dent/incdir_17010/orcl_ora_14604_i17010.trc
Corrupt block relative dba: 0x00000001 (file 6, block 1)
Bad header found during validating datafile for block range
Bad header found during validating datafile for block range
Data in bad block:
 type: 0 format: 0 rdba: 0x00000000
 last change scn: 0x0001.0000a20b seq: 0x80 flg: 0x01
 spare1: 0x0 spare2: 0x0 spare3: 0x0
 consistency value in tail: 0x00000000
 check value in block header: 0x0
 block checksum disabled
```

The information is repeated in the trace file mentioned, and from our work in *Chapter 3, Tracking the Bits and Bytes*, you know what most of the information refers to. From the alert log, you know the file number and block number. That identifies the segment to find the location of the corruption. Don't think this may be the only corruption that exists in this database—it is the one encountered due to a `create table as select` (CTAS) command. Read-only SQL statements won't necessarily find corruption. At this point, I would remove all access to this database and use the scripts mentioned on MOS to determine exactly the objects involved. At the same time, enter a Service Request on MOS and start to work on fixing things. Begin with this document on MOS: *Frequently Encountered Corruption Errors, Diagnostics and Resolution, [ID 463479.1]*.

Logical corruption

Logical corruption is some sort of inconsistency between the structures (both logical and physical) within the RDBMS, and is most often associated with software bugs. The following list contains some examples:

- Differences between the table row count and the corresponding index row count

- A table row is locked with a non-existent transaction

- The actual space used doesn't equal what the RDBMS has for the blocks

Extensive corruption information is written to the alert log once the database is aware of the issue. This happens during write access to the block or by certain Oracle utilities mentioned.

There are several Oracle database utilities that record any intrablock corruption by populating the views, V$DATABASE_BLOCK_CORRUPTION, V$COPY_CORRUPTION, or V$BACKUP_CORRUPTION.

The entries in these views are also automatically updated if the block corruption is repaired by the different methods of repair available—block media recovery, restoration of the datafile, recovery by an incremental backup, or block newing. Block newing occurs when the data block has no data associated with it. When there are deleted rows or a dropped table, Oracle will reuse that block by reformatting it.

Commands and utilities that detect corruption

The following SQL command identifies table and/or index consistencies (logical corruption) within a database. When the inconsistency is found, a trace file will be produced with detailed information.

```
SYS@SQL>Analyze table tablename validate structure cascade ;
```

Logical corruption or inconsistencies found in Locally Managed Tablespace are extents that may have overlapped using the same block or free extents that are reported as used. There are different methods, depending on whether the tablespace uses automatic or **manual segment space management (MSSM)**. Check the SEGMENT_SPACE_MANAGEMENT and EXTENT_MANAGEMENT columns in the view dba_tablespaces to determine if you are using auto or manual SSM.

- dbms_space_admin.tablespace_verify

- dbms_space_admin.assm_tablespace_verify

- hcheck.sql

Both of the `dbms_space_admin` SQL commands produce a trace file, which can be easily identified by giving the trace file a unique name like the following examples:

```
SYS@ORCL>execute dbms_space_admin.tablespace_verify('&tablespace_
name'); --Manual
oradebug setmypid
oradebug tracefile_name_for_Manual

SYS@ORCL>execute dbms_space_admin.assm_tablespace_verify('&tablespace_
name',dbms_space_admin.TS_VERIFY_BITMAPS) – Automatic
oradebug setmypid
oradebug tracefile_name_for_automatic
```

The Oracle-supplied Data Dictionary Health Check utility from *Chapter 4* is used for checking dictionary-managed extents or data dictionary inconsistencies, another type of logical corruption.

DBVERIFY

`dbv` is an external command-line utility that is most often used to determine if a backup database (or datafile) is valid. This utility can be used to validate any Oracle datafile, backup, or even user-managed backups. It is always best to use the command-line utility from the correct `$ORACLE_HOME` for a particular database. Dbverify can also be used to verify a table or index segment—it logs into the database to retrieve the segment location information within a datafile.

RMAN VALIDATE or BACKUP VALIDATE command

You can even validate individual blocks with the VALIDATE DATA FILE ... BLOCK command along with individual files, archivelogs, or the entire database, as shown below:

```
RMAN > Validate database  ;
RMAN > Validate data file <file no>,<file no>  ;
RMAN > Validate data file <file no> block <Block no> ;
RMAN > backup check logical validate database;
RMAN > BACKUP VALIDATE DATABASE ARCHIVELOG ALL;
RMAN > BACKUP VALIDATE CHECK LOGICAL DATABASE ARCHIVELOG ALL;
RMAN > restore database validate ;
RMAN > restore controlfile to '/u01/app/oracle/logs/' validate;
RMAN > restore archivelog from time 'SYSDATE-3' validate;
```

CTAS

The simple command to `create table as select statement` will show corruption issues. This is the statement I issued in the corruption example that gave an error about being unable to create the initial extent.

Export utility or Data Pump

Both of these utilities will populate the `v$block_corruption` view. I recommend checking the output from the periodic run of these utilities—shell scripting can scan for certain corruption related errors. When the script finds a certain error message, e-mail the entire output log to the DBA(s). It would also be good practice to keep these logs for historical reference, as it would be helpful to pinpoint when the corruption first appeared.

Which utility should be used?

It would not be overkill to use more than one corruption detection utility. That means scripting or scheduling the execution of RMAN validates commands as well as using the dbverify utility plus the `analyze table validate structure` SQL command. Every Level 0 RMAN backup would scan all blocks. But since a full backup only happens on a weekly basis, there would be gaps in corruption detection.

Setting the startup initialization parameter (the new `DB_ULTRA_SAFE` parameter can control several of these previously single parameters) `DB_BLOCK_CHECKSUM=TRUE` will prevent corrupt blocks from being read from disk. The RDBMS calculates a checksum for a block every time it is read or written to. The parameter `LOG_BLOCK_CHECKSUM` will calculate a checksum for redo log entries. This would prevent problems when trying to recover a database and encountering corruption. Another corruption-prevention database parameter is `DB_BLOCK_CHECKING`. This is always enabled for the system tablespace, no matter the setting (`FULL`, `MEDIUM`, `LOW`, `OFF`). All of these corruption-prevention parameters will use more CPU, due to the additional calculations. The amount of additional CPU can be substantial and would depend on the application workload. It is always recommended to prevent corruption in the first place instead of trying to restore or recover lost data.

Dbverify doesn't require a database login to scan the datafiles, but be aware that dbverify runs slower than RMAN due to the lack of a parallelism feature. The following query will spool a `dbv` command, and scripting this query and executing the resulting output will allow you to run dbverify simultaneously for all files. This is a viable workaround to the lack of a parallel feature for dbverify.

SYS@ORCL> select 'dbv file=' || name || ' blocksize='|| block_size || ' logfile=' || substr(name, instr(name, '/', -1, 1) +1) || '.' || file# || '.log' from v$datafile;

When you see an error about corrupted blocks, what should you do? The first thing would be to run one of the utilities or commands to identify the extent of the corruption. The alert log will have information about trace files that were produced when the database detected the corruption.

See the following documents for scripts to identify corruption by object as well as by blocks:

How to identify all the Corrupted Objects in the Database reported by RMAN [ID 472231.1]: Script to help identify those corrupt objects.

DBMS_REPAIR SCRIPT [ID 556733.1]: Check out this MOS document for the latest information on repairing corrupted data blocks.

What should I do if corruption is detected?

If you can, stop all current processing that would create transactions. I know this is bad, but it is better than losing data permanently. This means kicking off the end users. Once you know the type, extent of the corruption, and how to recover, then you can decide whether it is appropriate for them to proceed. Also, be aware that physical corruption is usually a sign of something **very bad** happening in the physical components, usually failing parts. The exception would be in a data warehouse environment with the standard method of loading data with NOLOGGING enabled to boost performance. Most often the data can be reproduced (or reloaded) from the original source. If failing parts aren't replaced, then the physical corruption will continue. Talk with your SA about OS testing of the hardware subsystem immediately.

If it is a physical corruption, then your best bet is to failover to a standby database, as advised in *Chapter 5, Data Guard and Flashback* on corruption prevention measures. Logical corruption may not require the end users to log off, as it may mean rebuilding an index, moving a table, or something less destructive.

Data Recovery Adviser

Oracle has the ability to create the script to repair the database. This is known as the **Data Recovery Adviser (DRA)**. If you need to introduce your own corruption for testing purposes, you could research on the Internet for examples. The following example is how the DRA was used to restore a corrupted datafile.

I removed all backups before starting this scenario. This means that the recovery came from the redo and any archived logs. Cool! See the restoration from the redo section for more about this.

1. RMAN backup command detects a problem and it doesn't mention the word "corrupt".

```
RMAN-03009: failure of backup command on ORA_DISK_1 channel at 01/22/2010 14:29:59
ORA-01122: database file 6 failed verification check
ORA-01110: data file 6: '/u01/oradata/orcl/testing.dbf'
ORA-01565: error in identifying file '/u01/oradata/orcl/testing.dbf'
ORA-27046: file size is not a multiple of logical block size
```

Notice that the alert log has the same date time stamp as the RMAN session, which detected the problem.

```
2010-01-22 14:19:24.420000 -07:00
create tablespace testing datafile '/u01/oradata/orcl/testing.dbf' size 10M
2010-01-22 14:19:26.761000 -07:00
Completed: create tablespace testing datafile '/u01/oradata/orcl/testing.dbf' size 10
M
2010-01-22 14:29:59.696000 -07:00
Checker run found 1 new persistent data failures
```

2. Using RMAN, I start investigating to see what RMAN knows about the problem.

```
RMAN> list failure;
List of Database Failures
=========================

Failure ID Priority Status    Time Detected Summary
---------- -------- --------- ------------- -------
982        HIGH     OPEN      22-JAN-10     One or more non-system datafiles are corr
upt
```

3. Using RMAN, I ask the DRA what I should do about this problem—this is
    known as the `advise failure` command.

```
RMAN> advise failure;
List of Database Failures
=========================

Failure ID Priority Status     Time Detected Summary
---------- -------- ---------  ------------- -------
982        HIGH     OPEN       22-JAN-10     One or more non-system datafiles are corr
upt
analyzing automatic repair options; this may take some time
allocated channel: ORA_DISK_1
channel ORA_DISK_1: SID=26 device type=DISK
analyzing automatic repair options complete
Mandatory Manual Actions
========================
no manual actions available

Optional Manual Actions
=======================
no manual actions available
Automated Repair Options
========================
Option Repair Description
------ ------------------
1      Restore and recover datafile 6
  Strategy: The repair includes complete media recovery with no data loss
  Repair script: /u01/app/oracle/diag/rdbms/orcl/orcl/hm/reco_539999020.hm
```

The contents of the repair script are included below:

RMAN>

```
# restore and recover datafile
  sql 'alter database datafile 6 offline';
  restore datafile 6;
  recover datafile 6;
  sql 'alter database datafile 6 online';
```

The Diagnostic Tool Set with 11g will create incidents automatically when a critical
issue is detected (such as corruption in this case). There are files that are meant to
be uploaded to Oracle Support personnel to help with an issue. They are located
in the diagnostic directories—`incident` and `incpkg`. Check the Oracle Database
Administrator's Guide for more information on how to package an incident,
specially-formatted trace files, and attaching them to a service request.

What does RMAN backup, restore, and recover?

Did you notice the addition of the word "restore" in the title of this section? Hopefully you did, as there is an important difference between restore and recover when it comes to Oracle. Restore is putting back the copy of the object (datafile, controlfile, spfile, archivelog) to a specific location. Recover is applying all of the transactions located in the online or offline (archived) redo and online undo segments to bring the database to a consistent state.

Consistency is where the checkpoint change numbers, for all datafiles agree with the checkpoint SCN of the database. That is your basic goal when doing database recovery. It is important to remember because anything that interrupts this process may result in lost transactions. Consistency is also important for the controlfile (it has its own checkpoint SCN), as Oracle takes a snapshot (read-consistent) of the controlfile if you back up the database when it is either mounted or open. The query below determines if the checkpoint change of the datafiles matches the checkpoint change of the database. If no row is returned, then everything is consistent:

```
SYS@ORCL>select name, file#, status, error, creation_change#, to_
char(creation_time, 'DD-MON-YYYY HH24:MI:SS') as creation_time,
to_char(checkpoint_change#, '999999999999999') as checkpoint_change#,
to_char(checkpoint_time, 'DD-MON-YYYY HH24:MI:SS') as checkpoint_time,
to_char(resetlogs_change#, '999999999999999') as resetlogs_change#,
to_char(resetlogs_time, 'DD-MON-YYYY HH24:MI:SS') as resetlogs_time,
to_char(bytes, '9,999,999,999,990') as bytes
 from v$data file_header
where status <> 'ONLINE'
or checkpoint_change# <> (select checkpoint_change# from v$database);
```

That is another key aspect of being in `archivelog` mode—you can use inconsistent backups, which means the database can still be open for read/write access by end users. Does this mean you can do backups anytime? No, backups generate redo activity while utilizing operating system resources to write the backup pieces. Backups should be done when the activity level is at its lowest. It is important to note that when a database is in `noarchivelog` mode, the only valid backup type is when that database has been taken down in a consistent manner—`shutdown immediate` is the one most often used.

While the commands `shutdown transactional` or `shutdown normal` are applicable, they aren't normally used, because it would require the database to wait until some or all of the transactions are completed (committed or rolled back) before shutting down. If your users are anything like mine, they probably won't log off unless they are forced to. There may also be certain processes that have something similar to a queue, like `DBMS_PIPES`, waiting for transactions to occur for processing. That type of database activity would also prevent the database from shutting down with the plain `shutdown` command.

So we are back to talking about what was covered in *Chapter 3*. As this is how Oracle tracks transact, it makes sense that point of recovery is actually the SCN. Even if you recover the database to a specific point in time, it is still SCN-driven. The following list is what RMAN can backup as well as restore to a device such as a local disk, optical drive, network-attached storage, or tape drive:

- Primary database
- Standby database
- Tablespace
- Datafile (current or image copy)
- Controlfile (current or image copy)
- Server parameter file (spfile) — another good reason to use them!
- Archived redo log file
- Backup sets

Don't assume that all backups are recoverable, as the media the backups are stored on can be temperamental. If you have the disk space, it would make sense to backup to a local disk, because that would make recovery faster. That backup to disk can then be migrated to tape for long-term offline storage.

There is an unwritten rule that DBAs keep at least three days of backups on local disks before migrating them to offline or near-line storage. Oracle 11g offers a few advanced features that can help with the lack of local disk storage for backups. For example, keeping the latest full incremental merge backup (combination of image copy but changed blocks) on disk along with duplexed archivelogs is a simplistic yet robust backup and recovery strategy.

Possible interruptions to the recovery process

Well, the first in the following list is self-explanatory but is worth mentioning. Make sure backups are occurring on a regular basis. The rest of the list will show you what may or may not prevent the recovery of lost data:

- No backups.
- No RMAN catalog: Controlfile will contain the most recent backup information.
- Commands such as Resetlogs, Inconsistent Database startup, and/or shutdown as well as using No Logging data loading procedures.
- No DBID available: This is required for certain types of restores. Look at the filename of controlfile autobackup; write a procedure to write this information to the alert log.
- Missing online REDO or UNDO: Depends on how database was shut down if recoverable.
- Missing temp: No issues with this one; just recreate or restart database.
- Missing read-only tablespaces: Restore from older backups or can use logical backups to recreate.
- Missing archivelogs: Can't recover any gap in transactions; possibly use LogMiner if not corrupt.
- Missing controlfile: Restore, recreation may result in lost transactions or longer restore time.
- Missing password file: Restore or recreate; if changed, this will require a database recycle; must match database `sys` password.
- Missing spfile: Restore or recreate by making a pfile first.

What doesn't RMAN backup, restore, and recover?

The following files are still considered critical, so here are a few comments on what their role is in the overall backup and recovery strategy for your organization.

- **Online redo**: Redo is archived for recovery
- **Online undo**: Usually not needed for recovery
- **Temporary tablespaces**: No need to backup; only used during queries

- **Binaries**: Multiple $ORACLE_HOMES and standbys provide some redundancy
- **Password files**: Can be recreated; requires database cycle if password is changed
- **Parameter files (pfiles)**: Can be recreated or a temporary one put into place
- **Diagnostic destination**: Restore from OS backups
- **SQL*Net files**: Can be recreated; may need to recycle database
- **Block change tracking file**: File recreated the next time RMAN is run
- **User-initiated RMAN backup logs**: E-mail to DBA; retain on disk for historical comparisons

Online redo: Key to consistency

One of the biggest misunderstandings for a new DBA is assuming that it is safe or reasonable to backup the online redo logs; this is usually attempted with a user-managed backup command. If your database is in `noarchivelog` mode, then the only type of backups that you should perform are closed, consistent, whole database backups. The files in this type of backup are all consistent and do not need recovery, so the online logs are not needed. You may accidentally restore backups of online redo logs while not intending to, thereby corrupting the database. As a side note: RMAN won't let you back up online redo logs.

The online redo can even recover datafiles that have never been backed up. See the following simplified scenario for a database in archivelog mode. Some of the output was shortened to save space. This illustrates the importance and role of online redo in the recovery process, as in the following example. I started by verifying that a full backup was available.

I created a new table segment in a new tablespace and switched log files to make sure data was flushed to disk. These steps are shown in the following output window:

```
SYS@ORCL> show parameter create_file
SYS@ORCL> db_create_file_dest      string        /u01/oradata
SYS@ORCL> create tablespace tbs_1;
SYS@ORCL> alter user dbuser quota unlimited on tbs_1;
SYS@ORCL>alter user dbuser default tablespace tbs_1;
DBUSER@ORCL> create table tbs_test as select * from dba_tables;
SYS@ORCL> alter system switch logfile;
```

The new tablespace was taken offline and verified the offline status. Next, the actual datafile was removed from the operating system.

```
SYS@ORCL> ALTER TABLESPACE tbs_1 offline immediate;
SYS@ORCL> select tablespace_name,status from dba_tablespaces;
SYSTEM                          ONLINE
UNDOTBS1                        ONLINE
SYSAUX                          ONLINE
TEMP                            ONLINE
CONVERSION                      ONLINE
TBS_1                           OFFLINE

SYS@ORCL> select name,status from v$data file;
/u01/oradata/ORCL/system01_ORCL.dbf    SYSTEM
/u01/oradata/ORCL/undotbs01_ORCL.dbf ONLINE
/u01/oradata/ORCL/sysaux01_ORCL.dbf    ONLINE
/u01/oradata/ORCL/conv01_ORCL.dbf      ONLINE
/u01/oradata/ORCL/data file/ol_mf_tbs_1_5nz5261s_.dbf   RECOVER

> ls -altr
total 102532
drwxr-xr-x 3 oracle dba      4096 Jan 14 15:01 ..
drwxr-x--- 2 oracle dba      4096 Jan 14 15:01 .
-rw-r----- 1 oracle dba 104865792 Jan 14 15:14 ol_mf_tbs_1_5nz5261s_.dbf

oracle@nodename:/u01/oradata/ORCL/data file[ORCL]
> rm *.dbf
```

An RMAN connection was started to the target controlfile to start a restore and recovery session. As there wasn't a recent backup to this new datafile, RMAN has no record of this datafile but the controlfile does.

If you go and look at the operating system level, after the restore command but before the recovery, the datafile will not exist.

```
RMAN> restore tablespace tbs_1;

Starting restore at 14-JAN-10
starting full resync of recovery catalog
full resync complete
allocated channel: ORA_DISK_1
channel ORA_DISK_1: sid=147 devtype=DISK
allocated channel: ORA_DISK_2
channel ORA_DISK_2: sid=139 devtype=DISK

creating data file fno=27 name=/u01/oradata/ORCL/data file/ol_mf_tbs_1_5nz5261s_.dbf
restore not done; all files readonly, offline, or already restored
Finished restore at 14-JAN-10
starting full resync of recovery catalog
full resync complete

RMAN> recover tablespace tbs_1;

Starting recover at 14-JAN-10
using channel ORA_DISK_1
using channel ORA_DISK_2

starting media recovery
media recovery complete, elapsed time: 00:00:03

Finished recover at 14-JAN-10
```

I made the tablespace accessible again to the end users by bringing it online. I also verified that the table segment existed as well as the status of the datafiles.

```
SYS@ORCL> alter tablespace tbs_1 online;
Tablespace altered.
SYS@ORCL> select tablespace_name,status from dba_tablespaces;

SYSTEM                          ONLINE
UNDOTBS1                        ONLINE
SYSAUX                          ONLINE
TEMP                            ONLINE
USERS                           ONLINE
CONVERSION                      ONLINE
TBS_1                           ONLINE

SYS@ORCL> select name,status from v$data file;
/u01/oradata/ORCL/system01_ORCL.dbf SYSTEM
/u01/oradata/ORCL/undotbs01_ORCL.dbf ONLINE
/u01/oradata/ORCL/sysaux01_ORCL.dbf ONLINE
/u01/oradata/ORCL/conv01_ORCL.dbf ONLINE
/u01/oradata/ORCL/data file/o1_mf_tbs_1_5nz5z6g4_.dbf  ONLINE
```

This recovery came completely from the transactions located in the online redo logs, as no backup was taken after the point where the tablespace was created, and no archivelogs were applied during the recovery process.

User-managed backups

There are quite a few third-party backup GUI-based utilities that use the RMAN utility API to backup databases (including OEM); they aren't in this category but are something to be aware of. If backups are done with SQL*Plus that is known as the user-managed type. Backups (RMAN or user-managed) can be done in two different ways: hot (inconsistent, open, archivelog mode) or cold (consistent, closed). If you have a reason to track these types of backups, RMAN can scan the file headers and catalog their existence, but RMAN cannot validate or verify that these backups are valid for recovery purposes.

The RMAN CATALOG command can be used to:

- Add user-managed backup pieces and image copies
- Record a datafile copy as a level 0 incremental backup, which can be used as the starting point for an incrementally updated strategy

To backup a binary copy of the controlfile without using RMAN:

```
SYS@ORCL> alter database backup controlfile to '/disk/control01.ctl';
```

To catalog that same copy of the controlfile, you can connect to either the controlfile or RMAN repository catalog for the same database:

```
RMAN> catalog controlfilecopy '/disk/control01.ctl';
```

To utilize RMAN in conjunction with user-managed backups, there are a few issues to be aware of:

- The target database has to be open or mounted during RMAN commands
- It can only be a datafile copy, controlfile copy, archived log, or backup piece
- It must be accessible on disk storage
- It can't be used to catalog backups between different databases like physical standbys and a primary

That is as much as you are going to find in this book about user-managed backups, just enough to make you aware of their existence. You may find a viable business need for such a procedure, but don't depend on this for your day-to-day backup and recovery strategy.

> *Using a Hot User-Managed backup to copy a database to a different Server –*
> *How To Make A Copy Of An Open Database For Duplication To A Different*
> *Machine [ID 224274.1]*

What do I do before starting a restore and recovery?

Hopefully, you have taken the time to practice several different types of recovery scenarios before having to do this for real in a production situation. This can be extremely nerve wracking. So take some time to settle down before starting, as you will need to think clearly. Don't leave the scene of the crime until things are normal, even if it turns out badly. Here are some generalized steps on how to proceed when the database goes down:

- Determine what is actually wrong before continuing

   Error messages don't always point to exactly what is wrong. They can be vague or general unless some sort of tracing is enabled. First, start with the database alert log and check for the existence of core dumps. Oracle has designed an RMAN-directed Failure Adviser that can be used in conjunction with manual procedures, but the adviser won't replace any of the steps in this list.

Run the `recovery_status.sql` script provided for this chapter. That might help to figure out the level of restorability you are working with. There is an example output file for what a normal database should look like (see `recovery_status.lst`).

- Backup current database

  This may or may not be possible depending on how extensive (is the server still up and running?) and actual type of data loss. Understand that taking a backup at this point may take longer than the actual recovery process. Also, make a copy of the controlfile (both binary and text-based) and the parameter files if they are still available.

  Check that you have archivelogs available. You may need more disk space than usual in a recovery situation, as this may require several backups at key points to minimize data loss. Keep the special backups in a different location than normal to keep confusion to a minimum.

- Put in an Oracle Support Request

  You may not need this help, but it is worth it even for a debriefing session on what you could have done differently. There is usually more than one way to fix a problem, which is why the next point is important.

- Research different scenarios

  DBAs constantly disagree on the best way to accomplish a task. There may be multiple approaches to the same problem. This may be the time to ask for advice.

- Practice the restore/recovery in a test database first

  This goes hand in hand with taking a deep breath before changing anything. It will give you some confidence that you can fix this problem correctly the first time and not cause additional unnecessary outages. Yes, things can become worse than they currently are!

- Document all of the actual steps

  This is really important, especially if you can't fix the problem yourself. Executing an RDA might be a great starting point to document the state of things before you start changing anything.

- When using RMAN set echo on, set debug I/O on as well.

```
RMAN> set echo on;
RMAN> run {
        allocate channel t1 type disk;
        debug io;
        backup database;
        debug off;
}
```

- Log RMAN at the command line and save all of the output

  The example command below starts RMAN, which connects to the target database controlfile using the RMAN-specific commands found in the file `restoresomething.rcv` and logs all output to `restoreout.txt` by appending to the existing log file.

  ```
  rman target / cmdfile backupsomething.rcv log /u01/app/oracle/
  logs/backupout.txt append
  ```

  All of the logging can help when diagnosing errors and double-checking what was actually typed during RMAN sessions: the output can scroll past quickly. If needed, run RMAN sessions in debug trace mode (`rman target / catalog trace rman.trc debug`). Normal backup activity should have the `set echo on` command as well as using the `log` command for historical and auditing activities.

  Use RMAN to test the backup validity before restoring with the following command:

  ```
  RMAN> restore validate database;
  ```

  Monitor the RMAN job by running the following query every two minutes to check that the `% Complete` column is increasing. Then query `V$SESSION_WAIT` to see what event the database might be waiting on if there is no change.

  ```
  SYS@ORCL>SELECT sid, serial#, context, sofar, totalwork,
                  round(sofar/totalwork*100,2) "% Complete"
         FROM v$session_longops
         WHERE opname LIKE 'RMAN%'
         AND opname NOT LIKE '%aggregate%'
         AND totalwork != 0
         AND sofar <> totalwork;
  ```

Find the most recent controlfile backup

This might be a challenge. Where was the latest one backed up to? This information isn't written to the diagnostic destination, but is located in the controlfile itself. As we aren't using a catalog, there isn't any other way to find out which one was the latest than to look at the operating system file date (if it is located on a locally-accessible filesystem). We can cheat a little by taking a look inside the snapshot controlfile created automatically when using RMAN, as it contains some backup information—date timestamp, configure commands, backup types, and locations.

Simply run the strings command; the default location for this file is $ORACLE_
HOME/dbs and the default name is snapcf_ORACLE_SID.f. Remember, there is a
configure command that can change both the name and location of this file. If you
run the strings command on the controlfile backup file, it will contain most of the
information found in the snapshot controlfile, but none of the configure commands.
I would highly recommend setting both the controlfile backup and snapshot backup
to a local file destination (not the FRA), as neither takes up a lot of room. If you want
to keep the snapshot version, you would need to rename the file, preferably with a
date timestamp, or it will be overwritten by any configure commands.

This is the information found in the text version of the snapshot controlfile:

- $ORACLE_SID
- TAG20100113T170027 — time stamp
- List of datafiles
- List of tablespaces
- Any configure commands run
- List of archivelogs
- Datafile backup location
- Controlfile backup name and location

Find the backup you want to restore

How do you find this information? RMAN backup logs or peeking inside the
snapshot controlfile will have the backup location. This is one of the items not
automatically dealt with by Oracle, the valuable output when running the actual
RMAN backup.

The RMAN log will have both the location of the controlfile backup as well as the
spfile, datafiles, and any archivelogs you backed up.

Online redo logs and temp files are recreated automatically by RMAN when a
resetlog is issued because online redo is not backed up.

```
RMAN>SET DBID 320066378;
RUN
{
SET CONTROLFILE AUTOBACKUP FORMAT
FOR DEVICE TYPE DISK TO '/disklocation/autobackup_format';
RESTORE SPFILE FROM AUTOBACKUP;
}
```

RMAN syntax has changed over the different versions of Oracle, which includes enclosing commands in the RUN { } block. You will see this older syntax used in a lot of the RMAN documentation and example scripts. It was included in this chapter for that reason. In current versions of Oracle, the RUN {} is more associated with a stored RMAN script, either user-created or Oracle-provided. For example, the RMAN duplicate command is a stored script that works in conjunction with your inputs.

Within the RMAN backup log, you will see that the controlfile is backed up last.

```
including current control file in backup set
including current SPFILE in backup set
channel ORA_DISK_1: starting piece 1 at 2009/01/01 12:00:00
channel ORA_DISK_1: finished piece 1 at 2009/01/01 12:00:02
piece handle=/recovery_area/V11/backupset/2009_05_0 /o1_mf_ncsnf_TAG20090506T11_501tr
0h7_.bkp tag=TAG20090506T11 comment=NONE
channel ORA_DISK_1: backup set complete, elapsed time: 00:00:02
```

If you do not have an RMAN backup log, simply locate the last file RMAN backed up. This should contain the controlfile backup if you have the auto controlfile backup turned on.

Restoring the controlfile

If there is no spfile then start a RMAN session to restore. RMAN is already aware, due to the stored configuration, of the file naming format for the autobackup command. This allows RMAN to search for it without connecting to the catalog repository in order to restore the spfile, as shown in the following output:

```
including current control file in backup set
including current SPFILE in backup set
channel ORA_DISK_1: starting piece 1 at 2009/01/01 12:00:00
channel ORA_DISK_1: finished piece 1 at 2009/01/01 12:00:02
piece handle=/recovery_area/V11/backupset/2009_05_0 /o1_mf_ncsnf_TAG20090506T11_501tr
0h7_.bkp tag=TAG20090506T11 comment=NONE
channel ORA_DISK_1: backup set complete, elapsed time: 00:00:02
```

At this point, you can restore the spfile from a user-specified location or the autobackup location:

```
RMAN> restore spfile from '/recovery_area/orcl/2009_05_05/o1_mf_ncsnf_
TAG20_501tr0h7_.bkp';

RMAN> shutdown immediate;
```

If spfile exists or has been restored, restore controlfile it's time to restore the controlfile: this command restores it from a specified location. If desired, the autobackup location would work as well—`restore controlfile from autobackup`. After you have started the database (`startup nomount` command) with the restored spfile, RMAN can restore the controlfile from an autobackup.

```
rman > target /
RMAN> restore controlfile from '/recovery_area/orcl/2009_05_06/o1_mf_ncsnf_TAG2009050
6T113947_501tr0h7_.bkp';

Starting restore at 2009/05/11 11:01:26
allocated channel: ORA_DISK_1
channel ORA_DISK_1: SID=151 device type=DISK

channel ORA_DISK_1: restoring control file
channel ORA_DISK_1: restore complete, elapsed time: 00:00:01
output file name=/oradata/orcl/control01.ctl
Finished restore at 2009/05/11 11:01:27
```

In the example above the controlfile has been restored to the location, as shown by the output log: `'/oradata/orcl/control01.ctl'`.

Restoring the database

Mount the database now that the parameter files and controlfile have been restored:

```
RMAN> alter database mount;
```

After you mount the controlfile, the RMAN repository is available and RMAN can restore the datafiles and find the archived redo logs. There are two different basic methods, depending on the time period of data you want recovered.

The assumption is that you have all of the archivelogs needed for either type of operation: full or point-in-time recovery.

Full recovery

Perform a full restore and recovery. This works if all of the datafile and archivelog backups are in the same location as when you used RMAN to backup.

```
RMAN> run {
restore database;
recover database;
alter database open resetlogs;
}
```

Point-in-Time Recovery

A **Point-in-Time Recovery (PITR)** would be used to restore a database to a particular point in time. It is often used for some sort of logical or physical database corruption that has occurred at a certain identifiable date and time, or by SCN.

```
RMAN> run {
set until time "to_date('Jan 10 2010 12:00:00','Mon DD YYYY HH24:MI:
SS')";
restore database;
recover database;
sql 'alter database open resetlogs';
}
```

The resetlogs command recreates the redo logs, overwriting whatever files that may currently exist. The information for the location, name, and size of the online redo logs comes from the combination of the restored controlfile and database parameters.

Verifying that the recovery is complete

Check to see that all of the datafiles, tempfiles, and logfiles exist:

```
SYS@ORCL>select name from v$datafile;
SYS@ORCL>select name from v$tempfile;
SYS@ORCL>select member from v$logfile;
```

Do you have the same number of objects you started with?

```
SYS@ORCL>select count(*) from  dba_objects;
```

You can also run the `recovery_status.sql` script provided in the code section for this chapter to verify that the database recovery is complete.

That is as basic as it gets for restoring and recovering a database. There are all sorts of problems that can arise when advanced scenarios come into play. Several scenarios that are worth practicing:

- No RMAN catalog
- Spfile and controlfile not restorable
- Uncataloged backups that have been crosschecked and expired
- Recovering from a user-specified location
- Recovering from online redo loss
- Recovering from temp tablespace loss
- Recovering loss of a tablespace
- Recovering loss of a read-only tablespace
- Recovering through a resetlogs operation (incarnations)

Remember the simplified steps: restore the parameter file, restore the controlfile, restore the database, and recover the database. Practice will help you keep a cool head when disaster strikes because some of the RMAN commands are complicated and can become quite convoluted. Start simple and add changes to your RMAN backup and recovery scripts gradually. It will take more time, but you will have more success in the long run.

Simplified recovery through resetlogs

During the *resetlogs* operation, the information in v$log_history and v$offline_range records is no longer cleared as in earlier versions of Oracle. There are two new columns in both of the views (v$log_history and v$offline_range), which indicate the database incarnation. The archivelog records belong to resetlogs_change# and resetlogs_time. The incarnation number of a database can be changed with several different methods—original database creation, NID operation, and a resetlogs operation. See the following SQL command to identify which set of archivelogs belongs to which incarnation of a database. If resetlogs or NID operation is not executed, then only the original incarnation DBID will show up in the results:

```
SYS@ORCL> select recid, thread#, sequence#, resetlogs_
change#,resetlogs_time from v$log_history;
```

In previous versions of Oracle DBAs, we often had bad experiences when trying to restore a database after a resetlogs operation. It was like a point of no return; there wasn't an easy way to recover transactions from archivelogs from a previous incarnation of a particular database. Once you passed that resetlogs point, your database was very vulnerable, because all previous backups were now obsolete. The latest method has the following advantages over the earlier one:

- There's need to perform a full backup after an incomplete recovery, as you can recover again.

- There's need to recreate a new standby database after a failover operation, which does a resetlogs operation to open the standby.

- Functionality is built into the newer version; there's no new RMAN command.

- It doesn't make any previous incarnation of an image-type backup obsolete for an incrementally merged strategy.

- Block media recovery can recover the corrupted blocks through a resetlogs operation on a parent incarnation.

- Newly generated archivelogs are usable with an earlier incarnation of the database.

Oracle 10g introduces a new format specification for archived log files. This new format avoids overwriting archived redo log files with the same sequence number across incarnations as in previous versions. One of the best features built into the 11g RMAN is that it automatically searches for archivelogs to apply during a recovery operation, looking into the known archive destinations. In the past, DBAs had to rerun commands multiple times a day to catalog the archivelogs being produced, in case they were needed for recovery. See the section on recovering using REDO only for examples on how to test this automatic retrieval of the archivelogs.

RMAN cloning and standbys—physical, snapshot, or logical

In 11g, all databases are now identified uniquely by DBIDs. In earlier versions, every database copy made by a method other than the duplicate command had the same DBID. In previous versions of Oracle, you would use the NID utility to change the DBID and ORACLE_SID for certain cloning procedures to a test database. You couldn't do this for standby databases because changing the DBID or ORACLE_SID would invalidate the configuration and the Data Guard process would not work. This is no longer needed—RMAN can now duplicate a production database for any reason. There is just a small difference in the commands run for the different types.

It is very easy to create a copy of a production instance with RMAN using the duplicate command. Most often this is to refresh a database for testing environments. Duplicating a database for a standby is slightly different, but the basic concepts are the same. What is great about doing this process on a regular basis is that it is a reproducible test of your backup and recovery strategies. It will tell you exactly how long it takes to recover a full database backup; apply the archivelogs to restore a copy of the production database to a consistent state.

There are two different types of duplicates—live database duplication and backup duplication. Live database duplication is producing an exact copy of a production database without taking a backup. This shouldn't be done during heavy production database use, as the process will consume resources to accomplish these steps. The backup duplication process uses existing backups to create the database. You might need a clone or a standby—physical, snapshot, or logical. A clone is just a copy of production, with no more updating of the information from the primary to the new copy until you recreate it. Most often DBAs set a schedule for cloning from the primary database to refresh the testing environments and keep the data fresh for the programming staff to test against.

Clones, DBIDs, and incarnations

You can clone a database with the older method of user-managed backups, but it is easier to do this with RMAN. That is because RMAN changes the DBID and ORACLE_SID (using the utility NID). This is another step you would have to do manually if you used the user-managed type of cloning a database. The following RMAN query will show the current DBID as well as any incarnations:

```
RMAN> list incarnation;
```

The following query will also find the current DBID:

```
SYS@ORCL> select to_char(dbid) from v$database;
```

DBID is also a part of the controlfile autobackup filename with the format of %F = c-<dbid>-<yyyymmdd>-<sequence number> like the following file:

```
c-3416182518-20100115-01
```

A script is provided as the code section for this chapter that gives you a quick way to duplicate a database to another server using RMAN. This script would result in exactly the same ORACLE_SID and DBID—called rman_diff_server.sql. If you want a different ORACLE_SID and DBID, then investigate the use of the NID utility. Also, be aware that if you backup both databases with the same DBID using an RMAN catalog repository, then the information in the repository is going to get replaced each time the catalog does a resync command. A way around these types of issues is to give each database a different tag as part of the backup and recovery commands, making each backup identifiable.

Creating a cloned database

This is what needs to be in place to accomplish the following task:

- Backups exist in the same location as taken on primary
- All directories for the datafiles already exist
- Either a pfile or spfile exists for CloneDB

- CloneDB has already been started with `no mount` command

```
oracle@nodename:/u01/app/oracle[CLONEDB]
> rman
connect target sys/password@PRIMARY
connect catalog rman/password@RMANCATALOG
connect auxiliary /
run {
set until time = "to_date('01/08/10:2:57:00','MM/DD/YY:HH24:MI:SS')";
allocate auxiliary channel ch1 type disk;
allocate auxiliary channel ch2 type disk;
allocate auxiliary channel ch3 type disk;
duplicate target database to CLONEDB
        logfile '/u01/oradata/CLONEDB/redo01a_CLONEDB.rdo' size 100m,
                '/u01/oradata/CLONEDB/redo02a_CLONEDB.rdo' size 100m,
                '/u01/oradata/CLONEDB/redo02b_CLONEDB.rdo' size 100m,
           '/u01/oradata/CLONEDB/redo03a_CLONEDB.rdo' size 100m,
           '/u01/oradata/CLONEDB/redo01b_CLONEDB.rdo' size 100m;
}
```

There is a text file in the code for this chapter that contains the normal errors (`cloning_errors.txt`) that occur during a cloning procedure. These errors are seen during the recovery phase, as the database is mounted, but before the resetlogs command. This is normal because the alert log entries are informing us that something is wrong (missing online redo logs) at this point that we are already aware of. These errors are okay to ignore. But if they continue past this particular time, then something else is wrong.

There is also a text file (`clone_output.txt`) that shows what should happen during a normal successful cloning operation. If the cloning process seems to be hanging near the end (see the following code section), turn off the GC Intelligent Agent temporarily because this has been an issue for my environment, especially before GC 10.2.0.5.

Now where do the datafiles, redo, undo, and temp files get created during a clone? They are put in exactly the same place as the production database, which is considered the `target` in a cloning operation. There is more than one way to put all of the assorted files in a different location—database parameters or using the `set newname` as part of the cloning script. A line for each data and temp file would need to be included as part of the script if using the `set newname` method:

```
set newname for datafile 23 to '/u01/oradata/CLONEDB/work01_CLONEDB.
dbf';
```

Using the database parameters to change the location of the database files on a different server is easier to maintain over time. Be careful cloning multiple databases on a single server—you could accidentally overwrite database files.

```
db_create_file_dest   --creates everything in one location
db_file_name_convert  -converts location for data,temp,redo to another
log_file_name_convert  -converts location for archivelogs to another
```

Post-cloning tasks

Here is a list of suggested housekeeping tasks for a newly cloned database. This is to clean up after a previous copy of the database has been removed. These steps are intended for a copy of production for testing use, not for a standby:

- Remove old trace, dump, audit files, alert logs
- Obsolete and expire old backups, exports, data pump files
- Remap database directories
- Adjust database links
- Revisit auditing, programmer access
- Register the database with RMAN catalog
- Rerun RMAN configure commands
- Turn off archiving if not needed

Creating a standby database

This section covers the use of RMAN when creating standby databases, whether it is a physical snapshot or logical type. There are other methods of creating standbys, but using RMAN is easier because several tasks are consolidated into a single command.

Physical standby

The following script is the simplest method of creating a physical standby. It is assumed that all of the primary database backups and all of the archivelogs since those backups are stored in the same location on the standby server. That is where the restored controlfile and RMAN catalog repository expects them to be. There are several steps that are needed to get to the point where you actually run the script:

- Physical standby spfile required
- Physical standby has started in nomount mode

```
rman target / auxiliary sys/change_on_install@STBY

Recovery Manager: Release 11.2.0.1.0 - 64bit Production

(c) Copyright 2008 Oracle Corporation.  All rights reserved.

connected to target database: STBY (DBID=3261937922)
connected to auxiliary database: STBY (not mounted)


RMAN> duplicate target database for standby dorecover;

Starting Duplicate Db at 09-APR-02
using target database controlfile instead of recovery catalog
allocated channel: ORA_AUX_DISK_1
channel ORA_AUX_DISK_1: sid=17 devtype=DISK

printing stored script: Memory Script
{
   restore clone standby controlfile to clone_cf;
   replicate clone controlfile from clone_cf;
   sql clone 'alter database mount standby database';
}
```

To create a snapshot or logical standby, refer to the *Oracle Data Guard Concepts and Administration* guide, as all of the standbys start out as physical and are then converted.

There is a script in the code section for this chapter that illustrates a live duplicate of a standby, that is with no existing backups of the primary. See the file named live_duplicate_standby.sql.

There is a formula for calculating the correct number of **Standby Redo Logs** (SRL). SRL is for improving the performance of a physical standby using the feature known as REAL-TIME APPLY, with little to no impact on the primary database. The transactions are transferred to the standby's online redo logs and applied to the standby instead of waiting for the archive process to write to primary online redo and then transfer. This reduces the number of transactions that could be lost to a bare minimum, especially for the MAXIMUM_PERFORMANCE mode. There is an Oracle-provided formula for the number of standby redo logs, as that is an important part of performance to discuss in the next chapter:

SRL = (maximum number of log files for each thread + 1) * maximum number of threads

For example, if the primary database has three log files for each thread and two threads, then eight standby redo log file groups are needed on the standby database.

Scheduled maintenance/cataloging of archivelogs

In earlier releases of Oracle, there were problems using RMAN to backup standbys or standby archive destinations, as stated in *Chapter 5*. More of the issues related to backing up standbys have been resolved in 11g, with unique DBIDs for all databases—no matter the type.

If there is a delay in writing an archived log to the standby site, it would show up as a wait on the primary database. If the FRA on the standby is full, waits labelled LNS wait on SENDREQ begin to register on the primary database. Each wait has a length of 10 ms. That may seem like a very short time to wait (milliseconds), but with an intensive OLTP database, multiple waits can add up affecting end user response time. The following output will show the errors from the standby alert log when the FRA is full on a standby.

```
Errors in file /u01/app/oracle/admin/RSTBY/udump/rstby_rfs_21481.trc:
ORA-00270: error creating archive log /backup/flash_recovery_area/RSTBY/archivelog/20
10_01_12/o1_mf_1_3228_%u_.arc
ORA-19809: limit exceeded for recovery files
ORA-19804: cannot reclaim 145510912 bytes disk space from 214748364800 limit
```

The problem may result from using the FRA for a standby archivelog destination. There are some techniques to configure Oracle for this type of situations. The one that most DBAs aren't aware of is that the FRA needs to be sized so that space pressure to remove obsolete backups is triggered when space_used is greater than or equal to the space_limit. The space_limit must be less than actual disk space available. If you consistently run out of room on a standby with FRA and it is very close in size to the actual disk space, try reducing the size of the FRA.

Rolling forward a standby using incremental

The RMAN command BACKUP INCREMENTAL FROM SCN will allow you to create a backup that begins with the current SCN of the standby. This incremental is posed at the right place to then roll forward the standby so that the standby and the primary are now in sync. This takes much less time than recreating the entire standby from a full backup again. See the following document for more details: *Rolling a Standby Forward using an RMAN Incremental Backup in 10g [ID 290814.1]*.

Rolling incremental for monthly updates to data warehouses

RMAN default backup strategy of rolling incremental updates into full backups can be used for updating a read-only data warehouse. Often a DBA needs to add last month's data that is much smaller in size than the entire database. This means there is no need to recreate the entire database just to add another month's work. The utilities data pump or the older export/import may take longer than expected for this monthly task. See the following document for updating an existing Transportable Tablespace Set with Incremental Backups: *Using RMAN Incremental backups To Update Transportable Tablespaces [ID 831223.1]*.

The DBMS_BACKUP_RESTORE package

The DBMS_BACKUP_RESTORE package is the system package created by dbmsbkrs.sql and prvtbkrs.plb. This package, along with the package DBMS_RCVMAN, is installed during the catproc.sql run. This is the interface between database server and the OS that provides the I/O services for backup and restore operations, as directed by RMAN.

In the package header, you can see the versions that this database version will support using RMAN—8.0.4.0 is the minimum for Oracle Database Version 11.1.0.7.

> *How to extract controlfiles, datafiles, and archived logs from SMR backupsets without using RMAN [Note:60545.1]*: This article is for using the DBMS_BACKUP_RESTORE package directly without the RMAN utility; it's useful for restoring from uncataloged tape backups.

Summary

You should have figured out by now that RMAN is a highly advanced tool in your arsenal of weapons against things that may attack the database. It even helps protect the database against the DBA, the most powerful being that it is sworn to protect but is also the greatest threat.

One of the most important things you should take away from this chapter is to maintain a constant vigilant eye on the database alert log. Errors may occur within SQL*Plus or other clients that actually mask a much larger issue such as corruption.

In order to provide the best possible service to your customers while keeping outages to a minimum, RMAN is one of the best tools for database backups and recovery. Remember the following list because these are important to backup and recovery as part of the MAA in addition to using RMAN:

- Running in archivelog mode—gives the ability to recover more transactions.
- Multiple copies of the controlfile—redundancy on different mount points.
- Multiple copies of online redo logs.
- Multiple archive destinations—can include standbys.
- Backups are happening on a regular basis—both physical and logical.
- Testing restores—by cloning or duplicating as well as creating standbys.
- Turn on block checking—worth the performance hit.
- Check password policy for data pump and/or export user—it may expire unexpectedly.
- RMAN—used for corruption detection and validating backups.
- One datafile to one backup piece—saves time during partial, small, or tape restores.
- No RMAN repository—make sure controlfile keep time is correctly timed for your retention policy. Catalog is required for Data Guard implementations.
- RMAN catalog maintenance—remove obsolete backups outside your retention policy; recatalog backups if needed.
- Make autobackup of controlfile persistent.
- Keep historical records of backup logs in case of complete loss.
- Record incarnations with the corresponding DBID—write to alert log, keep logs.
- Rethink the policy of delete all input for archivelog backups.

Testing for this chapter was done with the 11g versions 11.1.0.6.0 and 11.2.0.1.0 on several different servers: Linux 64-bit Red Hat 4 and 5, Linux 32-bit Red Hat 4 and 5, Windows Server 2003 32-bit.

While RMAN is great, it is only a tool that will be used, sharpened, dulled with use, and then sharpened again. Even DBAs that have been using it for a while need to reorient themselves with the newest features that will allow their applications to achieve even higher levels of uptime. That brings us to the next chapter on Migrating to 11g, as we introduce you to the shortest amount of downtime for upgrades—*Rolling Upgrades with a Transient Logical Standby.*

7

Migrating to 11g: A Step-Ordered Approach

How do you upgrade to the next release of Oracle without incurring extended periods of downtime and at the same time minimize possible disruptions? The information on how to accomplish this started back at the beginning of this book in *Chapter 2*, and was expanded further in *Chapter 4*. From using multiple Oracle Homes to using Data Guard standbys, all of the previous information is applicable and a buildup of knowledge for accomplishing large migration projects is required.

As a new DBA, it is important to realize that the binary upgrade and the database upgrade are two different events, most often executed at different times. A binary upgrade is the ORACLE_HOME software that is installed, upgraded, and maintained using Oracle-provided tools. A database upgrade is basically updating the data dictionary from one version to another. There are a myriad different ways (or migration paths) to accomplish both tasks, which is what this chapter is about.

Breaking up a large task into smaller chunks gives you multiple safe fall back positions for each shorter outage window. If something in one of the smaller steps doesn't work, back it out, reengineer, and redeploy. This will allow you to accomplish more in the long run, with less chance of failure and all the while installing confidence in your abilities. You will see how this approach works with each of these topics:

- What Oracle components are backwards compatible?
- Recommended order of migration.
- Patching, upgrades, and migrations—tips and techniques.

There are several migration paths available that can utilize the different technologies available in Oracle. There isn't a right answer as to which one to choose, I can't make that choice for you. Only the DBA in charge of a database should make the final decision on how to proceed. Most often it is the physical or application-specific limitations that dictate the path taken—hardware, software, outage window restrictions, and of course the most important one, the budget!

Most Oracle shops also look into replacing the hardware at major Oracle upgrades. This makes some of the transition easier, as the preparation steps take place on a server that isn't in production yet. Look at upgrading the operating system to the next release at the same time as migrating onto new hardware. That will save you downtime later to do the second migration. The basic limit to this type of migration—migrating to new hardware—is based on the size of the database. For a larger database it may take longer, depending on the method used, more upfront prep work, and even some creative thinking to accomplish with limited downtime.

Here is a list of the database upgrade technologies that will be covered in this chapter. An in-place upgrade will most often be performed on an existing database, as compared to migrating to 11g with a new database. You can expect to see tips scattered throughout.

- Manual upgrades—in-place
- **Database Upgrade Assistant (DBUA)**—in-place
- RMAN restore of backups for a manual database upgrade—in-place
- **Transportable Tablespaces (TTS)**—new
- Physical and/or Snapshot standbys—new
- Transient logical standby; rolling upgrades with minimal downtime—new
- Export/import or data pump—new

In the past, there were only manual upgrades and then the DBUA utility came along. RMAN gained more functionality for upgrades and then Data Guard standbys were introduced. The final lone method of migration—export/import or data pump, is really a last method of migration, which should only be chosen when the database is small or all other migration paths have been ruled out.

Migrating to a newer Oracle Database version doesn't have to be confined to a single outage period. Several interim steps can be done ahead to some of the compatible components, saving valuable time. Some of the components detailed in this chapter are parts of any Oracle Database edition—some are licensed requiring the Enterprise Edition of Oracle and others are completely separately installed Oracle software.

In a general sense, Oracle is backwards compatible for making that transition from an earlier version to a later one. The following components can be upgraded to 11g Release 2 (11.2.0.1 current patchset at the time of this writing) while still being compatible with earlier versions of Oracle Database:

- Oracle Net Services: LISTENER.ORA, SQLNET.ORA
- Clients (SQL*Net, JDBC, ODBC)
- RMAN Binary, Catalog, and Database
- Grid Control Repository Database
- Grid Control Management Agents
- ASM (Automatic Storage Management) and CRS (Clusterware)

The utilities that will have specific compatibility issues between Oracle versions include both export/import and data pump. See the following support documents for the latest up-to-date information:

- *Compatibility Matrix for Export And Import Between Different Oracle Versions [Doc ID: 132904.1]*
- Export/import data pump parameter version—*Compatibility of Data Pump Between Different Oracle Versions [Doc ID: 553337.1]*

As stated in Chapter 2, design your environment to be adaptable to change. This means that you should be comfortable with multiple Oracle Homes keeping each environment cleanly separated from the others. Install the 11g version in a different Oracle Home. Use the tools that Oracle provides, such as the oratab and oraenv file, to dynamically set environmental variables based on the ORACLE_SID as stated in *Chapter 2, Maintaining Oracle Standards*. See the section later on in this chapter on how to manually clone an existing ORACLE_HOME to apply patchsets.

Helpful troubleshooting and tracing for several of the utilities used in this chapter.

MOS Note 577775.1, "DBUA or Migration Is Hanging What to do?" and MOS Note 428118.1 "How to enable Java code tracing for DBUA, DBCA and NETCA?"

Oracle net services

As a DBA, controlling the environment is key to preventing disruptive events during migrations. Using the database parameter, LOCAL_LISTENER for each ORACLE_SID on a separate port allows the DBA to turn off or on access to that database without affecting other ports and/or ORACLE_SID(s). If you use port 1521, dynamic registration will happen for each instance on that node, and hence that port is avoided to maintain control.

Oracle recommends having multiple listeners running in multiple Oracle Homes (see *Note: 429074.1*), but experience has taught me that the highest version listener executable will work for any single-version, down-level database installed on a single node while preventing conflicts. You can use any combination of multiple ports and multiple listeners, but the executable comes out of only a single ORACLE_HOME location, as shown in the following listing of Unix processes:

```
oracle@nodename:/u01/app/oracle[]
> ps -ef | grep lsn
oracle    18762     1  0 03:28 ?        00:00:17 /u01/app/oracle/product/11g/bin/
tnslsnr listener_ordg -inherit
oracle    22802     1  0 2009 ?         00:00:01 /u01/app/oracle/product/11g/bin/
tnslsnr listener_orcl -inherit
```

The key to using a higher level listener is the variable TNS_ADMIN, which overrides the default Oracle net services location for the LISTENER.ORA, TNSNAMES.ORA, and SQLNET.ORA configuration files. Refer back to *Chapter 4* for more detailed information on modifying the *.ora files.

Cancel out the Oracle software installation when it starts to configure Net Manager (refer to the following screenshot). Cancelling out the step just stops any sort of listener starting in the new ORACLE_HOME. After the installation session is over, manually edit the *.ora files in preparation for switching to a new listener during off-peak hours. Switching to a new listener is basically turning off the old version and starting the new one. Manually configuring all listeners out of a single ORACLE_HOME would also prevent any possible conflicts such as hanging or the auto registration of port 1521.

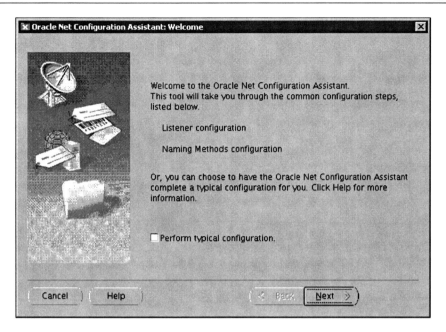

Client compatibility (SQL*Net, JDBC, ODBC)

In a general sense, client compatibility is supported on a minimum release (usually what is known as the terminal or last release for older products). In other words, a higher-level client can work with a lower-level database. This configuration will most often see a performance boost as well as other known client-specific issues resolved by upgrading the client before the database. The clients in the following list that have an asterisk (*) will have little to no issues with a single version down-level database, others have a comment related to the support:

- ODBC *
- SQL*Plus, Instant Client, SQL Developer *
- JDBC, JDK—Application specific
- Precompilers—Application specific
- Export/import or data pump—MOS article, very strict guidelines
- Database links*
- 32/bit to 64/bit—SQL*Plus, C, Cobol, database link
- PL/SQL features compatibility—New release features will be associated with the lowest version client

- Features availability — New release features will be associated with the lowest version client

- BEQUEATH connections are not supported between different releases — Unix-specific Oracle protocol that connects without a listener.

Oracle ODBC version compatibility mirrors compatibility for Oracle client software, as it is part of the client installation and tested as a bundle.

If you start with Oracle Database 10.x, there will be fewer issues than starting with any of the older versions. There are also few compatibility issues when dealing with a terminal (or final) release of an Oracle Database. See the following MOS and OTN documents for the latest updated information on client compatibility between all versions:

- *Client / Server / Interoperability Support Between Different Oracle Versions [ID 207303.1]* `http://www.oracle.com/technology/tech/java/sqlj_jdbc/htdocs/jdbc_faq.htm#02_02`

- *JDBC, JDK and Oracle Database Certification [Note 401934. 1]*

RMAN binary, virtual/catalog, and database

The RMAN executable version (binary) should be the same as the target database. This dictates using the same `ORACLE_HOME` to run RMAN scripts. Most sites with multiple databases connect to a remote RMAN repository catalog database. The RMAN repository catalog schema version must be greater than or equal to the RMAN executable with the built-in backward compatibility for earlier releases. Upgrade the catalog using RMAN commands as follows:

```
RMAN> upgrade catalog
RMAN-06435: recovery catalog owner is rman
RMAN-06442: enter UPGRADE CATALOG command again to confirm catalog upgrade
RMAN> upgrade catalog
```

This will not upgrade the database that houses the RMAN catalog to 11g. This upgrades the RMAN schema to be compatible with the higher release of RMAN. Upgrading the catalog allows you to backup any other 11g databases as well as previous versions. You can go ahead and also upgrade the RMAN catalog repository database to 11g at this point, using any of the standard methods: DBUA, EXP/IMP, EXPDP/IMPDP, Transportable Tablespaces, or a Manual Upgrade.

The RMAN catalog database should not be housed in the same place as your production database. It should be a separate database on a different server. It would be wise to test upgrading the catalog on a test copy of your RMAN repository. It is also customary to backup the RMAN catalog database on a regular basis, in case you need to restore backups or controlfiles from tape. *Chapter 6* indicated that there are limits when restoring from tape once they are removed from the RMAN repository (controlfile or catalog).

The RMAN catalog repository database is critical enough for an enterprise-wide utility for those organizations that have multiple databases and multiple DBAs. Some organizations use multiple RMAN schemas (catalog owners) for different Oracle releases and/or databases. 11g RMAN brings new functionality for handling different DBAs using multiple databases called the Virtual Private Catalog. It provides a fine-grained control mechanism for giving certain DBAs access to a subset of databases. This provides more flexibility than the previous method of multiple schemas for managing DBA backups.

 See *MOS Note 73431.1 RMAN Compatibility Matrix* for information on RMAN compatibility between releases.

Grid Control—database repository and agents

Many DBAs keep their RMAN Catalog and Grid Control repository in the same database because of their related DBA functionality. Grid Control 10.2.0.4+ is compatible with 11.1.0.6 version of the database, but I would recommend GC 10.2.0.5 with 11g as the repository database due to migration issues.

Migrating the Grid Control repository database to 11g was mentioned earlier in the book in Chapter 4. There is quite a bit of information on several migration methods included in that chapter.

Grid Control management agents are compatible with upper level Oracle Enterprise Management servers.

ASM, CFS, and RDBMS within an Oracle Grid infrastructure

Oracle Grid Infrastructure 11g Release 2 is a packaged software installation type that integrates ASM, ASM Cluster File System, Oracle Database, and Oracle Restart. It is designed to push the deployment of the different components of a highly available database into two different operating system accounts—ASM+ CFS and RDBMS. At the same time this allows multiple people to administer their respective components—the system administrator configures hardware and storage, the network administrator configures all network components, and the DBA is in charge of the database.

SYSASM and SYSDBA are privileged accounts associated with an ORACLE_HOME. The SYSASM account has privileges (for performing specific tasks) granted to an ASM ORACLE_HOME with a SYSDBA account with privileges to a Database ORACLE_HOME. Currently, both ORACLE_HOME types (ASM and Database) can exist in the same ORACLE_HOME installation directory.

See the following link in the Oracle forums for more specific information on current implementations and to find out how recent migrations have progressed:

`http://forums.oracle.com/forums/forum.jspa?forumID=62` (RAC, ASM, and CRS forum).

Oracle is proposing that in future releases there will be no SYSDBA privileges in an ASM instance. This is where Oracle is really pushing the separation of duties, but as DBAs know, in most shops there is not a clear separation of duties. These are some of the features that are meant to facilitate the separation of the ASM home from an ORACLE_HOME. These features in the following list are included in this chapter because the implementation details facilitate Advanced Migration Paths:

- Oracle Clusterware has a requirement to be installed in its own ORACLE_HOME

- ASM can be installed separately as of 10gR2. Features will be available on the lowest release in the combination of ASM home and Database home

- The ability to separate SYSASM and SYSDBA at the OS level by using different Unix accounts

- One-off patches have two components—one for Clusterware and another for the RDBMS

- As of 11gR2, ASM has the ability to perform a rolling upgrade while leaving the database still available

Often the DBA makes the judgment calls about the RDBMS as well as ASM, while CRS on CFS is more easily handed off to a system administrator who happens to know all the details of storage implementations. Here is Oracle's proposed separation of accounts and privileges. There are slight differences depending on which document is referenced:

OS Group	Oracle group		Privilege
OINSTALL	(group only)		OraInventory
OSASM	GRID	SYSASM	All ASM
OSOPER	OPER	SYSOPER	Startup, shutdown
OSDBA	ORACLE	SYSDBA	All RDBMS

Different operating system accounts provide a clear separation of file system privileges, which also delineates the ability to perform certain tasks. Along with different operating system accounts, it makes sense to have different ORACLE_HOME(s) for the Grid Infrastructure—both ASM and CFS in one home, RDBMS in the other. The Grid Infrastructure install can support either RAC or a standalone database.

Oracle ASM+CFS is always considered an out-of-place upgrade (a similar concept to the out-of-place patchset instructions later in this chapter). The older version of the software is installed at the same time as the newer version in different ORACLE_HOME(s), but only one home is being used. One-off cluster patches will have two components—Clusterware and RDBMS. There is also the promised capability for ASM to accomplish a rolling upgrade while still allowing full database access.

See the following documents for more information:

Oracle Clusterware (formerly CRS) Rolling Upgrades [ID 338706.1]

How to Change ASM Home on a Node in RAC [ID 558508.1]

Applying one-off Oracle Clusterware patches in a mixed version home environment [ID: 363254.1

Recommended order of migration

It is assumed that you, the DBA, would attempt multiple variations of a migration project in a non-production or standby environment first (See *Chapter 5* for testing scenarios) for several weeks to months before even attempting any changes to production. As you should notice, the database is not the very last thing to migrate; it is the optimizer. You aren't really migrating the optimizer, as you will be enabling the newest features of the optimizer by manipulating the related database parameters. In reality, you are migrating the statistics (see *Chapter 8* for more details).

Changes that survive testing are migrated to production gradually so that disruptions are kept to a minimum. The entire migration process should begin when a new version is first released, even while in beta. That would give a long period of time to test a new major release of Oracle. Often a year or more will pass before it is fully tested for production use. The following is a personal recommended listing of the order of implementation. By all means adjust it for your needs. I would recommend waiting until the product is out of beta testing before applying any of the following components in a production environment:

1. Listener
2. RMAN version as part of a Catalog Repository
3. RMAN Catalog Repository Database
4. Grid Control Database
5. Grid Control Agents
6. Clients—SQL*Plus, Instant client, ODBC, JDBC, among others
7. ASM and/or CRS
8. Database
9. Optimizer

The next section deals with the actual tasks that are done first, installing the newer version of Oracle Database software with some tips on how to automate this task.

Installation of major versions, maintenance releases, and patches

There is a difference when installing Oracle software, depending on whether it is a major release, maintenance release, or some sort of patchset. A new major release, for example, will go from 10.x to 11.x. A maintenance release is the second set of numbers, for example, going from 11.1 to 11.2. Review *Chapter 2, Maintaining Oracle Standards*, for the numbering convention for Oracle releases and some recommendations related to installing patchsets.

Release installation

If you are planning to do a release upgrade, either major or maintenance, then install the newer version in a new ORACLE_HOME. Remember to set the environmental variable ORACLE_BASE. Which version should you install? Find the most current one even if it has just been released, since you are installing this first in a test environment. Don't forget to patch this new ORACLE_HOME with the latest CPU or PSU patch if it is available. Check back on MOS for patchset availability for this newer version of Oracle Database on a regular basis. This section contains some of the tips you might need to install a newer release of Oracle Software.

There are three different modes when installing Oracle Software—interactive, suppressed, and silent. I recommend doing at least one interactive installation of a new major or maintenance release for a trial run. This trial run can also be used to record the installation routine, as shown by the following code. This recording can then be used as the response file for doing the subsequent installations silently (without human intervention). The resulting response file can easily be edited for any desired changes. The suppressed mode is a combination of interactive and silent.

```
> setup -record -destinationFile C:\install_oracle11gR2.rsp (on Windows)
oracle@nodename:/u01/app/oracle/softwareinstalldir
> ./runInstaller -record -destinationFile /tmp/install_oracle11gR2.rsp (on UNIX)
```

When interactively installing for the first time, do a custom install of the binaries only. I recommend not creating or upgrading a database at this time. The creation and upgrading tasks can be easily done later with a command-line utility on their own. **Database Creation Assistant (DBCA)** allows you to interactively create a database or save a set of scripts to edit and run manually for database creation. This chapter contains all of the different methods for actually upgrading an existing database to a newer release besides just using the DBUA.

ASM as well requires some prerequisites before it can be fully configured and utilized. As mentioned in the SQL*Net Services section of this chapter, a custom install also allows you to cancel out of the NET Configuration Assistant utility.

 Oracle Universal Installer (OUI) FAQ [ID 458893.1] will give great information that is not found in the standard Oracle Documentation.

A custom install will also allow you to monitor what is installed by default, particularly what optional components will be installed. Remember, optional means the additional licensing required. Review what licenses your organization actually owns because the database now monitors when an optional component is actually used, as shown by the example query below:

```
SYS@ORCL>select name from dba_feature_usage_statistics where detected_
usages > 0;
```

It is easy to determine what is an option when looking at the following URL for the different editions. It would not be an easy task to determine the different licensing options by using a query. http://download.oracle.com/docs/cd/E11882_01/license.112/e10594/editions.htm#CJACGHEB

The default installation of certain optional components are shown in the next screenshot; this comes from the 11.2 Oracle Universal Installer (OUI):

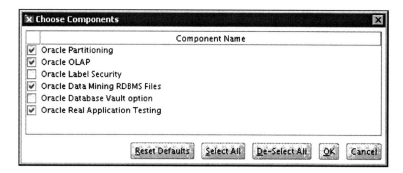

PatchSet installation—cloned ORACLE_HOME

Cloning is the easiest method for creating a copy of an ORACLE_HOME in order to apply further patchsets.

It is recommended to have at least two $ORACLE_HOMEs — one for production and another for testing patches at all times. The database can only be opened and used in a single ORACLE_HOME. The other homes not currently being used are upgraded and configured in advance of any database changes required in a new release. That is the last step in migration to a new release applying the database changes. Often I will have at least three ORACLE_HOMEs on a server at any one time — current production, patchset of production, and the new major or maintenance release home. Cloning or creating another new ORACLE_HOME for patching is called an out-of-place patchset apply in the Oracle documentation.

Follow these steps to clone an existing ORACLE_HOME:

1. As the root user, copy the existing lower-level ORACLE_HOME to the new upper-level ORACLE_HOME location.

```
ROOT@NODENAME:/u01/app/oracle[]
> cp -pr /u01/app/oracle/product/11.2.0/db_home1 /u01/app/oracle/product/11.2.0/
db_home2
```

2. Make sure the only differences between the ORACLE_HOME(s) are log-type files.

```
ROOT@NODENAME:/u01/app/oracle[]
> diff -q -r /u01/app/oracle/product/11.2.0/db_home1 /u01/app/oracle/product/11.
2.0/db_home2
```

3. Now that the new location has been copied, register the new ORACLE_HOME in the appropriate Oracle Inventory by using the clone.pl script provided by Oracle. The Unix tee command is a handy method for collecting large outputs to a file while still allowing you to see the output in the command window at the same time. Notice how I set the ORACLE_HOME by exporting the environmental variable. This makes sure the clone.pl script can find all other scripts needed for this process to complete successfully.

```
echo "Clone started `date`" | tee -a clone11gR2P2.log
oracle@nodename:/u01/app/oracle/product/11.2.0/db_home1
> export ORACLE_HOME=/u01/app/oracle/product/11.2.0/dbhome_1
> perl /u01/app/oracle/product/11.2.0/dbhome_1/clone/bin/clone.pl ORACLE_HOME=/u
01/app/oracle/product/11.2.0/dbhome_2 ORACLE_HOME_NAME=11gR2P2 ORACLE_BASE=/u01/
app/oracle
...............all output removed for brevity.............
>echo "Clone ended at `date`" | tee -a clone11gR2P2.log
```

4. Log in as the root user to run the newly created $ORACLE_HOME/root.sh.

5. Install the patchset, in this case 11.2.0.2, to the newly cloned ORACLE_HOME (/u01/app/oracle/product/11.2.0/db_home2). This upgrades the binaries only, not any databases that you want to upgrade to 11.2.0.2. After the binaries are upgraded, you may upgrade the database using any of the procedures described in the *Database upgrade methods* section of this chapter.

At this writing, the patchset 11.2.0.2 was not actually available. It is only used as an example in this case.

See the *How To Clone An Existing RDBMS Installation Using OUI [ID 300062.1]* document for more information about cloning `ORACLE_HOME`(s).

Now you have the higher-versioned Oracle Software (called binaries) installed with the separately upgradeable components. Higher-versioned components (such as the listener, clients, ASM + CRS) that exist on the same server as the database are intended to be installed, configured, and working in a separate `ORACLE_HOME` than the lower-level database home. The other components that are a separate install on a different server are assumed to have already been installed by this point as well: RMAN repository catalog, GC repository, and agents.

See the compatible components as listed in the *Recommended order of migration* section. We are now at upgrading the database. Making the database a completely separate step allows this whole process to be a step-ordered migration. There are several methods for upgrading the database—DBUA, manual, RMAN, TT, standbys, EXP/IMP, or data pump. The one you choose depends on several different things: size of database, amount of the downtime allowed, co-migration to new hardware, application-specific concerns, or technical obstacles.

Database upgrade methods

As stated earlier in *Chapter 2*, there is a MOS document called *Oracle 11gR2 Upgrade Companion* [see *ID 785351.1*], which I personally think is a misleading title. It implies that this is a utility of sorts, but it is only a very long document on everything you would ever want to know about upgrading. It applies to every installation type (see the following list of configurations, this is the same list mentioned in *Chapter 2* in the *Recommended Patches* section) and can be very confusing to new DBAs.

Targeted configurations in the upgrade companion:

- Generic
- Real Application Clusters and CRS
- Data Guard (and/or Streams)
- Exadata
- Oracle e-business suite

The upgrade companion seems to be a document taking all of the possible things that could go wrong with an upgrade all bundled up in one place. I would recommend downloading the companion, and copying all of the text in a document to which you can then add comments or amend as needed. Take out the information that doesn't apply to your environment or is intended for other targeted configurations.

How long does the database upgrade take?

Technical considerations are usually the most important concern when the DBA is weighing the different options for upgrading the database itself. End users will be more concerned with the downtime due to this upgrade. There is only one way to determine how long a process will take. Run it in a test environment that mimics production as close as possible.

Whether you use the DBUA or the manual method, there really isn't much difference, as both will result in about the same amount of downtime. That is because the step that takes the longest time to complete is the actual conversion of the data dictionary from one version to another. Here are some things to keep in mind for keeping an upgrade window as small as possible:

1. It takes less time to migrate the data dictionary from a 10.x database to 11.x than it would take to start with an older version; there are just fewer data dictionary changes.

2. All PL/SQL becomes invalidated, so databases that contain more objects that require compiling would take longer. Compile using the parallel compile package `utlrcmp.sql` instead of the standard `utlrp.sql`. For a server with multiple CPUs, the degree of parallelism is recommended to be set to the number of CPUs plus two. Remember to account for multi-core CPUs.

3. Collect statistics (or import desired statistics) on all objects prior to performing the upgrade. See the next chapter for more information on collecting and importing statistics.

4. Make all other tablespaces other than SYSTEM, SYSAUX, UNDO, ROLLBACK SEGMENTS, and SYSAUX offline. Two different commands would work for this task, OFFLINE NORMAL or even READ ONLY, as the data in application-specific tablespaces isn't changed during an Oracle upgrade. Any ordinary READ ONLY tablespace will need to be made READ WRITE temporarily after the upgrade, so the data file headers can be updated and then restored to READ ONLY status. See the MOS document *Increasing Migration Performance and Recovery time using offline Tablespaces [ID 780318.1]* for more details. It would be necessary to check that there are no SYS-owned objects in any off-lined tablespaces.

   These same steps would also save time if you need to downgrade or restore the database from a failed upgrade attempt.

Database Upgrade Assistant (DBUA)

This is the new kid on the block—it used to be widely avoided, but is now dependable enough to be used by even the most hardcore command-line DBA. Useful for saving time and avoiding some of the mistakes most often encountered with the manual method. This method would be worthwhile attempting, first in a test environment to see what steps are required for a particular upgrade that would otherwise be done manually. The DBUA can let you know if the required database parameters are correct and whether there is enough room in the system tablespace, as well as enable version-specific features that are all assorted housekeeping tasks.

The following upgrade options page indicates some of the recommendations for speeding up the database upgrade itself—parallel compiling (see comments about `utlrcmp.sql` later in this chapter) and turning off the archive process.

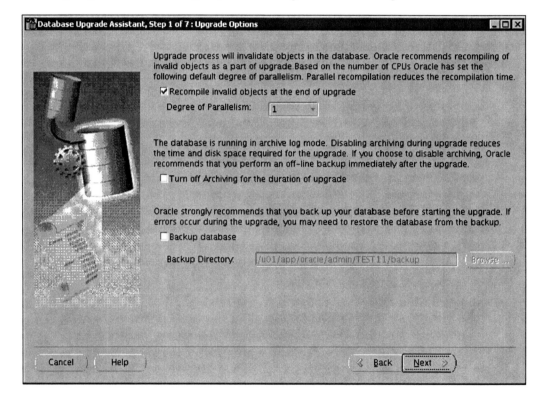

RMAN

Did you think the previous chapter was finished? Nope, I just ran out of room in that chapter, so here we go again. RMAN can be used as part of a manual migration strategy, either by restoring a copy of an older database to a new server or using the transportable tablespace method of upgrading. At the end of this section, some tips on using RMAN catalog repository with multiple Oracle Database versions are also included.

Using RMAN as part of a manual upgrade process

RMAN is configured so that a higher release is able to restore a lower release (upgrade) or vice versa (downgrade). Think of the following exercise in two parts—using RMAN to restore and recover a database, and then upgrading the database manually to 11g. This method will work for a database either in a noarchivelog mode with a consistent RMAN backup, or an archivelog mode with an inconsistent RMAN backup. You will also need additional archivelogs for the `recover until time` command. Because both topics (using RMAN for the database migration and manual upgrades) are being covered, I won't reiterate the manual upgrade steps later in this chapter, as they are well documented in Oracle's Upgrade Companion.

The overall steps for this example of upgrading a database from 10.2.x.x to 11.2.x.x are slightly different from the cloning section of *Chapter 6* in this book because it doesn't involve the duplicate command. You will find more information on this process in the book *Oracle Database Backup and Recovery User's Guide 11g* (*Chapter 19, Performing RMAN Recovery: Advanced Scenarios*). Look for the section labeled, **Restoring a Database on a New Host.** Also, follow the instructions in the Oracle Database Upgrade Guide as well. Here, in the chapter titled *Upgrading a Database to the New Oracle Database 10g Release,* see the section labeled **Upgrade the Database Manually**.

I recommend not connecting to the RMAN catalog repository for this type of recovery because it will change the information about the original database while executing the restore and recovery commands. These changes may include the automatic deletion of flashback logs, filenames and location changes, and the new incarnation due to the resetlogs command. It is assumed that all of the steps are being executed on a different server than the one that hosts the original database being copied.

1. Install the required 11g software along with the appropriate PSUs or CPUs on a different server. Create an entry for the database to be restored in `/etc/oratab` on the new server (see the following example entry). The `ORACLE_SID` has to be the same as the original. You can use the utility NID to change both the `ORACLE_SID` and DBID after the last step.

    ```
    ORCL:/u01/app/oracle/product/11.2.0/dbhome_1:N
    ```

    You can always come back later to change the `N` to a `Y` in the oratab for this entry to enable Oracle's method of auto startup and shutdown routines. See the Oracle documentation for your operating system.

2. Create any required directories for data file locations, `diag_dest`, audit destinations, and so forth on the new server. At this point, you can change the datafile locations, but that has to be accounted for in the RMAN restore command by `SET NEWNAME`.

3. Run the Pre-Upgrade Information Tool on the existing database to see what may need to be changed for this upgrade to be completely successful. This tool also does some housekeeping chores for this upgrade, as the following output demonstrates—timezone fixes—and may completely fail the entire backup if not run in advance, as shown by the error below:

```
DOC>    - "ORA-01722: invalid number"
DOC> if the pre-upgrade utility (utlu112i.sql) has not been run to:
DOC>a) create and update registry$database table to include the current database
 timezone file version used in the old release; or
DOC>    b) do inserts into sys.props$.
DOC>
DOC>    o Action:
DOC> Shutdown ABORT and revert to the original ORACLE_HOME.  Then run
DOC> utlu112i.sql to populate registry$database with the database DOC>timezone f
ile version used by the lower version database and to DOC>populate sys.props$ wi
th Day Light Saving Time (DST) properties i
DOC> OR
DOC>    - An "ORA-01722: invalid number"
DOC>if the old release uses a timezone file version newer than 8 (shipped with 1
1.2) but the new release has not been patched yet.
DOC>    o Action:
DOC>Shutdown ABORT and patch new ORACLE_HOME to the same timezone file version a
s used in the old ORACLE_HOME.
DOC>#
    TO_NUMBER(value$) != (SELECT tz_version from registry$database))
                                        *
ERROR at line 6:
ORA-00904: "TZ_VERSION": invalid identifier
```

If you happen to skip this step creating the error file above, I would recommend going back to the original database and starting over. Run the Pre-Upgrade Information Tool, then run another RMAN backup on the original server and a restore/recovery session on the new server. Reverting to an older timezone file on a new ORACLE_HOME gives me an uncomfortable feeling that this step may somehow impact the ability to successfully complete patching and upgrades in the future.

4. Any backups must be available on the new server. If migrating to 11g on the same server, look into using transportable tablespaces instead. The backup files may be copied to the same disk location made available on tape, or use an alternate location. See the `catalogfilecopy` command for how to catalog existing backups in a different location.

5. Set the DBID and start the database instance in nomount mode. The DBID can be retrieved from the controlfile autobackup filename as well as the RMAN backup log itself (you should be logging the commands and saving the output)

```
RMAN> CONNECT TARGET /
RMAN>SET DBID 3417997090;
RMAN>STARTUP NOMOUNT
```

6. Recover the spfile or create a new pfile. Most often you don't want exactly the same parameter file as the original database, so creating a new pfile just for this recovery session makes sense. After the recovery is complete, adjust the pfile and create an spfile for permanent use. In this case, I would recommend setting the database parameter DB_UNIQUE_NAME for the restored database as something different from the original. In your 10.2.0.4 backup, there is no inclusion of the spfile when the controlfile is automatically backed up. So you can't restore both automatically in this migration from 10g to 11g exercise.

7. Recover the controlfile and mount the database.

```
run {

SET CONTROLFILE AUTOBACKUP FORMAT FOR DEVICE TYPE DISK TO '/
backuplocation/%F';

restore controlfile from autobackup;

alter database mount;

}
```

8. Restore the datafiles and recover the database. In this case, I recovered to a certain point in time.

```
RUN

{

set until time = "to_date('02/05/10:16:00:00','MM/DD/YY:HH24:MI:
SS')";

  # restore the database and switch the datafile names

RESTORE DATABASE;

SWITCH DATAFILE ALL;

RECOVER DATABASE;

}
```

In the example above, I did not include the use of NEWNAME to change the location of the datafiles. This is well documented and easy to add to the script.

9. Open the recovered database with resetlogs along with the special parameter meant for upgrading. This does several housekeeping chores so that the process can complete successfully.

```
SYS@ORCL>  alter database open resetlogs upgrade;
```

10. Upgrade the database manually—this consists of running several scripts to complete the version-changing process. This process changes the data dictionary to the new version, replacing any changed system packages and procedures. Some features will not require any database parameter changes; these are enabled by default. Other database parameters become obsolete (no longer used) or deprecated (scheduled to be removed in a later release).

```
SYS@ORCL> SPOOL upgrade_to_11gR2.log
SYS@ORCL> @catupgrd.sql
```

In earlier releases of Oracle, there was a shutdown command that has now been moved to the end of the `catupgrd.sql` script. A clean shutdown flushes all cache, clears out buffers to make sure the database is consistent for the next startup command. You will have to exit the closed SQL*Plus session and start a new one for the startup command to be successful.

```
SYS@ORCL> STARTUP
```

11. Use the Post-Upgrade Status Tool to make sure all the installed components were successfully upgraded. This script (tool) changes name according to the exact release you are upgrading to, this example is the 11.2.x version. I provided some of the output, which is confusing because it says everything is valid, yet also contains errors. It's time for some research on My Oracle Support. Usually, you will encounter the same errors in a test environment for an upgrade. That is the time to enter an Oracle Service Request, as in this case only the Oracle XML error was a known issue at the time of this writing.

```
SYS@ORCL> @?/rdbms/admin/utlu112s.sql
Oracle Database 11.2 Post-Upgrade Status Tool
   Component                            Status      Version
   Oracle Server                        VALID       11.2.0.1.0
   JServer JAVA Virtual Machine         VALID       11.2.0.1.0
Oracle Workspace Manager
.   ORA-00942: table or view does not exist
.   ORA-06512: at "WMSYS.OWM_MIG_PKG", line 1575
.   ORA-06512: at "WMSYS.OWM_MIG_PKG", line 1592
.   ORA-06512: at line 1              VALID       11.2.0.1.0
Oracle XDK                              VALID       11.2.0.1.0
Oracle XML Database
.   ORA-04043: object XDB_DATASTORE_PROC does not exist
.   ORA-04043: object XDB_DATASTORE_PROC does not exist
                                        VALID       11.2.0.1.0
Oracle Database Java Pack               VALID       11.2.0.1.0
Oracle Multimedia                       VALID       11.2.0.1.0
Oracle Expression Filter                VALID       11.2.0.1.0
Oracle Rules Manager                    VALID       11.2.0.1.0
Gathering Statistics

Total Upgrade Time: 00:29:13
```

12. There is a new post-11g database upgrade script called `catuppst.sql`, which performs several tasks that don't require the special upgrade mode. This keeps downtime to a minimum because the upgrade mode prohibits any connections other than the SYS as SYSDBA account.

    ```
    SYS@ORCL> @?/rdbms/admin/catuppst.sql
    ```

13. Run `utlrp.sql` or `utlrcmp.sql` to recompile any remaining packages that are invalid.

    ```
    SYS@ORCL> @?/rdbms/admin/utlrp.sql
    SYS@ORCL>SELECT count(*) FROM dba_invalid_objects;
    SYS@ORCL>SELECT distinct object_name FROM dba_invalid_objects;
    ```

Several scripts and output files are provided in the code package for this section. See `Restore_to_newHost1.rco` and `Restore_to_newHost2.rco` that are the RMAN scripts used for this exercise. You will have to change them as noted inside the files for your environment. There are the accompanying `*.1st` files to show a successful run. There is also the output from the Pre-Upgrade Tool for this database—`predupgradetool.1st`.

Downgrading with RMAN

While the process is similar to doing a manual upgrade, this chapter doesn't fully cover everything you need to know about stepping back to an earlier version of Oracle Database. Use the Oracle Documentation and the detailed documents listed below for more information. It would be worth your while learning about and practicing in a test environment how to downgrade the database. This makes sure there aren't any unknown technical obstacles. Think of it as one of the many possible backup and recovery exercises that need to be practiced—just another part of the Maximum Availability Architecture.

See the following documents for more information on downgrading:
How To Downgrade From Database 11.2 To Previous Release [ID 883335.1]
Complete Checklist For Downgrading The Database From 11g To Lower Releases [ID 443890.1]

When might using the RMAN manual method for upgrades/downgrades be useful?

- Migrating between one-off operating system levels.
- Migrating a database to new hardware that is not eligible for TT method.
- Changing the database word size (32-bit versus 64-bit).
- In saving some work in having to install the older ORACLE_HOME on a new server as well as a few of the manual migration steps.
- For a trial restore of production in a test environment.
- The downgrade option is usually done after a failed database upgrade. This is usually due to an unanticipated technical limitation.

Refer to *Answers To FAQ For Restoring Or Duplicating Between Different Versions And Platforms [ID 369644.1]*.

Transportable Tablespaces (TTS)

There are several different Oracle-provided utilities or packages that a DBA can use with transportable tablespace(s). What TTS brings to an Oracle database is a method of compartmentalizing the physical database objects (tables and index segments) into a moveable entity. Export/import, data pump, DBMS_FILE_TRANSFER, and RMAN can all move a TTS by changing all of the datafile headers associated with the logical entity known as a tablespace.

Since Oracle10g database, a tablespace can be transported to another database with the same or higher database parameter compatibility setting, and the databases can be on the same or different platforms as well.

Segments that are in the **system** tablespace and any objects owned by SYS will not be transported. This includes all of the users, privileges, PL/SQL stored procedures, Java classes, callouts, views, synonyms, dimensions, DBA directories, and sequences as part of the data dictionary, plus any objects you have created that are owned by SYS. This also means that anything SYS-owned should not reside in the application data tablespaces to be transported.

Several different migration scenarios that can utilize TTS include:

- Restoring an unrecoverable database
- Upgrading a database
- Migrating to a different operating system
- Migrating or consolidating ASM datafiles

While you may not have a good use for TTS today, there is always the possibility of needing to use TTS in the future. I would highly recommend pre-certifying your database(s), making sure they can be used before you actually have to use the TTS procedure. It also makes sense to keep the physical objects in a database that have similar use and lifespan in an appropriately grouped tablespace, keeping things neat and tidy.

Preparatory steps for TTS migrations

If a database has multiple end user applications using the records contained within, it is recommended to keep the schemas or application owners in different tablespaces separate from each other. This separation provides more control over any housekeeping or maintenance tasks like TTS so that you can take down a single application while still providing access to others.

The tablespace name in the target database cannot have the same name as a tablespace in the source database. Since the 10g release, you can use the rename tablespace procedure to solve this problem, which can be performed either on the target or the source database.

```
SYS@ORCL>ALTER TABLESPACE USERS RENAME TO USERSQUERY;
```

However, there are a few limitations to this procedure that need to be understood:

- OMF created datafile names have to include their tablespace name; even if renamed they will retain the original tablespace name.

- Put read-only tablespaces into read-write mode temporarily after the rename or TTS procedure so that the datafile headers are updated to reflect the changes.

- Remember that there is a database parameter UNDO_TABLESPACE that will have to be changed if that tablespace name is changed. After altering the parameter and if you are using a static parameter file, it will have to be updated manually for the next database restart.

- Any recovery process with the old tablespace name won't cause issues: old recovery — old tablespace name; newer recovery — new tablespace name.

- You cannot rename the SYSTEM, SYSAUX, or any offline tablespaces.

There are several scripts included in the code section for this chapter that have to do with qualifying a database for TTS. See a script called transport_violation_check.sql, which identifies tablespaces that aren't self-contained. You will need to provide a list of tablespaces, which identify objects from the transport_set_violations view that reference objects in the tablespace to be transported. There is another view pluggable_set_check that checks from the other direction — objects that will no longer be able to reference objects from the tablespace you want to transport. See the provided script named tts_reference_violations.sql.

If objects don't currently qualify as transportable, then it is time for some homework, which may include:

- Moving SYS-OWNED objects to the SYSTEM or SYSAUX tablespace
- Moving application segments to be self-contained

TTS violations that occur aren't always just physical segments. There often will be constraints or views that will normally cross tablespaces due to application needs or business rules. These items will be easy to recreate on the new database with an export or data pump dump file after the tablespaces have been transported.

Using TTS for upgrades

What an elegant solution to upgrading for larger databases — keeping the datafiles in the same location and running an `imp` or `impdp` command to change the appropriate metadata for the datafiles. This would reduce the amount of downtime because the application datafiles are not moved.

If the upgraded database is on a different server (or platform), then the datafiles need to be copied over after they are made part of a transport set. If the actual datafiles exist on a storage device that is accessible from either the source or target server as a local device, then that would decrease the amount of downtime incurred when copying datafiles as part of the TTS procedure.

TTS cookbook

The TTS procedure really just uncouples the datafiles from the older database, modifies the datafile headers, and reconnects them to the other database. ORCL is the source database of ORACLE_SID whereas NEW is the target database of ORACLE_SID.

The following is a simplified checklist for moving the data in the users' tablespace:

1. Double check the platform on the source database.

    ```
    SYS@ORCL>SELECT platform_name FROM v$database;
    ```

2. Check endian compatibility for both source and target. This will be of the lowest level database compatibility setting:

    ```
    SYS@ORCL> show database compatible.
    SYS@ORCL>SELECT endian_format FROM v$transportable_platform where

    PLATFORM_NAME like '%&your_server%';
    ```

3. If the endian format is not compatible, then RMAN will need to be used for the conversion process. The files that need to be converted will be any that have application data; add your additional tablespaces to this query:

    ```
    SYS@ORCL>SELECT file_name FROM dba_data_files
     WHERE tablespace_name IN ('USERS');
    ```

4. Check to see if the tablespaces are self-contained. Fix any that are moveable; plan migrating any unmoveable objects by other means, usually data pump or export.

```
SYS@ORCL>EXECUTE DBMS_TTS.TRANSPORT_SET_CHECK('USERS''user',TRUE);
SYS@ORCL>SELECT * FROM transport_set_violations;
SYS@ORCL> SELECT * from PLUGGABLE_SET_CHECK where TS1_NAME='USERS'
or TS2_NAME='USERS';
```

5. Pre-create the target database (NEW) (it can be an existing database) along with any users that own objects in the TTS being migrated.

6. Make the source TTS tablespaces read only.

```
SYS@ORCL>ALTER TABLESPACE users READ ONLY;
```

7. Export the self-contained transportable tablespace as a transport set.

```
> expdp system/password DIRECTORY=TTS_DUMP DUMPFILE=exptts.dmp
LOGFILE=expTTS.log TRANSPORT_TABLESPACES=users
TRANSPORT_FULL_CHECK=Y
```

8. Convert using RMAN from one platform to another on the source database. If on the same platform, this conversion step is not necessary. Yours may be a different platform conversion.

```
rman> CONVERT TABLESPACE users TO PLATFORM 'AIX-Based Systems
(64-bit)' FORMAT '/tmp/%U';
```

9. Transfer the data pump dump file and all of the copied or converted datafiles in binary mode to the target server.

10. Plug in the tablespaces by running the appropriate data pump on the target database (you can use the older version of import if you used the older export on the source database):

```
> impdp system/password DIRECTORY=TARGETTTS DUMPFILE=expTTS.dmp
LOGFILE=impTTS.log TRANSPORT_DATAFILES=('/=(/u01/oradata/new/
users01.dbf')
```

11. Change the newly transported tablespaces back to read write.

```
SYS@ORCL>ALTER TABLESPACE users READ WRITE;
```

Some special limitations to TTS are as follows:

- The source and target database must use the same database character set and national character set

- In Oracle9i and Oracle8i, the source and target database must be on the same hardware platform

Recreating an unrecoverable database with TTS

This is a great way to recreate a database that can't be recovered or recreated with any other method than the export/import or data pump utilities. It is assumed that this database can be opened, as that is part of the TTS procedure. A certain type of data dictionary corruption that is unrecoverable is an example that would qualify for this procedure. While this discussion is more suited for the RMAN chapter, it is included here because the information is specific to the TTS process. This process is worth mentioning because it drastically reduces the amount of downtime due to two different reasons:

- It only exports the metadata for the objects in a particular tablespace and not the physical data (rows)
- Indexes don't have to be recreated

A few technical limitations would exclude certain types of migrations:

- Both the source database and target database are required to be on the same operating system and Oracle Database version
- The database and national character sets must be the same on both databases

Some additional steps may be required for using this procedure across the network or changing filenames or locations of datafiles.

Using TTS to add skipped read-only tablespaces during duplication

Usually read-only tablespaces are skipped during a RMAN duplicate database procedure to save time. The duplicate procedure changes the DBID of the target database to be different than the source, which in turn changes the datafile headers and prevents the use of a read-only or normal offline tablespace. The following three different alternatives can be used to add a read-only tablespace during the RMAN duplicate procedure:

- Export or data pump dump file can be used with TTS to move the objects by following the TTS procedure for the read-only tablespace by itself. The same steps should be followed as in the TTS cookbook section.
- `DBMS_FILE_TRANSFER` procedure can move the read-only data from one database to another. This procedure is discussed in the next section.

- Clone the database rather than doing `duplicate` database. This creates a new incarnation but the same DBID. This makes it easy to add back a read-only or offline normal tablespace. This cloning process was discussed in the previous chapter.

Using TTS to merge two ASM databases into one

Another method of migrating data between databases is by using the procedure `DBMS_FILE_TRANSFER` package for anything that can be stored in ASM groups. `DBMS_FILE_TRANSFER` can be used for moving archivelogs, RMAN backups, datafile copies, spfiles, Data Guard configuration files, change tracking file, flashback logs, cross platform transportable tablespaces, and data pump files.

In this example, we are looking at creating a transport set (TTS) to merge ASM datafiles from one database to another. `DBMS_FILE_TRANSFER` transfers the metadata across a database link, so the necessary SQL*Net resolution would need to be in place for this process to be successful. The following are the generalized steps that are different than the cookbook provided earlier. Step 5 is where the two processes start to become different. Steps 1 through 4, which are preparation steps, can stay the same.

1. A new database doesn't have to be created unless that is your situation; this can work for existing databases or a combination of new and existing ones.

2. This step of making the tablespaces read-only is moved farther down on this list.

3. Create a database link between the source and target database.

   ```
   SYS@ORCL> create database link FTLINK connect to system identified
   by password using 'NEW';
   ```

4. Create an ASM-based directory in the source database (ORCL) to hold the metadata dump file, logfile, and current datafiles slated for transport.

   ```
   SYS@ORCL> create directory ttsdump as '+DATA/';
   SYS@ORCL> create directory ttsdumplog as '/exportlogs/tts_log/';

   SYS@ORCL> create directory ttsdumpdatafile as '+DATA/datafile/';
   ```

5. Grant read/write access to the directories created.

   ```
   SYS@ORCL> grant read, write on directory ttsdump to system;
   SYS@ORCL> grant read, write on directory ttsdumplog to system;
   SYS@ORCL> grant read, write on directory ttsdumpdatafile
   to system;
   ```

6. Repeat steps 7, 8, and 9 on the target database. It is assumed for this example they will have the same ASM names.

7. Make the source tablespaces read only for transporting.

```
SYS@ORCL> ALTER TABLESPACE TRANSPORT1 READ ONLY;
SYS@ORCL> ALTER TABLESPACE TRANSPORT2 READ ONLY;
```

8. Export the metadata for the tablespaces slated for transport on the source server.

```
> expdp system/password directory=ttsdump dumpfile=transport1.dmp
logfile=ttsdumplog:transport1.log transport_tablespaces=transport1
,transport2 transport_full_check=y
```

9. Use DBMS_FILE_TRANSFER to send the metadata dump file and datafiles to the target server. Notice how we can change the data filenames in the process.

```
SYS@ORCL> begin
 dbms_file_transfer.put_file
 (source_directory_object => 'ttsdump',
 source_file_name => 'transport1.dmp',
destination_directory_object => 'ttsdump',
destination_file_name => 'transport1.dmp', destination_database =>
'NEW');
 end;
/
SYS@ORCL> begin
 dbms_file_transfer.put_file
 (source_directory_object => 'tts_datafile',
 source_file_name => 'transport1.29.570721319',
 destination_directory_object => ' ttsdatafile',
 destination_file_name => 'tts1_db1.dbf',
 destination_database => 'db2');
 end;
 /
SYS@ORCL> begin
dbms_file_transfer.put_file
(source_directory_object => 'tts_datafile',
source_file_name => 'transport2.29.586721335',
destination_directory_object => 'ttsdatafile',
destination_file_name => 'tts2_db1.dbf',
destination_database => 'db2');
end;
/
```

If the endian formats are different, then you must use the RMAN convert after transferring the datafiles to the target server.

Example code:

```
RMAN> CONVERT DATAFILE
    '/u01/oradata/tts1_db1.dbf',
    '/u01/oradata/tts1_db1.dbf'
    TO PLATFORM="Solaris[tm] OE (32-bit)"
    FROM PLATFORM="HP TRu64 UNIX"
    DB_FILE_NAME_CONVERT=
    "/u01/oradata/", "+DATA"
    PARALLELISM=5;
```

10. On the target server, it is time to import the metadata using data pump:

```
>impdp directory=ttsdump dumpfile=transport1.dmp
logfile=ttsdumplog:transport1.log TRANSPORT_DATAFILES='+DATA1/
tts1_db1.dbf','+DATA1/tts2_db1.dbf'
keep_master=y
```

11. Turn the tablespaces back to read-write mode:

```
SYS@ORCL> ALTER TABLESPACE TRANSPORT1 READ WRITE;
SYS@ORCL> ALTER TABLESPACE TRANSPORT2 READ WRITE;
```

This is only an introduction to the DBMS_FILE_TRANSFER procedure. There are many other ways of using this package for migrating ASM objects.

Here is another migration scenario utilizing TTS: *How to Avoid Long Refresh Time Required to Initialize Materialized View Data? [ID 734596.1]*

Sharing read-only tablespaces between different databases with TTS

There is an interesting article that mentions a scenario to share a single tablespace between two databases, but both databases would be using the tablespace in read-only mode. A reasonable use for this tactic would be to offload read-only queries to another database for tuning and performance reasons. The single-most limiting factor is that the tablespaces would have to be read-only in both databases. There are some other limitations (same block size) and requirements for accomplishing this task.

For more details, see *How to Share Tablespace Between Different Databases on Same Machine [ID 90926.1]*.

Now consider the case study that used the USERS tablespace between two databases on a single server — source ORACLE_SID (ORCL) and target ORACLE_SID (NEW). Both databases used the same block size and ran the same Oracle version.

It was made sure that there were no tablespaces of the same name in NEW, and the existing USERS tablespace was renamed to USERS1. That still left the same username in the NEW database, SCOTT. A new user named SCOTT2 in the NEW database was created.

```
SYS@NEW> alter tablespace users rename to users1;
Tablespace altered.
SYS@NEW> create directory imptts as '/backup/exportdp/ORCL';
Directory created.
SYS@NEW> create user scott2 identified by password;
```

In the source database ORCL, the USERS tablespace was made read-only and it was double checked that it was transportable.

```
SYS@ORCL>EXECUTE DBMS_TTS.TRANSPORT_SET_CHECK('USERS',TRUE);
SYS@ORCL>SELECT * FROM transport_set_violations;
SYS@ORCL> alter tablespace users read only;
```

Then the USERS tablespace was exported as a transport set.

```
> expdp system/password directory=DATA_PUMP_DIR dumpfile=tts.dmp logfile=exptts.
log transport_tablespaces=USERS transport_full_check=y
Copyright (c) 2003, 2007, Oracle.  All rights reserved.
Connected to:Oracle Database 11g Enterprise Edition Release11.1.0.6.0-Production
Starting "SYSTEM"."SYS_EXPORT_TRANSPORTABLE_01":  system/******** directory=DATA
_PUMP_DIR dumpfile=tts.dmp logfile=exptts.log transport_tablespaces=USERS transp
ort_full_check=y
Processing object type TRANSPORTABLE_EXPORT/PLUGTS_BLK
Processing object type TRANSPORTABLE_EXPORT/TABLE
Processing object type TRANSPORTABLE_EXPORT/INDEX
Processing object type TRANSPORTABLE_EXPORT/CONSTRAINT/CONSTRAINT
Processing object type TRANSPORTABLE_EXPORT/INDEX_STATISTICS
Processing object type TRANSPORTABLE_EXPORT/CONSTRAINT/REF_CONSTRAINT
Processing object type TRANSPORTABLE_EXPORT/TABLE_STATISTICS
Processing object type TRANSPORTABLE_EXPORT/POST_INSTANCE/PLUGTS_BLK
Master table "SYSTEM"."SYS_EXPORT_TRANSPORTABLE_01" successfully loaded/unloaded
********************************************************************************
Dump file set for SYSTEM.SYS_EXPORT_TRANSPORTABLE_01 is:
  /backup/exportdp/ORCL/tts.dmp
********************************************************************************
Datafiles required for transportable tablespace USERS:
  /u01/oradata/ORCL/users01_ORCL.dbf
Job "SYSTEM"."SYS_EXPORT_TRANSPORTABLE_01" successfully completed at 07:13:09
```

Because this was on the same server, I kept the staging directory in the same location as the dump location. Notice the location of the dump file and the datafile in the output of the expdp command above.

Now import the transport set into the target database NEW—the REMAP_SCHEMA command was used to make SCOTT2 the owner of the imported objects.

```
oracle@nodename:/u01/app/oracle[NEW]
>impdp system/password directory=imptts dumpfile=tts.dmp transport_datafiles=('/
u01/oradata/ORCL/users01_ORCL.dbf') remap_schema=SCOTT:SCOTT2

Import: Release 11.1.0.6.0 - Production on Tuesday, 16 February, 2010 7:32:38
Copyright (c) 2003, 2007, Oracle.  All rights reserved.
Connected to: Oracle Database 11g Enterprise Edition Release 11.1.0.6.0 - Produc
tion
Master table "SYSTEM"."SYS_IMPORT_TRANSPORTABLE_01" successfully loaded/unloaded
Starting "SYSTEM"."SYS_IMPORT_TRANSPORTABLE_01":  system/******** directory=impt
ts dumpfile=tts.dmp transport_datafiles=(/u01/oradata/ORCL/users01_ORCL.dbf) rem
ap_schema=SCOTT:SCOTT2
Processing object type TRANSPORTABLE_EXPORT/PLUGTS_BLK
Processing object type TRANSPORTABLE_EXPORT/TABLE
Processing object type TRANSPORTABLE_EXPORT/INDEX
Processing object type TRANSPORTABLE_EXPORT/CONSTRAINT/CONSTRAINT
Processing object type TRANSPORTABLE_EXPORT/INDEX_STATISTICS
Processing object type TRANSPORTABLE_EXPORT/CONSTRAINT/REF_CONSTRAINT
Processing object type TRANSPORTABLE_EXPORT/TABLE_STATISTICS
Processing object type TRANSPORTABLE_EXPORT/POST_INSTANCE/PLUGTS_BLK
Job "SYSTEM"."SYS_IMPORT_TRANSPORTABLE_01" successfully completed at 07:32:40
```

Finally, I verified that the tablespace USERS (transported in), and the renamed USERS1 tablespace existed and the datafiles were accessible.

```
oracle@nodename:/u01/app/oracle[NEW]

SYS@ORCL> select file_name, tablespace_name, status from dba_data_files;

/u01/oradata/NEW/system01_NEW.dbf
SYSTEM                          AVAILABLE

/u01/oradata/NEW/undotbs01_NEW.dbf
SYSAUX                          AVAILABLE

/u01/oradata/NEW/sysaux01_NEW.dbf
UNDOTBS1                        AVAILABLE

/u01/oradata/NEW/users01_NEW.dbf
USERS1                          AVAILABLE

/u01/oradata/ORCL/users01_ORCL.dbf
USERS                           AVAILABLE

5 rows selected.
```

Think of this sharing tablespaces as a poor-man's version of the logical standby database or Active Data Guard, which are both methods of offloading read-only queries to standby databases. This shared database environment would be a little more difficult to handle technically and with very little documentation, but may be worth some investigation to see if it works for you. Reasons to use this offbeat method may include both the ability to utilize the often-underused CPU power of a single server while at the same time minimizing Oracle licensing costs required for running Oracle Databases on multiple servers.

Cross-platform migrations with a transportable database

The TTS section above is one example of using RMAN for converting datafiles when migrating across different endian platforms by the `convert datafile` command. This section deals with converting the entire database from one platform to another (cross-platform migrations). There are two major types of cross-platform migrations using what is called Transportable Database with RMAN—source host conversion and target host conversion.

For the transportable database (RMAN CONVERT DATABASE command), the documentation will tell you to convert all datafiles. Actually this type of migration is only required for datafiles that contain undo data. This includes all SYSTEM tablespace datafiles, any datafiles that contain ROLLBACK segments, and of course all data files that are part of any UNDO tablespaces. Eliminating the application data from this conversion process would reduce the amount of downtime considerably.

Starting with 10gR2, skipping the conversion process on application data is only possible with the target platform conversion, not the source type. Target platform conversion happens on the server you are migrating to, not the one you are migrating from. This would be using the RMAN CONVERT DATABASE ON TARGET PLATFORM command.

Usually during a target platform conversion, datafiles are copied to a temporary staging directory. Then a convert script is run, which places the datafiles in their final location. In this modified procedure, only the data files that contain undo data are copied to the staging area. The application data files that are not run through the conversion process will need to be copied (by SCP or FTP) or made accessible on the target server by NFS or SAN storage devices.

The following are some general steps:

- Identify data files that contain undo data on the source database:

```
SYS@SOURCE>select distinct(file_name)
from dba_data_files a, dba_rollback_segs b
where a.tablespace_name=b.tablespace_name;
```

Use the transportable database procedure as documented in the Oracle Database Backup and Recovery User's Guide:

- Start up nomount target database
- Run the modified convert script after removing the application datafiles and fixing any path changes
- Run the transport script that creates the target controlfile, open the target database, and recompile all PL/SQL

Please refer to the documentation for complete details. The MOS note mentioned in the box below has a case study for cross-platform migration. Be aware that this note doesn't contain the instructions for skipping application datafiles for reducing conversion downtime.

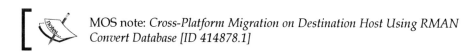

[MOS note: *Cross-Platform Migration on Destination Host Using RMAN Convert Database [ID 414878.1]*]

Physical and/or snapshot standbys

Starting with10gR2, standbys are a very dependable solution from Oracle for accomplishing upgrades. There is a downside to using a physical or snapshot standby: what happens to all of the redo data (transactions) occurring in the production database? That redo stream will no longer work across different versions of Oracle. Once the standby is upgraded, no more transactions can be applied from the primary database. So that means if you use a physical standby for your migration, then the primary would need to be made unavailable or read-only during the upgrade. Once the upgrade on the physical standby is finished, then you would fail over the clients.

The hardest part of this process is moving the clients; it's completely different at individual organizations, depending on all of the applications and third-party products involved. Downtime can be kept to a minimum by scripting or automating the failover steps as much as possible.

Why would you use this method? Well, if there was a problem with the upgrade due to some untested or unforeseen problem, there is the possibility of failing the clients back to the earlier version of Oracle. Any transactions that occurred while on the new version would have to be accounted for and migrated separately. And because you migrated the client components of Oracle 11g before the database (as outlined in this chapter), then you have a certain comfort level knowing they will work for all versions involved in this migration. Now you can see some of the reasoning for doing a step-ordered approach—it gives you a back out plan.

Failing back to original version

There are several save points in this entire process at which you could revert to the previous version if there is an unrecoverable failure:

- **Backups**: This would be to restore the older ORACLE_HOME. But since you are following the advice in this book, older ORACLE_HOME still exists on your server. This would simply mean that at the appropriate time in the Downgrade or Flashback procedures, you would switch back to the older ORACLE_HOME.

- **Flashback database**: Using Flashback + Guaranteed Restore Point on the logical standby to revert to the earlier version of Oracle is the fastest method, albeit also taking a lot of resources (flashback log storage) at the disk level.

- **Downgrade procedure**: If you didn't use Flashback, then you would have to downgrade the database to get it back to the original version you started with. If you have also let normal production use occur creating transactions during the upgrade window, then the downgrade procedure is the only option for you.

If you plan on using a physical standby, then you would leave the original version of Oracle untouched, shut down the database, or keep it idly waiting and removed from the Data Guard configuration. You would wait to upgrade the old primary to the newer version and restart the redo stream once it has been determined that the newer version is stable for production use. The next section deals with using standbys for upgrades without stopping the redo stream during the migration.

Transient logical standby: Rolling upgrades with minimal downtime

Oracle promises the least amount of application downtime of any database upgrade or migration method—it's reported to reduce to a bare minimum of two minutes required for the switchover from the logical back to the primary. This is a process that promises the world, but it requires something in return—extensive testing and practice, two databases (different servers), and a gutsy DBA.

Transient is the operative word for this procedure—the logical standby can't already exist; it must be a new logical standby created just for this upgrade. The commands are done without Data Guard. In fact, you will need to remove all Data Guard configurations.

There are a couple of differences in the process depending on the Oracle version you are starting with and the ending version. The basic difference is that the 10g to 11g Migration is easier to accomplish with less commands, which is similar in the functionality changes for Data Guard from 10gR2 to 11g. This section will concentrate on the rolling upgrade example from 10gR2 to 11g, as that would help more DBAs who are not on 11g in production yet. Executing a rolling upgrade from 10.2.x to another higher 10.2 version would also be done using the same steps. There is a difference in the white paper that you would follow, in this case *Database Rolling Upgrade Using Transient Logical Standby-Oracle Database 10g Release 2* from the MAA website. The basic conversion steps are as follows:

- Convert an existing physical standby to a logical standby
- Perform a rolling upgrade of the logical standby from a lower version to a higher one
- Revert the logical back into the physical
- Switch over the clients to the new primary

What seems to be a simple process actually details many different subtasks that take advantage of all of the features of an MAA environment for disaster recovery to accomplish the least amount of downtime for upgrading a database. This graphic assumes these databases are on different servers that may or may not be the case in your setup. The databases are color-coded according to the role they play at any particular point in the process.

I recommend running this conversion using two different servers for performance reasons, as the conversion process on a logical standby needs all of the horsepower that is ordinarily reserved for standard production use. Having your production database and the in-process logical standby on the same server would be competing for the same CPU, memory, and I/O, causing contention.

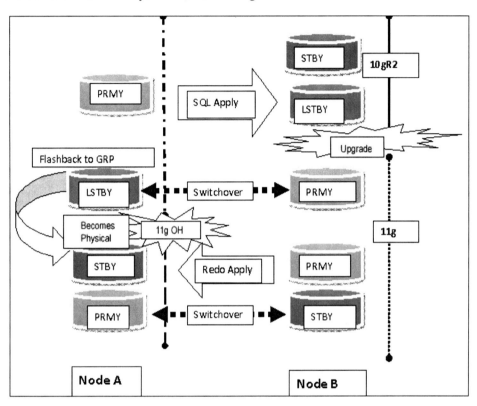

There are quite a few preliminary steps required to pull this off and you have already surmised additional resources. There are several limiting factors that will help you decide if this approach will work in your situation. As you learned from the chapter on MAA, the logical standby doesn't support all data types. The following queries will help you determine which database objects (DDL and DML) are supported or not supported.

This first one determines which schema (object owner) is skipped and the second ascertains which individual objects are unsupported:

```
SYS@ORCL>SELECT OWNER FROM DBA_LOGSTDBY_SKIP WHERE STATEMENT_OPT =
'INTERNAL SCHEMA';
SYS@ORCL>SELECT DISTINCT OWNER, TABLE_NAME FROM DBA_LOGSTDBY_
UNSUPPORTED;
```

Why would particular objects or schemas be skipped? Remember the upgrade's primary purpose is to change the data dictionary and these internal schemas are part of that dictionary. If these weren't skipped, any changes on the primary side would overwrite the version being upgraded on the transient logical side. Unsupported objects are just a version-specific feature—each new Oracle Database version that is released has provided additional datatypes that are supported. How might you work around the issue of unsupported data types?

- Temporarily suspend any DDL or DML changes to the unsupported tables for the upgrade window.

- Perform the upgrade at a time when users will not be making changes to the unsupported tables. You could limit access to the database by only allowing SYS or SYSTEM to connect. The first command is done before starting the upgrade, the second after the upgrade is finished:

  ```
  SYS@ORCL>alter system quiesce restricted;
  SYS@ORCL>alter system unquiesce;
  ```

- Capture unsupported transactions by executing the following on the primary database before starting the upgrade:

  ```
  EXEC DBMS_LOGSTDBY.APPLY_SET('MAX_EVENTS_RECORDED',DBMS_LOGSTDBY.
  MAX_EVENTS);
  EXEC DBMS_LOGSTDBY.APPLY_SET('RECORD_UNSUPPORTED_
  OPERATIONS','TRUE');
  ```

Once the upgrade is over there are several different ways to make sure the unsupported transactions are applied. See the MAA documentation for how to use the DBMS_LOGSTDBY.INSTANTIATE_TABLE procedure to bring the entire table from the primary to the logical standby. This step would need to be done after the upgrade, but before you switch the logical standby back into a physical standby database. See the image provided in this section. There is also the standard method of moving data besides the dbms_logstdby procedure—across a database link, export/import, and/or data pump.

Export/import or data pump migration

This is a good exercise for any DBA, but a tedious method of migrating a database from one version to another. Usually, it's the last resort with a difficult or unusual migration path such as different operating systems with incompatible and unconvertible endian(s) types or a characterset conversion. The larger the database, the longer the amount of time it takes to complete, and it requires the database to be down (or provide the end users with a read-only copy) during the conversion process.

Now who should have the `exp_full_database` privilege, which is required for performing exports and import tasks? The system user has the DBA role by default, which contains the export privilege among other advanced privileges. Most DBAs use the system account for executing dump tasks, but you may want to create a dedicated user account for these types of tasks. This change most often comes from a security requirement to lock down the standard accounts like system. Don't get caught in the trap of using the DBA's personal username and password to schedule tasks at any point in time; this is not a good practice.

Choosing which Oracle Database user account to run dump file tasks was mentioned due to the lesser-known fact that you will not get a consistent dump file of the database when executing the task as SYS as SYSDBA. Exceptions to this rule include the following situations:

- Exporting a transportable tablespace set with export (Oracle9i and Oracle8i)
- Importing a transportable tablespace set with import utility (Oracle10g, Oracle9i, and Oracle8i)

The `SYS` user cannot do a transaction level consistent read (read-only transaction). Any queries by `SYS` will show all changes made during the transaction even if `SYS` has set the transaction to be `READ ONLY`. This inconsistency is the technical, detailed reason why you shouldn't use the `SYS` account to create dump files. Well you could, but they wouldn't be consistent.

You cannot use data pump on any files created by the export or import process or vice versa because they are incompatible. The export utility is deprecated, but import will be kept around so that older versions of Oracle Database can be imported into a newer version. You should be using data pump for much more than just a logical (DDL) backup utility, it provides advanced functionality not available in the older utilities.

Be aware that there will be redo created during a data pump job due to the creation of the job table that gives you the ability to monitor, change priority, resume a stopped job, and so on. The resulting data pump file will be larger than the older export file for the same database and versions of the utilities involved. See the following listing for a comparison:

```
-rw-r-----  1 oracle oinstall 30156615680 Feb 10 09:53 export.dmp   --EXPORT
-rw-r--r--  1 oracle oinstall 35358236672 Feb 10 11:04 expdp.dmp    --DATAPUMP
```

The compatibility level of the data pump dump file set is determined by the compatibility level of the source database and that information is stored in the header of the dump file. Use the Export Data Pump parameter version in case the target database has a lower compatibility level than the source database, for example, version=10.2.

If you need more information about a particular dump (either export or data pump) file, there is more than one way to get the information from the header part. One way is to run the `impdp` command with a non-existent table name with tracing (100300) enabled, as shown below:

```
> impdp system DIRECTORY=DATA_PUMP_DIR dumpfile=exp.dmp nologfile=y sqlfile=imp.
sql tables=notexist trace=100300

Import: Release 11.1.0.6.0 - Production on Wednesday, 10 February, 2010 11:21:10

Copyright (c) 2003, 2007, Oracle.  All rights reserved.
Password:

Connected to: Oracle Database 11g Enterprise Edition Release 11.1.0.6.0 - Produc
tion

ORA-39002: invalid operation
ORA-39166: Object NOTEXIST was not found.
```

It does return an error, but the resulting trace file with all of the same information will be located in 11g in diagnostic destination `../rdbms/trace` directory. In earlier versions of Oracle Database that trace file would show up in the `BACKGROUND_DUMP_DEST`.

It requires creating a procedure (supplied by Oracle) that makes a user-friendly output instead of using the `DBMS_DATAPUMP` and `GET_DUMPFILE_INFO` directly. See `create_showdump.sql` for the code supplied for this chapter to create the package `show_dumpfile_info`. The following output was executed on an 11.1.0.6 32-bit Oracle Database to view the header of a 64-bit 10.2.0.4 Oracle data pump file. Note how the compatibility setting of the database is included, highlighted by an arrow below:

```
ORCL11> SET serveroutput on SIZE 1000000
ORCL11>  exec show_dumpfile_info('DATA_PUMP_DIR','exp.dmp');
------------------------------------------------------------------
Purpose..: Obtain details about export dumpfile.        Version: 19-MAR-2008
Required.: RDBMS version: 10.2.0.1.0 or higher <===10.2.0.1.0 due to database co
mpatible is =10.2.0.1.0

.            Export dumpfile version: 7.3.4.0.0 or higher
.            Export Data Pump dumpfile version: 10.1.0.1.0 or higher
Usage....: execute show_dumfile_info('DIRECTORY', 'DUMPFILE');
Example..: exec show_dumfile_info('MY_DIR', 'expdp_s.dmp')
------------------------------------------------------------------
Filename.: exp.dmp
Directory: DATA_PUMP_DIR
Disk Path: /backup/exportdp/UPPRD
Filetype.: 1 (Export Data Pump dumpfile)
------------------------------------------------------------------
...File Version....: 1.1 (Oracle10g Release 2: 10.2.0.x)
...Master Present..: 1 (Yes)
...GUID............: 7F41E2B14F0D12F3E040FA860E051435
...File Number.....: 1
...Characterset ID.: 873 (AL32UTF8)
...Creation Date...: Wed Feb 10 09:08:10 2010
...Flags...........: 2
...Job Name........: "SYSTEM"."SYS_EXPORT_FULL_02"
...Platform........: x86_64/Linux 2.4.xx
...Language........: AL32UTF8
...Block size......: 4096
...Metadata Compres: 1 (Yes)
...Data Compressed.: 0 (No)
...Metadata Encrypt: 0 (No)
...Data Encrypted..: 0 (No)
...Job Version.....: 10.02.00.04.00
...Max Items Code..: 20
```

Compatibility settings decide which features are available and which objects can be imported without error between versions, and is considered the dump file version. In the case above, version 10.1.0.1.0 is highlighted. This version 10.1 comes from the database initialization parameter known as compatible.

Here is the output from the same database for the older type export dump file. Sorry it may be confusing, but I simply put an export file in the same directory as the earlier data pump example. That was due to the show_dumpfile_info requiring a directory name. I know it is the older export type because the Filetype line in the example below refers to it as Original. This is not as much information as the header from data pump, but this informs me that an environmental variable is not what I expected. It should show a character set of AL32UTF8 and not the one listed below (WE8MSWIN1252):

```
ORCL11> SET serveroutput on SIZE 1000000
ORCL11> exec show_dumpfile_info(p_dir=> 'DATA_PUMP_DIR', p_file=> 'exp.dmp');
------------------------------------------------------------------------
Purpose..: Obtain details about export dumpfile.           Version: 19-MAR-2008
Required.: RDBMS version: 10.2.0.1.0 or higher
.          Export dumpfile version: 7.3.4.0.0 or higher
.          Export Data Pump dumpfile version: 10.1.0.1.0 or higher
Usage....: execute show_dumfile_info('DIRECTORY', 'DUMPFILE');
Example..: exec show_dumpfile_info('MY_DIR', 'expdp_s.dmp')
------------------------------------------------------------------------

------------------------------------------------------------------------
Filename.: exp.dmp
Directory: DATA_PUMP_DIR
Disk Path: /backup/exportdp/UPPRD
Filetype.: 2 (Original Export dumpfile)
------------------------------------------------------------------------
...Characterset ID.: 178 (WE8MSWIN1252)
...Direct Path.....: 1 (Direct Path)
...Export Version..: EXPORT:V10.02.01
------------------------------------------------------------------------
```

It is possible to extract all of the DDL statements from a data pump file with a matching and higher level data pump client version. While it is also possible to use a single maintenance release lower-level data pump client, it is not recommended. The following example will extract all of the DDL statements, but the resulting file (impdp11g.sql in this case) is not usable exactly as is. That's usable in the sense that you could run the SQL statements in the file, successfully creating the database objects.

```
oracle@nodename:/u01/app/oracle/product/11gR2[ORCL11]
   >impdp system/manager DIRECTORY=DATA_PUMP_DIR DUMPFILE=expdp10.dmp \
NOLOGFILE=y SQLFILE=impdp11g.sql FULL=y
```

You will need to edit the file directly (back up the original first) and replace the lines with ALTER SESSION SET CURRENT_SCHEMA ... and any lines with -- CONNECT ... with a correct CONNECT statement. Also place two dash characters (which comments out the line) in front of the anonymous PL/SQL blocks that may appear within the logfile for any database options that are installed.

Data pump can be executed over a database link with two different release levels between the source and the target database with a single major release difference being supported. Network transfers with data pump can be used to facilitate the migration of data to new hardware or remote sites. This may be used more for convenience rather than performance because the speed of the network between sites is usually slower.

Most often database objects are migrated separately using data pump or export/import to speed up the process for larger databases. These objects are usually imported into the new database in this order:

- Creating datafiles and/or tablespaces.
- Importing DDL (this includes user accounts but not indexes or constraints).
- Importing actual data, recreating indexes, recreating and enabling constraints.

The process usually starts with extracting the DDL statements as shown earlier in this section. Don't edit the resulting file from the single full SQL extract file. Extract each set of DDL separately in different runs—tables, indexes, constraints, data, among others.

If you need to change the physical location or storage parameters of certain objects, see the following data pump parameters. Be aware that if you have REUSE_DATAFILES as Y, then there is the possibility of overwriting a data file inadvertently.

- TRANSFORM: Metadata transform to apply to applicable objects
- REMAP_DATAFILE: Redefine datafile references in all DDL statements
- REMAP_TABLESPACE: Tablespace objects are remapped to another tablespace
- REUSE_DATAFILES: Tablespace will be initialized if it already exists (default is N)

When upgrading a database with this method, it is normal to have quite a few errors on the actual import process, as well as objects that won't compile afterwards. There is no one list on what errors you will encounter, as they are often specific to your application deployment methods, migration path, versions involved, and so on. The following are some of the few error types with a recommended fix or preventive tip:

- Missing grants from the SYS user: There are grants from SYS that will not be imported as they might overwrite or be invalid for the newer version of Oracle.

  Fix: Grant execute on DBMS packages to the appropriate application owner as well as the appropriate users.

- Import errors related to Plan tables like DBMS_XPLAN.

  Fix: Drop and recreate the newer version of Explain Plan. See the next chapter on Tuning for more information. An upgrade would also affect the STATSPACK schema — most often the user named PERFSTAT (see *Chapter 8* on the newer Automatic Workload Respository, which requires an additional Management Pack license).

There will be specific grants and privileges missing if the SYS or SYSTEM accounts were used instead of the application owner (schema) for their database object. Make it a practice to use the schema owners for grants to their objects and not the SYS or SYSTEM accounts. See the script from the code section for this chapter — grants_ from_sys.sql. This script is meant to be run on the source database before the export process to capture any grants that might be needed. It is an all-inclusive script, which will need to be edited to eliminate database object types that you aren't interested in preserving.

 If you are stuck with export/import as your only migration path, check out the following free GNU-licensed software that can parallelize the process (much faster migration) using Unix named pipes.

http://pepi.sourceforge.net/

Character set selection—UTF8

Whenever it is time to migrate to a newer version of Oracle, it is also time to rethink the character set selection. As more and more businesses declare an international presence on the Internet, the storage of multiple languages is becoming even more important. Many DBAs simply use the default character set for the particular Oracle Database version they are installing. It's better not to follow what everyone else does blindly!

Unicode (UTF8) is a universal character-encoding scheme that allows the storage information from any major language using a single character set. Unicode is a definition that controls the code points, properties, standard scripting behaviors, and algorithms for use with other coding software standards.

Do you occasionally see upside-down question marks or other tics or offhand characters on printed material or data displayed within an application? That can come from different sources, but they most often point to problems with the storage of extended characters (not 7-bit ASCII) within the database, or conversion issues that have happened somewhere between the application (browser, software, SQl*Plus, and so on) and the database.

If at all possible, migrate to a superset of your current character set that will add several extended characters that your application can choose to store data with. Migrating to a superset will most often causes little to no issues, but it does add downtime to the database to ensure consistency and integrity during the conversion process, if you are looking to choose a character set in the following list. Oracle recommends choosing the superset that comes after that character set in this list, with a longer term recommendation to move to UTF8:

- US7ASCII: Better to migrate to WE8MSWIN1252 or WE8ISO8859P15
- WE8ISO8859P1: WE8MSWIN1252 is a superset
- UTF8: Better to migrate to AL32UTF8
- ZHS16CGB231280: ZHS16GBK is a superset
- ZHS32GB18030: Better to migrate to AL32UTF8
- KO16KSC5601: KO16MSWIN949 is a superset
- ZHT16BIG5: ZHT16MSWIN950 solves various problems of ZHT16BIG5

This is how to check what current character set your database has:

```
SYS@ORCL>  select nls_characterset from nls_database_parameters;
```

Converting a database from one character set to another can be a daunting process, so it is time to become familiar with NLS basics, Oracle's character scan utility called CSSCAN, and the CSALTER procedure. What's just as important is determining what character conversion is happening between the client application and the database.

 For extensive information on this huge topic, more than you wanted to know about character sets, see *AL32UTF8 / UTF8 (Unicode) Database Character Set Implications [ID 788156.1]*.

To gain familiarity with migrating issues as well as the day-to-day functionality of a Unicode database, it might be worth your while to migrate some of the accessory databases to an AL32UTF8 character set. Both Grid Control and RMAN catalog repositories can be AL32UTF8, and they have no issues working as designed with other databases of different character sets.

Post-11g upgrade tasks

There is the standard post-upgrade task list as part of the version-specific Oracle Database Upgrade Guide documentation. The difference between the documentation and the step-ordered approach is that some of these steps can be done in advance. See the following partial list from the Upgrade Guide along with comments:

- Update environment variables (Linux and Unix systems only) — from *Chapter 2, Maintaining Oracle Standards*, only need to edit a configuration file instead of a multitude of scripts.

- Upgrade the recovery catalog — already done earlier according to step-ordered approach.

- Upgrade **Automatic Storage Management (ASM)** — step-ordered approach is to upgrade ASM instance (different home) before any databases, keeping it at the same compatible level. After all databases serviced by this ASM are migrated to 11g, then advance the ASM compatible parameter to 11g to enable the new features.

- Add new features as appropriate — wait at least a week before changing any database parameters; add changes gradually.

- Set threshold values for tablespace alerts in the OEM console — important as these start out as a null value.

- Configure Oracle Data Guard broker — a major change that affects all redo traffic; broker property `InitialConnectIdentifier` is being changed to `DGConnectIdentifier`.

- Don't forget to apply any post-upgrade one-off patches, patchsets, CPUs, or PSUs changes to the database. These patches may or may not have multiple parts that require installation — software updates, manual operating system changes, and database changes in the form of a SQL script to run. Following the step-ordered approach the software updates would have already been installed in an `ORACLE_HOME`. The database changes have to be done to all databases that were upgraded, no matter the method used.

- Cost-based optimizer upgrade and statistics — see the next chapter.

There is an Oracle-supplied script to show up some issues related to upgrades that aren't covered in any of the upgrade documentation supplied by Oracle — duplicate objects owned between SYS and SYSTEM accounts, JVM installation verification, and various errors that may occur depending on your migration path.

Migration path refers to the starting version for a particular database and all data dictionary versions applied since. It will show which option was installed at a particular version as well. This may not seem important right now, but there have been bugs associated with the migration path which may present a technical obstacle for certain types of database upgrades.

I would recommend running this script on a test copy of the database before you upgrade, and then search MOS for any bugs related to the migration path indicated. See *Script to Collect DB Upgrade/Migrate Diagnostic Information* (dbupgdiag.sql) *[ID 556610.1]*. There is output from a run labeled db_upg_diag_ORCL.log in the code section for this chapter.

One of the biggest changes in 11g is the default profile and hardened security features. Passwords are now case sensitive by default; that is something to plan for:

- Migrating current end user passwords—as they expire, the new ones will be case sensitive.

- Expiring current passwords to change to new case sensitive format when they log on to 11g for the first time.

- Changing everyone's password will need a mechanism to inform end users of the newly reset passwords. Its different than pre-expiring.

The SYSTEM password expires with the default profile, which may be a problem if this account is used for any scripting or scheduled database maintenance tasks.

Password failure can occur between the primary and physical standbys as well as streams because of the new security features in 11gR1. The fix for the resulting ORA-16191 error is to set the case sensitivity database parameter SEC_CASE_SENSITIVE_LOGON=FALSE. It also requires you to recreate the password file on all servers with ignorecase=Y to orapwd utility. Also, remember that if you recreate the password file, you will have to recycle (restart) each database involved to reread the newly created password.

Summary

For using 11g on a daily basis for accessory databases such as Grid Control and RMAN, listeners for databases and clients will require regular exposure to the new version. This should increase your skill level and confidence in the new release while reducing the possibility of disruptions.

As a new DBA, it is important to realize that the binary upgrade and the database upgrade are two different events that most often executed at different times. Taking apart a large project and cutting it up into more manageable components brings stability to what can be an overwhelming process to someone new to Oracle.

Hopefully, this chapter opened up the possibility of a creative migration path that you hadn't considered before. Oracle expands the features of each version while still including compatible components to earlier as well as later versions, providing you with multiple paths for upgrades.

It is interesting that the final point for our migration path in this chapter is about migrating or upgrading the optimizer. We will cover that in the next chapter.

8
11g Tuning Tools

Here we are, at the last chapter of this book. It is intended to be the culmination of all the knowledge from the previous chapters. What this chapter provides is details on how to start tuning as a DBA—what is most important to know, how to find that information, and what tools are provided in 11g for preventing and resolving performance issues. The new SQL Plan Management features are covered, along with a recommended migration path for upgrading the query optimizer while keeping performance disruptions to a minimum.

There are two components to tuning: proactive and reactive. Proactive tuning includes an assessment of the current conditions—end user response time, server resources, automatic or manual tuning jobs, and startup initialization parameters. Reactive tuning includes continued assessment after adjusting resources, whether they are server, network, or database-based. Expect this chapter to just be a quick introduction to tuning, as entire books are dedicated to just this one topic.

The topics covered in this chapter include the following:

- Hardware load testing and forecasting
- Proactive monitoring tools
- Reactive diagnostic and tracing utilities
- Automatic Database Diagnostic Monitor
- Automatic Workload Repository
- Active Session History
- SQL Advisors
- Adaptive Cursor Sharing and Bind Peeking
- Statistics Gathering
- SQL Plan Management
- Upgrading the Optimizer in 11g

Unless your database is tiny (something close to the default install size of 4 GB), it is easy to state that all databases will benefit from tuning. And that chore of tuning the database will never go away. Why? Because:

- Data changes over time (more rapidly in an OLTP environment)—such as inserts, updates, deletes. Changing data affects the way the data is stored in a block, extent allocation, index leaf splits, and so on.

- Applications will change with client upgrades, new or revised queries, business needs, or even the adoption of new technology.

- Oracle upgrades change the data dictionary—new features, statistics gathering, Optimizer changes, Oracle kernel changes.

First in the order of business is identifying what needs to be tuned. Then you can use different methods of tuning to speed things up—whether it is system-wide or a single, specific query. It is imperative that you go over any concepts that you don't understand as you read through this chapter. I recommend starting with the *Oracle Database 2 Day + Performance Tuning Guide* of the Oracle documentation for the version you are interested in. Move on to the *Oracle Database Performance Tuning Guide* as part of the Oracle documentation when you are well-versed in the basic terminology of tuning.

Hardware load testing and forecasting

There are several open source (free) utilities that help in predicting when the current operating system and database resources will eventually run out—known as forecasting. It is a worthwhile exercise whether you are testing new hardware, determining the amount of time left on the existing servers, or trying to test different I/O configurations. You will need to find a tool that provides different load simulators for different database types—OLTP, a web-based application, or a data warehouse. These tools are designed to put extreme loads on a system; be sure to test during off-times or on non-production systems.

I recommend using all of the free resources found on `http://www.orapub.com`. While it is a commercial company, they have a good reputation in the Oracle community. On their website, look for the link called **Tools / Products**. Using several of their free tools, I was able to determine that the new commodity hardware selected to replace an older proprietary server was suitable for our workload. Refer to Chapter 4 of this book for more details. See the following screenshots for a graphic representation of the testing results; the first screenshot is the older server we were trying to replace and the second is the newer commodity hardware.

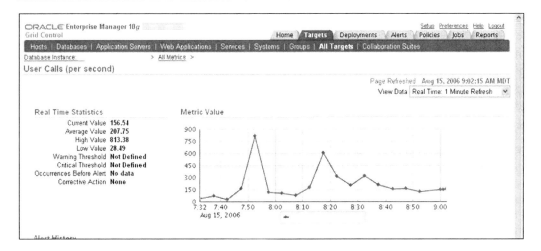

The basic numbers in the graphs came from measurements inside the database (v$sysstat view) while running a huge web load simulation test. I surmised that the second server using commodity hardware would perform as well or better than the older server. The values indicate a user calls/second rate. Now that the commodity hardware is in production, I can say that the prediction was correct.

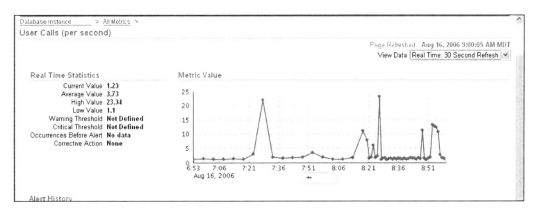

I recommend running several tests and comparing the output by type—OLTP, data warehouse, and application-specific. Only using a single test or benchmark won't give enough evidence. For example, a popular test is to create a table and insert a million rows; this one test is not adequate to simulate all the different workloads for a typical database application.

Using standard benchmarks (like creating a million row table) is important when talking about testing scenarios. There should be an assortment of different benchmarks when testing. One benchmark should be a simple query. This is a non-complex SQL query (that is, no partitioning, not a parallel query), which takes approximately 1 minute to complete when running properly. As part of the testing, compare the execution plan of the benchmark query for all runs.

There should be a representative benchmark for each of the varied tasks that a typical end user performs against the Oracle database being tested. Benchmarks allow you to compare the actual performance of one system or database against another. The benchmarks need to be easily reproducible, testable, and provide measureable results. One of the best tests for our OLTP application is a particular C program that generates large numbers of archivelogs.

Using a hardware testing suite that uses database statistics will also help test database-specific configurations. I ran the same set of tests for each startup initialization parameter change in a testing environment, until our heavy archivelog generator ran as quick as production. Database workload testing is particularly important when migrating to a new Oracle version.

The following screenshot is the graph output from the Oracle Enterprise Manager (OEM) console during the testing run from the earlier test between the two servers. Notice the extremely high amounts of Disk I/O being executed: its a combination of disk read and write operations. While the graph below seems to indicate high Instance I/O the entire time, it is due to the narrowness of the display area in the graph.

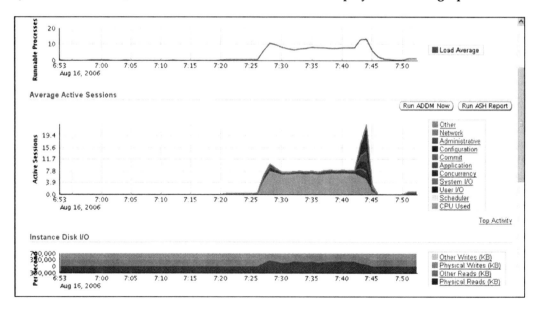

Orion—Oracle I/O numbers calibration tool

This is a tool most often used when there are large changes planned—new hardware, the filesystem configuration, or migrating to ASM. Check out the *Oracle Database Performance Tuning Guide* for the **Top ten mistakes found in Oracle Systems** list—I/O setup is on the list. Proper I/O configuration makes these types of tests critical for proactively or reactively tuning a database. The key features for Orion include the following:

- There is no need to create and run an Oracle database
- It uses the Oracle database's I/O libraries
- It simulates several different workload scenarios—OLTP and data warehouse

A simple test can be set up and executed quickly. I recommend creating a specific directory for all testing. Organize before you get started on what tests you want to perform with a directory for each—Small Random I/O, Large Sequential I/O, Large Random I/O, and Mixed Workload. The Orion tool is now included in the following location as part of the database installation on Linux, as shown in the following screenshot:

```
oracle@nodename:/u01/app/oracle/bk[NEW11]
> which orion
/u01/app/oracle/product/11.2.0.2/dbhome_1/bin/orion
```

The following example is for Linux:

 Orion doesn't require the use of the dd command for creating files, there is an example in the user's guide that uses dd to double check that a file is accessible. The one in the user's guide is a different version of the command. The command listed below is a quick way of creating a formatted file of a specific size on UNIX; you can also use actual database files to test with. You might want to test with data file sizes that are comparable to your production database.

1. Create a file that is a multiple of DB_BLOCK_SIZE with dd (a standard Unix command). There are two examples below; look for the difference in file size with both being a multiple of 8k:

   ```
   dd if=/dev/zero of=/u01/oradata/TEST_ORION.dbf bs=8k count=1024
   dd if=/dev/zero of=/u01/oradata/TEST_ORION02.dbf bs=8k
   count=531072
   ```

   ```
   oracle@nodename:/u01/oradata[NEW11]
   > dd if=/dev/zero of=/u01/oradata/TEST_ORION.dbf bs=8k count=1024
   1024+0 records in
   1024+0 records out
   8388608 bytes (8.4 MB) copied, 0.022851 seconds, 367 MB/s
   oracle@nodename:/u01/oradata[NEW11]
   > dd if=/dev/zero of=/u01/oradata/TEST_ORION02.dbf bs=8k count=531072
   531072+0 records in
   531072+0 records out
   4350541824 bytes (4.4 GB) copied, 21.8787 seconds, 199 MB/s
   oracle@nodename:/u01/oradata[NEW11]
   > ls -altr
   total 4260964
   drwxr-xr-x 6 root    root        4096 Oct 20 08:48 ..
   -rw-r--r-- 1 oracle dba        8388608 Mar 22 06:45 TEST_ORION.dbf
   drwxr-xr-x 4 oracle dba           4096 Mar 22 06:46 .
   -rw-r--r-- 1 oracle dba     4350541824 Mar 22 06:47 TEST_ORION02.dbf
   ```

2. Create a file with the full path of the file you want to test with. Most often you would use multiple files for testing I/O. In this simple example, we are using two files. Below, I have shown using the editor vi to create the file TEST_SmIO.lun with the required entries for this test:

   ```
   oracle@nodename:/u01/app/oracle/test[]
   >vi TEST_SmIO.lun
   ```

   ```
   /u01/oradata/TEST_ORION.dbf
   /u01/oradata/TEST_ORION2.dbf
   ```

3. Run orion with the file that you just created as part of the input—num_disks is the number of spindles; check with your system administrator on how the spindles are mapped to actual volumes.

   ```
   orion -run simple -testname TEST_smIO -num_disks 1
   ```

4. Check the output in the same directory that the executable was run; here is a listing of the files produced for this particular test run:

```
-rw-r--r--  1 oracle dba    62 Mar 22 07:12 TEST_smIO.lun
-rw-r--r--  1 oracle dba   353 Mar 22 07:13 TEST_SmIO_20100322_0713_summary.txt
-rw-r--r--  1 oracle dba   177 Mar 22 07:13 TEST_smIO_20100322_0713_trace.txt
-rw-r--r--  1 oracle dba   353 Mar 22 07:13 TEST_smIO_20100322_0713_summary.txt
-rw-r--r--  1 oracle dba     0 Mar 22 07:13 TEST_smIO_20100322_0713_mbps.csv
-rw-r--r--  1 oracle dba     0 Mar 22 07:13 TEST_smIO_20100322_0713_lat.csv
-rw-r--r--  1 oracle dba     0 Mar 22 07:13 TEST_smIO_20100322_0713_iops.csv
drwxr-xr-x  3 oracle dba  4096 Mar 22 07:34 .
```

5. The following screenshot is part of the file `*summary.txt` that was located in the directory above. Notice how all of the matching output files have a matching date timestamp. There are `csv` files produced so that you can view the results with the spreadsheet software. If you receive zero for the columns as shown in the screenshot, check the OS library configuration.

```
ORION VERSION 10.2.0.1.0
Commandline:
-run simple -testname TEST_SmIO -num_disks 1
This maps to this test:
Test: TEST_SmIO
Small IO size: 8 KB
Large IO size: 1024 KB
IO Types: Small Random IOs, Large Random IOs
Simulated Array Type: CONCAT
```

Here is the website for the User Guide and downloadable operation-specific executables. It is not required to install Oracle software and/or a database to use Orion: `http://www.oracle.com/technology/software/tech/orion/index.html`

Calibrate I/O

Oracle provides an I/O Calibration test, which requires a working Oracle Database using the `DBMS_RESOURCE_MANAGER.CALIBRATE_IO` procedure. This test is to narrow down a performance problem to determine whether it is the database or storage sub-system.

I recommend using this testing on your standby as suggested in Chapter 5. If you have a logical standby, that would also be excellent for testing, because the serialized SQL Apply process will perform differently depending on the I/O subsystem configuration.

Asynchronous I/O is required to be installed: it is native to Windows systems, so no additional work is necessary. Unix servers will need to be checked by the system administrator for the existence of specific libraries required for using ASYNCH I/O.

 The following documents are specific to Linux: *Enterprise Linux: Linux, Filesystem & I/O Type Supportability* [ID 279069.1] and *How To Check if Asynchronous I/O is Working On Linux* [ID 237299.1].

jMeter

This is another piece of free testing software that I have personally used. As with any of the free tools, there is a certain amount of work involved with installing, configuring, and interpreting the results. Once you have the GUI Interface running, most of your time will be spent designing the actual tests. There are a few test examples provided to help get you started, but they will be limited in scope.

What is nice about this tool is that you can remotely run tests using JAVA (OS independent) on multiple servers. Its primary focus is for testing web applications, but it can be used for other types. The software's main page can be found at `http://jakarta.apache.org/jmeter/`.

There is a specific section in the documentation that is meant to help design a Database Test Plan Module. Go to `http://jakarta.apache.org/jmeter/usermanual/build-db-test-plan.html`. I see this tool as being more suited to testing applications that run on databases but not the actual database or hardware subsystem.

Monitoring hidden or underlying problems

It may not always be the database that is the bottleneck or slowest component of all the collective pieces that exist between the client and the application. If testing shows the database to be operating within normal benchmark limits (properly tuned), then it is time to take a look at other most-encountered performance issues. Note that some of these are Oracle components, some of them are not. Get your system administrator involved early on whenever there is a system-wide slowness problem, such as:

- Slow or busy server
- Underlying network
- TNS Listener hanging (see MOS document in the box)
- Shared server (also known as Multi-threaded server)—related issues
- Properly functioning application
- Advanced networking option—encryption
- Transparent gateways
- Connection manager

 Refer to *TNSListener Hanging - Information to Get For Resolving or Troubleshooting [MOS Doc ID 230156.1]*.

Proactive monitoring

Here is where the proactive part of the DBA in regards to tuning begins. In the newest versions of Oracle, most of the background work is already done for you, including automatic statistics gathering and managing execution plans. The automatic tuning features should be used first to see if they work for your applications; most DBAs will adjust tuning based on what approximately 90% of the database performs best with. The other 10% (just an estimate) will consist of targeted problem queries or vendor-application SQL code that can't be changed to make it run more efficiently during execution.

Automatic Diagnostic Database Monitor (ADDM)

The ADDM report comes from the DBMS_ADVISOR package, whether generated by the OEM console as seen in the picture below, or by running the $ORACLE_HOME/rdbms/admin/addmrpt.sql script. There is an additional license cost to use the ADDM report, which will be discussed in the next section.

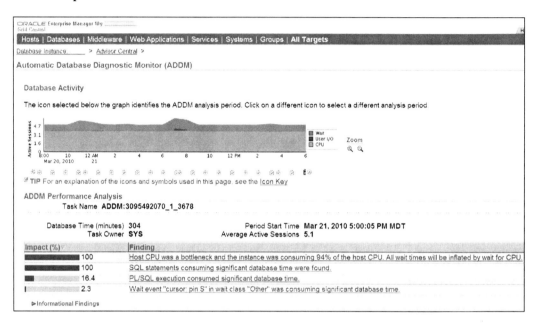

An ADDM report may produce a wrong recommendation as in this case. This report comes from a Logical Standby Database during the period of heavy activity on the production database. The fact that SQL APPLY serializes the application of the transactions, means it consumes large amounts of CPU. Adding hardware is not the answer in this situation, and neither is the use of a resource manager to throttle back the SQL APPLY process. This would only slow down the transactions that need to be applied on the standby. As the DBA, you will need to determine what recommendations are valid and applicable in a particular situation. In this example, I understand that SQL APPLY needs all of the CPU until the large transaction has been applied. The following screenshot is what the text version of the same report would look like:

```
          DETAILED ADDM REPORT FOR TASK 'ADDM:3095492070_1_3678' WITH ID 3725
          ----------------------------------------------------------------

                   Analysis Period: 21-MAR-2010 from 17:00:05 to 18:00:08
               Database ID/Instance: 3095492070/1
          Database/Instance Names:
                       Host Name:
                  Database Version:
                    Snapshot Range: from 3677 to 3678
                     Database Time: 18241 seconds
             Average Database Load: 5.1 active sessions


   ~~~~~~~~~~~~~~~~~~~~~~~~~~~~~~~~~~~~~~~~~~~~~~~~~~~~~~~~~~~~~~~~~~~~~~~~~~~~~~~~~~~~



   FINDING 1: 100% impact (18241 seconds)
   --------------------------------------
   Host CPU was a bottleneck and the instance was consuming 94% of the host CPU.
   All wait times will be inflated by wait for CPU.

      RECOMMENDATION 1: Host Configuration, 100% benefit (18241 seconds)
         ACTION: Consider adding more CPUs to the host or adding instances
            serving the database on other hosts.
         ACTION: Session CPU consumption was throttled by the Oracle Resource
            Manager. Consider revising the resource plan that was active during
            the analysis period.

      RECOMMENDATION 2: SQL Tuning, 75% benefit (13591 seconds)
         ACTION: Run SQL Tuning Advisor on the SQL statement with SQL_ID
            "7gxwhtkpmzzpg".
            RELEVANT OBJECT: SQL statement with SQL_ID 7gxwhtkpmzzpg and
            PLAN_HASH 754736028
```

Hourly snapshots are stored in the Automatic Workload Repository (discussed in the next section). The ADDM report is generated hourly after each Automatic Repository Workload snapshot. The results are calculated by comparing the performance between snapshots. The ADDM report link will not show up in the OEM console if there are no findings (problems), but it can still be manually run as needed within the console.

You may want to generate snapshots outside the 60 minutes for troubleshooting a specific SQL statement. Take a snapshot before the SQL statement starts and after it ends using the following code:

```
SYS@ORCL>DBMS_WORKLOAD_REPOSITORY.CREATE_SNAPSHOT('TYPICAL');
```

If you want to see the latest ADDM report, which is stored in the Automatic Workload Repository (AWR), use the following code. This returns a text version with all detailed findings (find this script `latest_adm.sql` in the code for this chapter):

```
set long 1000000
set pagesize 50000
column get_clob format a80
select dbms_advisor.get_task_report(
task_name, 'TEXT', 'ALL')
as ADDM_report
from dba_advisor_tasks
where task_id=(
select max(t.task_id)
from dba_advisor_tasks t, dba_advisor_log l
where t.task_id = l.task_id
and t.advisor_name='ADDM'
and l.status= 'COMPLETED');
```

There is a tunable parameter to ADDM—DBIO_EXPECTED. It is changed using the DBMS_ADVISOR package and is specific to your hardware. The default works unless you have either old hardware or the faster RAM hard drives.

It is time to talk about Oracle Licensing in this section, as several of the tuning features are enabled by default yet require an additional license for use. If your organization has not purchased the Diagnostics and Tuning Pack as part of the OEM, then the following steps need to be followed to adjust the default Control Management Pack Access.

In any of the 10.x database versions, the ADDM is enabled by default, running automatically after every AWR snapshot. There are different ways to disable this depending on the Oracle Version.

In Oracle 10g, set database parameter `statistics_level=BASIC`. This completely disables ADDM, but it also disables many of the other **free** tuning components. It is better to set the hidden database parameter (a hidden parameter starts with an underscore) as follows:

```
ALTER SYSTEM set "_addm_auto_enable"=false scope=both;
```

In Oracle Database 11g, the database parameter called `control_management_pack_access` is used to specify which of the OEM management packs should be active. There is a default value that is set to `"DIAGNOSTIC+TUNING"`. To disable ADDM, you can set the database parameter as follows:

```
alter system set control_management_pack_access = "NONE" scope=both;
```

There may be a situation where your organization owns the licensing for the Diagnostics and Tuning packs but has to keep the database parameter `STATISTICS=BASIC`, which turns off the tuning features as mentioned above. You can still utilize the features taking a snapshot manually like this:

1. Take a starting snapshot:

   ```
   SYS@ORCL> EXECUTE dbms_workload_repository.create_snapshot();
   ```

2. Take an ending snapshot, after the problem has occurred or been recreated:

   ```
   SYS@ORCL> EXECUTE dbms_workload_repository.create_snapshot();
   ```

3. Run the SQL scripts found in `$ORACLE_HOME/rdbms/admin` for the final reports:

   ```
   SYS@ORCL>@awrrpt.sql
   SYS@ORCL>@addmrpt.sql

   SYS@ORCL>awrddrpi.sql (compare periods report)
   ```

The running of these two scripts will ask for the snapshot IDs, which are conveniently listed for you after giving answers to several of the prompts.

If you are using OEM without purchasing any of the additional packs, there won't be as much functionality available. To view functionality, with and without the packs, go to the GC Setup Link, Management Pack Access. Adjust the access by clicking or removing a check mark and apply the changes. What happens is that the clickable links for that management pack are no longer accessible in the console.

Take the time to remove any that you don't have a license for and check the box agreeing to the pack access. Testing for a new functionality is fine with Oracle products, but it needs to be on a database with none of your production data. So if you need to test GG management packs, this will require a new install on a testing box with none of your production servers, databases, or application servers being monitored. Talk to your Oracle licensing representative for the exact details.

Automatic Workload Repository

Automatic Workload Repository (AWR) consists of the SGA-based in-memory statistics collection process (MMON), with snapshots taken at regular intervals. Depending on the Oracle Version and the appropriate database parameters, the RDBMS will schedule AWR snapshots automatically every 60 minutes. These snapshots will include the results of the last executed ADDM; these ADDM results are from the hourly snapshots of data.

The snapshot output is recorded in the data dictionary, which can be retrieved (using SQL or by the GC OEM console) for historical comparison over the retention period.

```
SYS@ORCL>SELECT * FROM dba_hist_snapshot ORDER BY snap_id;
```

Another useful search is identifying which execution plan (out of several) was executed at a certain time. This information comes from the AWR. The first query will find the SQL_ID needed for the subsequent queries.

```
SELECT tf.* FROM DBA_HIST_SQLTEXT ht, table
(DBMS_XPLAN.DISPLAY_AWR(ht.sql_id,null, null, 'ALL' )) tf
WHERE ht.sql_text like '%&PIECEOFSQL%';

select sql_id, PLAN_HASH_VALUE, to_char(timestamp,'DD-MON-YYYY HH24:
MI:SS') from DBA_HIST_SQL_PLAN where sql_id= '&SQLID';
```

For diagnosing issues or abnormalities in the AWR repository itself, see $ORACLE_HOME/rdbms/admin/awrinfo.sql. This script reports the total amount of database space that AWR occupies, estimated AWR growth, and Advisor Tasks information.

Active Session History (ASH)

Active Session History, an automated task, will identify currently running SQL for all connected and active sessions. While AWR and Statspack are important tools for diagnosing issues, they don't have the level of detail for individual SQL statements that ASH does. Here are the highlights of ASH:

- It retains seven days of history by default
- Statistical analysis of events, session, and waits
- It can dump to trace file
- SYS@ORCL11>alter session set events 'immediate trace name ashdump level 10'; — gives 10 minutes of history
- Sample every 10 seconds
- V$ACTIVE_SESSION_HISTORY or DBA_HIST_ACTIVE_SESS_HISTORY
- ASH report ($ORACLE_HOME/rdbms/admin/ashrpt.sql) or through EM console.

See the code for this chapter — ash_top_min.sql (Top SQL from the last minute) and ash_top_ios.sql (identified SQL that uses the most I/O).

If you don't own the management packs required for this utility, check out the following location for a freeware version called S-ASH: `http://ashmasters.com/ash-simulation/`. There are a couple of versions of S-ASH depending on your edition of Oracle installed.

SQL Advisors

In 11g, one of the automatic tuning tasks is what is known as Automatic SQL Tuning (`SYS_AUTO_SQL_TUNING_TASK`). By default, the task is configured and running in all of the maintenance windows that include the SQL Tuning Advisor (STA) and SQL Access Advisor (SAA). ADDM results may include the recommendation to run STA to improve a SQL statement.

Remember that whenever you run an advisor, the results are Oracle recommendations. The DBA needs to manually decide which recommendations are suitable for their application. I would compare the explain plans (easy to do with the OEM console) to see the actual differences in the costs associated with a recommendation.

The advisor may suggest collecting statistics, missing indexes, as well as an improved execution plan. The STA will collect statistics (for evaluation only) as well as account for any missing indexes to come up with a better plan. The improvements are saved as a SQL profile. A SQL profile is not an actual saved execution plan; it is a stored fix to any incorrect estimates due to index or statistics issues. The regular execution plan is used along with the SQL profile, resulting in an improved performance.

The default behaviour is not to automatically accept SQL profiles when they are generated by the automatic tuning task. In 11g, I recommend starting with SQL Plan Management and only using SQL profiles as a temporary fix for plan stability issues.

The SQL Access Advisor (SAA) suggests alternate access paths to the data using indexes or materialized views to improve performance. SAA can use a workload that comes from memory (`V$SQL`) or user-defined workloads (a particular schema(s) or SQL Transport Set). Evaluation includes any combination of new indexes, new materialized views, storage creation parameters, dropping unused indexes, or modifying existing indexes.

The SAA is not as useful as the STA—it may recommend dropping an important index that is not being used during the time you ran the advisor. To monitor which indexes are being used requires a longer process where you turn on monitoring for certain indexes, run a workload, and then stop monitoring. The complete steps are found in the MOS document: *Identifying Unused Indexes [ID 144070.1]*.

Monitoring Tools are one of the most important components for proactively tuning an Oracle Database. In this book, the overall monitoring GUI tool used is the OEM console. It provides a Graph Interface with real-time monitoring capabilities. In this chapter, the console is used with the Diagnostics and Tuning Management Pack. Everything in regards to tuning can be done without the Diagnostics and Tuning Optional License. This brings us to the next section, STATSPACK, the free version.

STATSPACK

The Statspack utility is a set of PL/SQL and SQL scripts that come included with an Oracle license. It is similar in functionality to AWR, in that it takes snapshots over a period of time, which can be compared to evaluate performance. The information in the snapshot comes from the dynamic performance tables as part of the data dictionary. The code itself can be modified or customized since it is not encrypted. It has to be installed, configured, and scheduled to be run by the DBA. While the actual install, scheduling, and maintenance of the Statspack utility is not difficult, it takes dedication and work to maintain over time.

Each Statspack version can be upgraded to keep existing snapshot data, but there is no downgrade available. The only way to restore is to de-install, and do a schema-level import of the data, usually the PERFSTAT schema. The original Statspack Documentation is found in the older 9i Oracle documentation at the following location: `http://download.oracle.com/docs/cd/B10501_01/server.920/a96533/statspac.htm#PFGRF019`

Updated information for the version you are interested in is located in `$ORACLE_HOME/rdbms/admin/spdoc.txt`. There are changes from 10.2 and 11.1, but no changes appear in the document to Statspack between 11.1 and 11.2.0.1.

While Oracle provides some diagnostic information when generating a report, it still requires some DBA experience to use Statspack successfully. The Oracle database has hundreds of wait events, statistics, and metrics that are used to report the time spent by a transaction and are dependent on the individualized workload for any one system. There are free or low-cost analyzers and viewers available for the standard text Statspack report. One that has been around for a long time and is still used can be found at: `http://www.oraperf.com`.

If you are migrating from Statspack to using AWR, beware that collecting both types of snapshots may interfere with each other. Since AWR is collected on the hour, if the database startup initialization parameter is `statistics_level = typical` (or `all`), move the Statspack collection to the half-hour to prevent conflicts.

There is more information on using Statspack with 11g at:

`http://kerryosborne.oracle-guy.com/2008/11/statspack-still-works-in-10g-and-11g/` `http://wiki.oracle.com/page/Oracle+Tuning+with+STATSPACK+and+AWR`

Reactive diagnostic and tracing tools

The utilities listed below may or may not be applicable, depending on your database version, operating system, Oracle support agreement, and/or management packs licensed. While several of these were listed in the proactive section above, they are still applicable for use when diagnosing a performance problem. The GUI OEM console has both real-time and historical charting capabilities that are valuable for both proactive and reactive activities.

The utilities native to Oracle Database or located in `$ORACLE_HOME` are as follows:

- PL/SQL Profiler: Discovering which PL/SQL line takes the most time—`DBMS_PROFILER`
- STATSPACK: Snapshots (`spreport.sql`)—check out the Statspack section in this chapter
- Events and Tracing: See the Tracing and Diagnostic Events Section
- Error/Crash Issues: Automatic Diagnostic Repository, Support Workbench, Advisors, and Checkers

 The Diagnostic and Tuning management packs are only available for the Enterprise Edition of Oracle. The features of the Tuning pack are dependent on the Diagnostic pack being installed.

Database—additional management packs required:

- SQL Tuning Advisor: Ranked improvement recommendations—`DBMS_SQLTUNE` or `$ORACLE_HOME/rdbms/admin/sqltrpt.sql`
- AWR (Automatic Workload Repository): Saves snapshots, benchmarking—report (`$ORACLE_HOME/rdbms/admin/awrrpt.sql`)
- ADDM (Automatic Diagnostic Database Monitor): Report (`$ORACLE_HOME/rdbms/admin/addmrpt.sql`)
- ASH (Active Session History): `$ORACLE_HOME/rdbms/admin/ashrpt.sql`
- SQL Incident Analysis: Severe enough for uploading to MOS for an SR
- SQL Failure Analysis: SQL failures that don't produce an incident

Database — available on MOS website:

- SQLTXPLAIN: extensive explain plan — *sqlt.zip [ID 215187.1]*
- TRCANLZR: analyzing raw SQL trace data — *trca.zip [ID 224270.1]*
- OPDG: Oracle Performance Diagnostic Guide
- *Troubleshoot an ORA-600 or ORA-7445 Error Using the Error Lookup Tool [ID 153788.1]*
- RDA: Remote Diagnostic Agent used with the DBPERF Profile

Operating System Utilities — available on MOS website:

- OS_Watcher: *Collect/Archive OS, Network Metrics, Windows version available [ID 301137.1]*
- LTOM: *Comprehensive Integrated Real-time Collector for OS and Database (Hang Detector, Data Recorder, Session Trace Collector) [ID 352363.1]*
- Procwatcher: *Script to Monitor and Examine Oracle and CRS Processes [ID 459694.1]*
- Stackx: *shell script UNIX, extracting Core/Stack Trace Files [ID 362791.1]*
- HangFG: *Hang File Generator — Unix scripts [ID 362094.1]*

Bind peeking and Adaptive Cursor Sharing

This section requires some basic knowledge of tuning, as it pertains to bind peeking and Adaptive Cursor Sharing. Before the 10g Version of Oracle Database, there were performance issues related to bind peeking. The query optimizer takes a quick look (peek) at user-defined bind variables the first time they appear in a cursor. A bind variable is a substitution variable instead of a literal — in this example as A: instead of the literal 100. That peek may or may not be the best value to base the execution plan of a query on. The next time the optimizer encounters that same cursor, no more peeking takes place no matter the bind value, because the cursor is shared among all the queries for the same information.

Why wouldn't the first peek be the best one to use? It depends on the mathematical distribution of the data. For example, a table with three column values — 1, 10, 100, contains 245 rows, 2 rows and 6 rows of each value respectively. There is a larger number of rows that contain the value 1 for the same column. The query optimizer may choose a particular execution plan based on whether a Full Table Scan or an Indexed lookup is more efficient. When that plan choice is based on the wrong peek, then a bad execution plan is the usual result.

Oracle Database11g introduced SQL Plan Management in order to control when an execution plan changes, whether it is due to bind peeking or any other reason for an execution plan to change. It is based on the ability to store multiple execution plans for a SQL_ID, comparing plans, and executing the top performing plan.

11g has also introduced Adaptive Cursor Sharing, which doesn't always take the first peek and shares the resulting execution plan for a particular cursor. There will be different execution plans generated for different bind variables of a cursor with the cursor marked as bind sensitive if a histogram is used. Adaptive Cursor Sharing may produce multiple cursors that result in multiple plans, with the optimizer choosing the best plan for the bind variables being used.

 See later in the next section for more on histograms. For an example case study on bind peeking in 11g, look up the following blog: http://oracletoday.blogspot.com/2007/08/bind-variable-peeking-in-11g.html.

The next section is about gathering statistics, which is important when as changes occur (data, system, or dictionary-related) to maintain an accurate count of the changing values as well as their distribution.

Gathering statistics

There is the Oracle-supplied package DBMS_STATS that will calculate statistics for a table (entire schema or the entire database), which is considered the replacement for the older (legacy) compute statistics command for calculating the cost of a query. Using the DBMS_STATS package will be your primary method for regulating statistics gathering on any database 10g and above, along with the startup initialization parameters of TIMED_STATISTICS and STATISTICS_LEVEL.

11g puts statistics gathering under the larger umbrella of **Automatic Maintenance Tasks Management** or **AutoTask**, which is used in conjunction with the resource manager so that jobs (like statistics gathering) are sure to complete successfully within the resource windows. These are the tasks automatically implemented:

- Optimizer statistics gathering
- Automatic Segment Advisor
- SQL Tuning Advisor

The first set of automatic tasks is where we will start in this section-Optimizer Statistics Gathering, which calls the `DBMS_STATS.GATHER_DATABASE_STATS_JOB_PROC` package. This task determines which objects (tables, column, index, or system) have missing or stale (data has changed beyond a certain threshold percentage) statistics. The monitoring for stale statistics comes from the `*_tab_modifications` view.

From the OEM Console, there are several tasks associated with statistics as seen in the screenshot below. All of the statistics tasks listed use the `DBMS_STATS` package:

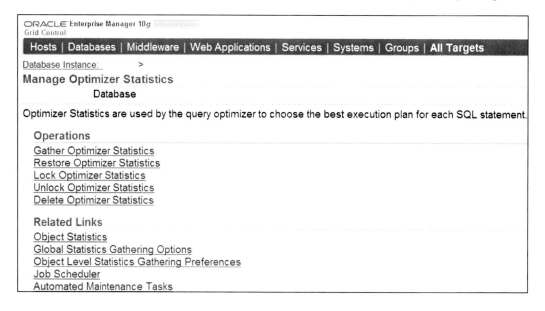

If you need to change statistics, the place to start is with the Global Statistics Gathering Options. Think of this as top-down tuning 90% of the database by making a few adjustments to the automatic statistics gathering job. The window that comes up when choosing that link is shown in the following screenshot:

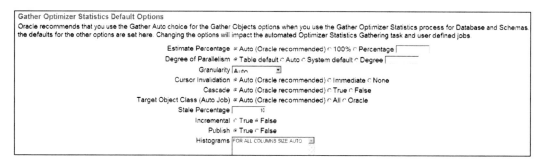

The field that most DBAs need to adjust (as it varies from application to application) is the Histograms box. This adjusts what is known as the METHOD_OPT argument of DBMS_STATS. Histograms are also known as column statistics; this is the statistic type that is important to gather when the data is not evenly distributed (known as skewed data) as mentioned earlier in this chapter.

METHOD_OPT has a default of FOR ALL COLUMNS SIZE 1 on Oracle 9i, which really means **no histograms**. The 10g and 11g versions default to AUTO, which means that the execution of the DBMS_STATS package is what decides in which columns a histogram may help to produce a better plan. When migrating an existing 10g database to 11g it is important to note that non-default values (such as METHOD_OPT) are not changed during the upgrade process.

Here are some general recommendations for gathering statistics by object type:

- Application schema objects—statistics gathered when stale as defined by the auto stats job.
- Data dictionary objects—gather full statistics once, unless there are large schema changes to the database or an Oracle upgrade.
- Fixed objects—dynamic performance tables, gather once during normal production workload.
- System performance stats—gather once with normal production workload. This needs to change if the workload, hardware, or system configuration changes drastically.

For the last two items in this list, if your workload varies widely, then stick to the defaults that Oracle provides.

What might need to be exempt from the automatic statistics gathering job are volatile, large bulk loads. These are dealt with by setting the values to a predetermined normal value and then locking the statistics. External tables statistics are also usually exempt from statistics gathering. If you completely turn off statistic gathering for all application schemas, Oracle recommends leaving statistics gathering active for the data dictionary. This also assumes that the system statistics and fixed object statistics have already been gathered.

 For more information on histograms and METHOD_OPT, take a look at work done by Wolfgang Breitling at http://www.centrexcc.com/.

Comparing statistics

Use the Oracle-supplied package `DBMS_STATS.DIFF_TABLE_STATS_*` to compare statistics from any combination of the following possible sources:

- User-created statistics table
- Current statistics in the data dictionary
- Point in history
- Pending statistics

Comparing statistics would be very useful in your database upgrade from 10g to 11g and eventual migration to SQL Plan Management. For migration purposes you are looking for the SQL statements where the statistics are the same from one database to another while the execution plan is different. Comparing the statistics would verify that they aren't the reason for the change in plans.

Restoring statistics history

There is a way to restore the statistics when performance degrades from the historical record of the statistics saved by default since Oracle Database Version 10g.

```
SYS@ORCL>select DBMS_STATS.GET_STATS_HISTORY_RETENTION from dual;  --
default of 31 days   for 11g

SYS@ORCL>select DBMS_STATS.GET_STATS_HISTORY_AVAILABILITY from dual;
--the oldest statistics that can be restored

  SYS@ORCL> select TABLE_NAME, STATS_UPDATE_TIME from dba_tab_stats_
history;  --indicates when statistics were gathered for each table.
```

There are several different ways to restore a particular set of statistics:

```
execute DBMS_STATS.RESTORE_TABLE_STATS ('owner','table',date);
execute DBMS_STATS.RESTORE_DATABASE_STATS(date);
execute DBMS_STATS.RESTORE_DICTIONARY_STATS(date);
execute DBMS_STATS.RESTORE_FIXED_OBJECTS_STATS(date);
execute DBMS_STATS.RESTORE_SCHEMA_STATS('owner',date);
execute DBMS_STATS.RESTORE_SYSTEM_STATS(date);
```

Here is an example showing how to restore the entire database statistics to a certain timestamp:

```
execute dbms_stats.restore_database_stats( as_of_timestamp => to_
timestamp_tz('2010-03-19 11:05:00 -6:00', 'YYYY-MM-DD HH24:MI:SS TZH:
TZM') );
```

There will be a difference in execution plans for the same SQL statements in different databases, due to a different set of gathered statistics.

 See the following note for how to transport statistics from one database to another for testing: *How to Use DBMS_STATS to Move Statistics to a Different Database* [Note: 117203.1].

Knowing what needs to be tuned

You are looking for what is doing more work than required (Full Table Scans instead of index lookups) or waiting for some sort of resource (latches, locks or I/O).

Find the database process(es) that is (are):

- Using the most CPU
- Performing the most disk I/O operations
- Executing the most number of times
- Taking the longest time to execute (which is known as elapsed time)

You need to fix the really bad performing SQL statements first, which is why it is most often deemed the TOP N SQL. These TOP statements will bring the most benefit from the time spent in tuning or optimizing. The TOP N SQL designation comes from what is listed in a STATSPACK and/or ADDM report output from the AWR for an Oracle database.

There are specific thresholds that the RDBMS uses to determine the top 10 most resource-intensive statements (see the script `top10.sql` provided for this chapter):

- Buffer Gets: 10,000
- Physical Reads: 1,000
- Executions: 100
- Parse Calls: 1,000
- Sharable Memory: 1,048,576
- Version Count: 20

Extensive information is gathered from the database, which shows in detail the time being spent on various activities. Overall end-user response time is a combination of CPU time and any waits that may be occurring.

Response Time = Service Time (CPU) + Wait Time (sum of all waits)

At different points in this chapter, it was mentioned what changes might cause a SQL statement to start performing badly — object statistics, schema, and/or data changes. Don't forget about bindpeek(ing) when talking about performance issues. Refer to Chapter 10 of the *Oracle Database Performance Tuning Guide* for "Instance Tuning Using Performance Views" for help in interpreting the ASH, ADDM, or Statspack reports.

Tuning a single query

Recommendations on what to change first should be based on doing the least amount of harm. Remember that you could possibly make changes that would affect database performance system-wide for the worse. The following are some suggestions for adjusting:

- 11g SQL Plan Management — in earlier Oracle versions, use Stored Outlines.
- Dynamic Sampling — different from normal statistics gathering.
- System Statistics — lets the optimizer know specifics about your hardware.
- Database Startup Initialization Parameters — system-wide change that may cause bad performance and can be specific to a vendor application.
- Hints — provides the optimizer with more information to pick a certain execution plan. See the OPT_PARAM type suggested below.

It is important to note that changing database parameters is one of the top ten mistakes in the *Oracle Database Performance Tuning Guide*. Adjusting database parameters are most often used when the entire database is performing badly for all SQL queries or when the application vendor recommends a specific parameter change. See the MOS Document: *Tuning Queries: 'Quick and Dirty' Solutions [ID 207434.1]. OPT_PARAM Hint [ID 377333.1]*: Introduced in 10g. Using a Hint to change optimizer settings; is especially useful for migrating from one Oracle version to another by either advancing or downgrading the compatibility version for specific SQL statements.

SQL Plan Management (SPM)

Making executions plans more stable plus adaptable to changes (system, dictionary, data) as they occur is the reasoning behind the SPM components of 11g. It is a major improvement to the stored outlines that have been a part of Oracle Database since version 8i. While stored outlines provided stability for a fixed optimized execution plan, it didn't have the features for storing, comparing, and verifying multiple plans. Hints, which are added to the actual SQL, are intended to provide guidance to the query optimizer for picking a certain execution plan. Hints will also require ongoing maintenance to prevent query regression as data changes.

This is the default SPM behavior:

- SQL Plan Baseline Capture (Automatic)
    - ○ `OPTIMIZER_CAPTURE_SQL_PLAN_BASELINES = true`
    - ○ First plan automatically accepted, new plans non-accepted
    - ○ If Stored Outline exists, are enabled, and `USE_STORED_OUTLINES=true`, then manually migrate new plans. Disable stored outlines to use newer plans.

- SQL Plan Baseline Selection (DBA run)
    - ○ `OPTIMIZER_USE_SQL_PLAN_BASELINES = true`
    - ○ Plan must have `ENABLED=YES` and `ACCEPTED=YES`

- SQL Plan Baseline Evolution (Scheduled or DBA run)
    - ○ Scheduled and run by DBA with procedure
    - ○ Bad plan stays non-accepted, better becomes accepted as part of plan baseline

The query optimizer chooses from accepted plans that are part of the SQL Plan Baseline. Creating the baseline can happen by either scheduling `DBMS_SPM` to verify all non-accepted plans or the DBA can manually designate which plan is the best. The following query will indicate which plans are accepted:

```
SYS@ORCL11> select sql_text, plan_name, enabled, accepted from
dba_sql_plan_baselines;
```

A particular plan is identified by the column `SQL_HANDLE` in `dba_sql_plan_baselines` view and is used for managing the plan history with the `DBMS_SPM` package.

SQL Tuning Advisor can also evolve plans and insert a newly tuned plan that is not in the plan history. See the section *Upgrading the Optimizer* for recommendations on migrating to 11g and using the SPM functionality for the first time.

All of the SPM features can be accessed by using either the OEM console or the DBMS_SPM package. Any end user who needs access to administer plan history will need the new 11g privilege ADMINISTER SQL MANAGEMENT OBJECT privilege assigned to them.

SQL Management Base

There is a repository (part of the data dictionary) containing all of the components of SPM for maintaining plans: statement logs, plan histories, SQL plan baselines, and SQL profiles. The repository is called SQL Management Base (SMB) and it is self-managing, with the default maxsize of 10% of the SYSAUX tablespace. There is a weekly scheduled purging task that removes plans not used for the last 53 weeks. If you exceed the default percentage maxsize, then only alerts are generated. It is up to you to do something about it by increasing the threshold, increasing the tablespace size, or manually purging SPM objects.

Tracing and diagnostic events

While researching SPM, I came across new tracing capabilities for SPM by setting an event. This is called the Universal Tracing Service, and it was mentioned in a single document — *Sql Plan Baseline Not always created [ID 788853.1]* — with the following code:

```
alter session set events 'trace [sql_planmanagement.*]';
```

Also, check out the document *SQL PLAN MANAGEMENT TRACING* [ID 789520.1] for tracing any SPM changes using the DBMS_SPM package.

What is an event ?

An event is an Oracle-supplied internal mechanism to signal (most often trace or debug sessions) when a certain change in database behaviour occurs. It also enables the collection of trace or debug information and starts certain error checking features.

When should I set an event?

An event should be set only after you understand the following:

- Exactly what the event will change
- It may or may not be applicable to the database version in use
- Oracle Support has requested you set an event
- Recommend setting in a test database first

What are the different event levels?

There are different event levels. That vary according to the event number and the Oracle version you are using.

For example, event Number 10046 has four tracing levels and is commonly used for researching specific SQL tuning cases:

- Level 1 is default and traces all activities until the trace session is terminated
- Level 4 = level 1 tracing + bind variables
- Level 8 = level 1 tracing + wait events
- Level 12 = level 1 tracing + bind variable + wait events

While other events will look more like the following, this example will be seen in the database initialization file (pfile):

```
event="10235 trace name context forever, level 65536"
```

A bad situation can get worse by setting events randomly without the exact level, causing core dumps or a database crash. This means you need to research carefully before setting any type of event. It may appear that setting an event is an ordinary thing because they are found in many Oracle-related technical sources, but it should not really be done unless you have a valid reason for doing so.

Specific Trace events for performance problems

Oracle diagnostic events and ORA errors share the same range of numbers from 0 to 65535 for their codes. The following are some examples of Trace events:

- 10046 Trace: Studying the performance specific to a certain SQL statement
- 10053 Trace: How the CBO operates for a hard parse situation
- 10032 and 10033 Trace: Tracing for Sort Conditions
- 10104 Trace: Trace Events for hash join problems.

For a listing of these error numbers, check out the following file: `$ORACLE_HOME/rdbms/mesg/oraus.msg`

Also, look up *Setup & Usage (Tracing) [ID 117736.1]*.

Events vary by version. Use the following query for comparing databases; this is a common method used by DBAs for this type of task. You will need to create a database link between the databases for this to work. This will also require the appropriate TNSNAMES.ORA entry for the query to work. See the `EventDiff.sql` file in the code section for this book that contains additional formatting commands to make the output easier to read:

```
SYS@DB11>select event#,event_id,name from v$event_name
  where event_id not in (select event_id
 from v$event_name@DB10g);
```

Interpreting the resulting Event Trace file

The Trace Analyzer, TRCANLZR, is a tool provided by Oracle, downloadable on MOS, that parses through a RAW SQL Trace generated by setting EVENT 10046. It processes the large trace file and places the analysis report into a staging repository area. It connects to a single database at a time but can be used for multiple databases for the single trace file analysis. Just be aware that data dictionary differences will result in a different analysis than where the trace file was first generated. The scripts in the `tra/dict` area can be copied from system to system to simulate the same data dictionary for multiple databases when used for a single badly-performing SQL analysis.

The report generated will include a huge amount of information that includes:

- Response time
- Summary of the database calls
- List of the top SQL by response time
- SQL with associated dependencies
- I/O wait summaries
- Most used or **hot** blocks
- Time gaps when no tracing activity occurred
- Transaction summary
- Any non-default database initialization parameters
- Row counts involved
- Explain plans

- Tables, indexes, partitions, sub-partitions, and indexed columns referenced by explain plans
- CBO statistics for tables, indexes, columns as well as histograms
- Bind variables involved
- The time analysis for the SQL statement

TRCANLZR analyzes more than TKPROF or TRCSUMMARY while providing additional report details, which makes it a more advanced tool for tuning a specific SQL statement. See the following for more information: *Note: 39817.1* and *Note: 224270.1 Interpreting Raw SQL Trace Files* and *TRCANLZR TKProf Interpretation (9i and above)* [ID 760786.1].

> Here are two blogs that have more information on the newer diagnostic events in 11g:
>
> http://blog.tanelpoder.com/2009/03/03/the-full-power-of-oracles-diagnostic-events-part-1-syntax-for-ksd-debug-event-handling/
>
> http://oraclue.com/?s=diagnostic+events

Upgrading the Optimizer

This section deals with the general steps of upgrading and enabling the features of the Optimizer from 10g to 11g. Upgrading also includes a migration of existing 10g versions of execution plans and statistics to the new SPM method. There are many different ways of accomplishing this task, depending on your current method of gathering statistics, automatic tuning tasks, and execution plan maintenance.

Here is a basic plan of attack:

- Capture and back up existing 10g Execution Plans and Statistics
- Upgrade the database to 11g
- Start the applications and allow the end users to log on to the 11g database
- Adjust the database startup initialization parameters once the new version has been stable for at least a week
- Capture new execution plans and new statistics
- Evolve or verify new plans that execute better than the 10g versions

Capturing and backing up execution plans and statistics

It is assumed in this section that your existing 10g database is successfully tuned with well-performing execution plans and updated statistics are available. If you don't have a well-performing 10g database, try testing an 11g upgrade using all of the new auto-tuning features, including SQL Plan Management. That can be simply done by adjusting the optimizer startup initialization parameters as first outlined in the SPM section in this chapter.

 Center of Excellence (COE) on MOS has a set of scripts to capture statistics from an Oracle database in preparation for an upgrade from 9i or 10g. Refer *Managing CBO Stats during an upgrade to 10g or 11g* [MOS Doc ID 465787.1].

SQL Tuning Sets

As a part of the Diagnostics Pack, SQL Tuning Sets (STS) is the recommended method of capturing execution plans for migrating to 11g. An STS includes the SQL statements, and execution plan, along with execution statistics (different than optimizer statistics). Oracle Version 10gR2 will capture the execution plan as part of an STS, but any version before that will not. If that is the case, then look to using stored outlines as in the next section.

To create an STS, use OEM or by the DBMS_SQLTUNE package as in the following example:

```
execute sys.dbms_sqltune.create_sqlset (sqlset_name => 'SPM_
STS',description => '10gPlan');
```

After creating an STS, load in the execution plans for use as an SPM baseline plan. The plans can come from the AWR, another STS set, or by what is currently in memory (known as cursor cache). It is recommended to skip the SYS schema, as there are data dictionary changes in 11g and the older execution plans migrated from a 10g database would no longer be valid.

Stored Outlines

Stored Outlines are a method of locking in execution plans. They are now deprecated but are another tool that can be used for migrating your current execution plans to 11g, even if you don't have any current outlines in use. They are good for testing because a stored outline can be disabled or re-enabled as needed. They can be done manually for specific SQL statements using the `create outline` command or bulk capture for all SQL statements as in the following case. It is assumed that you would only want certain schemas that are application data-specific.

To create and capture existing Stored Outlines, enable stored outlines with a valid description:

```
SYS@ORCL10> alter system set create_stored_outlines=10gPLAN;
```

Grant any schema owner the `create any outline` privilege:

```
SYS@ORCL10> grant create any outline to <schema_owner>;
```

Run a standardized workload by running the actual application in production or in a testing database.

Turn off the stored outlines capture after the workload is complete:

```
SYS@ORCL10> alter system set create_stored_outlines=false;
```

Double check the existence of Stored Outlines captured with the category of 10g PLAN for each application schema owner:

```
SYS@ORCL10> select name, sql_text, category from user_outlines;
```

These stored outlines are contained in the OUTLN schema, which can be exported as needed (use data pump or the Export/Import utility). This export file is an excellent form of backing up execution plans and can as well be imported into another database for testing.

Capturing and backing up Optimizer Statistics

Statistics have the greatest impact on the execution plan that the query optimizer chooses. It is assumed that an upgrade will be performed on an existing database with existing statistics. Making sure the statistics are gathered and backed up is paramount for the migration process.

Statistic gathering in the 10g database for the migration should be taken during what is known as peak load (greatest amount of database activity). In my OLTP database, this is usually around 3:00 pm when people are hurrying to complete tasks before leaving for the day. There may be other periods of time that are just as important to a particular application. Look for the Top N SQL statement(s) identified as critical, month-end processes as well as the usual SQL queries run as part of the normal reporting workload.

There are several methods to capture and back up statistics:

1. Maintain at least seven days of AWR snapshots history. Default settings retain the last eight days. Double check your current settings for `STATISTICS_LEVEL`, which may affect the length of retention. Use the `$ORACLE_HOME/rdbms/admin/awrextr.sql` to extract a designated number of days into a valid data pump directory as backup or to use in a testing situation. See the MOS Doc: *Transport AWR Data [ID 872733.1]*.

2. While using Statspack, run it at Level 7, which generates execution plans. Since Statspack is a schema (usually Perfstat), it is easy to back up and export the execution plans using standard Oracle Export/Import utilities.

3. Export the complete set for a particular schema into a stats table. That is done by first creating the table and then loading the statistics for a particular schema:

```
EXECUTE DBMS_STATS.CREATE_STATS_TABLE('SYSTEM','10g_STATS_TAB');
EXECUTE DBMS_STATS.EXPORT_SCHEMA_STATS('SCHEMA_NAME','10g_STATS_
TAB','10gSTATS');
```

It is easy to back up the stats table created above by using an export utility, as it is now a database table object. This is also a method of importing these same statistics into another database.

Just as in the execution plan example, you don't want the current SYS statistics, system statistics, or fixed object statistics, as all of these are no longer applicable when you upgrade. The new 11g Oracle version needs to calculate these statistics based on the new Oracle kernel and Optimizer.

Upgrade the database to 11g

Keep `optimizer_features_enable` in your older 10.x version for at least a week. Move the backed up execution plans into the SPM so that they start out as the SQL Plan baseline. Each plan, bulk loaded, will automatically be accepted or added to an existing baseline plan. Load execution plans by:

- SQL Tuning Sets

```
SYS@ORCL11> DBMS_SPM.LOAD_PLANS_FROM_SQLSET( -
sqlset_name => 'SPM_STS');
```

- Stored Outlines—the following code loads all previously captured stored outlines (see the earlier section on how to do the capture):

```
SYS@ORCL11> variable report clob;
SYS@ORCL11>execute :report:=DBMS_SPM.MIGRATE_STORED_OUTLINE(
attribute_name=>'ALL');
```

- Cursor Cache—meant for those statements not captured before the upgrade

```
SYS@ORCL11> DBMS_SPM.LOAD_PLANS_FROM_CURSOR_CACHE;
```

 See the following document for more details on loading plans from a staging table: *How to move 10gr2 Execution Plans and load into 11g spm [ID 801033.1].*

The most important thing is that you need to keep the existing 10g statistics; no automatic gathering should be in place. In the following diagram, there is a picture of the OEM screen used to disable the optimizer statistics gathering job.

ORACLE Enterprise Manager 11g
Grid Control

Hosts | Databases | Middleware | Web Applications | Services | Systems | Groups | **All Targets**

Database Instance   > Automated Maintenance Tasks >

Automated Maintenance Tasks Configuration
Global Status ⦿ Enabled ⦾ Disabled
   Task Settings
   Optimizer Statistics Gathering ⦿ Enabled ⦾ Disabled (Configure)
            Segment Advisor ⦿ Enabled ⦾ Disabled
     Automatic SQL Tuning ⦿ Enabled ⦾ Disabled (Configure)

Maintenance Window Group Assignment

Window	Optimizer Statistics Gathering	Segment Advisor	Automatic SQL Tuning
	Select All | Select None	Select All | Select None	Select All | Select None
SUNDAY_WINDOW	☑	☑	☑
MONDAY_WINDOW	☑	☑	☑
TUESDAY_WINDOW	☑	☑	☑
WEDNESDAY_WINDOW	☑	☑	☑
THURSDAY_WINDOW	☑	☑	☑
FRIDAY_WINDOW	☑	☑	☑
SATURDAY_WINDOW	☑	☑	☑

The following is the SQL method of disabling the optimizer statistics collection job. I recommend running this SQL as soon as the database upgrade is finished:

```
SYS@ORCL11>EXEC DBMS_AUTO_TASK_ADMIN.DISABLE('auto optimizer stats
collection', NULL, NULL);
```

The query below verifies that the auto optimizer stats collection has been disabled:

```
SYS@ORCL11> select client_name,status from Dba_Autotask_Client;
```

The following is a step to make gathering statistics safer. This allows testing to occur before the newly gathered statistics are used against the loaded execution plans as part of the baseline. Since the following doesn't change any additional global preferences, it will gather statistics using the 11g version but store as pending, not in effect.

```
SYS@ORCL11>DBMS_STATS.SET_GLOBAL_PREFS('PENDING','TRUE');
```

It's time to gather the 11g Dictionary Stats, fixed objects, and system statistics! See the recommendations for gathering statistics by object type in this chapter:

```
SYS@ORCL11>DBMS_STATS.GATHER_DICTIONARY_STATS (
        comp_id           => NULL,
        estimate_percent => 100,
        method_opt        => 'FOR ALL COLUMNS SIZE 1',
        cascade           => TRUE,
        statid            => NULL,
        options           => 'GATHER' );
```

- Gather Fixed Object Stats:

```
SYS@ORCL11> DBMS_STATS.GATHER_FIXED_OBJECTS_STATS;
```

- Gather System Stats—First use standard `noworkload` to gather statistics for baseline hardware measurements and then gather system stats with a start/stop predetermined workload over a period of several hours. This system-gathering step can be rerun after major hardware or workload changes.

```
SYS@ORCL11>DBMS_STATS.GATHER_SYSTEM_STATS (gathering_mode =>
'NOWORKLOAD');
SYS@ORCL11>DBMS_STATS.GATHER_SYSTEM_STATS (
    gathering_mode => 'START');
SYS@ORCL11> DBMS_STATS.GATHER_SYSTEM_STATS (
    gathering_mode => 'STOP');
```

- Gather 11g Application Statistics according to application party software recommendations. Application in this case means the particular schemas that have been installed in an Oracle database to support an application. There may be a recommendation to use different parameters than the defaults as in the following command:

```
SYS@ORCL11> execute dbms_stats.gather_schema_stats ('SCHEMANAME');
```

Test each individual SQL statement by changing the OPTIMIZER_USE_PENDING_ STATISTICS at the session level. This allows you to control the new statistics with existing loaded SQL Plan Baselines. See the following code:

```
alter session set optimizer_use_pending_statistics=TRUE;
```

Use the previously mentioned method of comparing statistics to eliminate changed statistics as the reason for an execution plan change. After investigating the differences in statistics, there are a couple of options to try to improve a bad execution plan:

- Try SPM to evolve and verify an execution plan instead of using the 10g loaded plan

- Keep the older 10g statistics by locking them in, preventing any new stats gathering

- Add a Hint (suggestion: use the new OPT_PARAM mentioned earlier)

- Change the SQL statement to perform better with the new statistics

Once all previously identified (and any newly identified) badly performing SQL statements have passed testing, it is time to implement the stable baseline execution plans with new 11g statistics for the entire database, as in the next section.

 An excellent method of extracting a SQL statement for moving a single reproducible test case to another database is using the package DBMS_SQLDIAG. The data pump extract contains DDL information plus statistics and an explain plan. Actual data rows are optional. See the following MOS Document: *How to create a SQL-testcase using the DBMS_SQLDIAG package [ID 727863.1]*. This package has only been available since Oracle 10.2.0.4.

Capturing new execution plans and new statistics

Turn on Pending Statistics and publish them using the following commands and SQL Plan Management will be in effect:

```
SYS@ORCL11>execute DBMS_STATS.SET_GLOBAL_PREFS('PENDING','FALSE');


SYS@ORCL11>execute dbms_stats.publish_pending _stats ();
```

It is time to re-enable the autotask job of gathering statistics, as shown below:

```
DBMS_AUTO_TASK_ADMIN.ENABLE(
client_name => 'auto optimizer stats collection',
operation => NULL,
window_name => NULL);
```

Evolving or verifying new plans that execute better than the 10g versions

While using Statspack, follow the instructions for upgrading if you haven't already done so. They can be found in `$ORACLE_HOME/rdbms/admin/spdoc.txt`. Be sure to set the snapshot levels to seven for the execution plans to be generated and scheduled for hourly executions. If AWR is being used, it is already running and executed hourly.

Compare the Top N SQL statements from before the upgrade and after. They should be similar; if not, the changes should be introduced one at a time to try and eliminate any bad execution plans.

Run the SQL Tuning Advisor—it may recommend a SQL profile, index changes, or statistics gathering. Research on MOS for any known bugs, issues, or configuration changes that might be relevant. Research and test Optimizer Hints. Create an Oracle Service Request and generate a complete, reproducible test case by using the DBMS_SQLDIAG package as mentioned earlier.

 Visit `http://optimizermagic.blogspot.com`, Oracle's own Optimizer Blog, which is great for checking out the latest, newly released features and tips on upgrading the optimizer. Look here for information on migrating from different versions to 11g.

Summary

This final chapter was meant to condense a lot of information into an easy-to-understand format, prioritizing the different elements along the way. This chapter will only get you started on the quest for the ever-elusive tuned database. It doesn't contain everything because the topic is vast and has to be customized to fit your environment—a unique mix of operating systems, application software, Oracle versions, and personnel expertise. A few tips were included for where to look when something else may be wrong; it isn't always the database (or the DBA) that is to blame.

This chapter was meant to get you started learning about how to set events, wading through trace output, collecting statistics, and analyzing explain plans with the different tools and utilities from Oracle. SQL Plan Management is a new feature intended to help with tuning issues both during an Oracle upgrade and afterwards.

Most of the research for this book came from the official Oracle documentation and My Oracle Support website. Participating in Oracle conferences, training sessions, e-mail lists, Oracle User Groups, and volunteer activities over the years all played a hand in forming the total collective knowledge. Start sharing the knowledge you have gained over the years with others. Don't worry about giving away what you consider to be prized information. It's only by opening up to others that you will receive something in return.

Index

My Oracle Support (MOS) 15
My Oracle Support website 63, 64

N

NETCA 12
nid 12
no mount command 228
noprompt command
  about 203
  expired backups, need for 203

O

OEM 12
OEM database control 12
OEM Grid Control Intelligent Agent 29, 31
OFA
  about 11
  11g differences 27
  about 26, 27
  GUI displays 28
  XWindows software 28
oidca 13
OME 197
OMF 122
OMS, GC
  keeping, highliy available 146
online redo logs 123
OPDG 300
operating system differences
  reducing, with common tools 52
Optimal Felxible Architecture. *See* OFA
Optimal Flexible Architecture (OFA) 11
Optimizer upgradation
  about 311
  database, upgrading to 11g 315-317
  execution plans and statistics, backing up 312
  execution plans and statistics, capturing 312
  new execution plans, capturing 318
  new statistics, capturing 318
  Optimizer Statistics, backing up 313
  Optimizer Statistics, capturing 313
  SQL Tuning Sets 312
  stored outlines 313
  verifying 318

Oracle
  backup strategy 196
  DRA 210
  incremental merge backup 188, 190
  incremental merge backup, controlfile 191
  net services 238
  Standard Edition 149
Oracle-provided Unix commands
  about 39
  Dbhome 39
  Dbshut 39
  dbstart 39
  oerr 39
  Oraenv 39
  Sysresv 39
  Tkprof 39
  trcasst 39
  wrap 39
ORACLE_HOME 23
Oracle Database 11g version
  database states 164
Oracle Database High Availability
  optimizing 111
Oracle Database High Availability
        optimization
  about 112, 113
  alternate archive destination 114
  archivelog mode 112
  archivelog space, monitoring 114, 115
  auditing 125
  control files 122
  database compatibility parameter, with pfile 115-117
  database compatibility parameter, with spfile 115-117
  data dictionary healthcheck 131
  data files, autoextending 124
  data storage, implementing 118
  different disk device, using for archivelogs 114
  hard drive space, monitoring 114, 115
  multiple archive destinations 113
  storage, dealing with 118
Oracle Enterprise Manager. *See* OEM
Oracle Grid Infrastructure 11g
  about 242
  ASM 242, 243

read-only tablespaces, sharing between different databases 264-267
snapshot standby, using 268
transient logical standby 270-272
unrecoverable database, recreating 261
using, for upgrades 259

U

Unix commands 51
Unix environment 39
Unix scripting 39
unused block compression 187
user_dump_dest parameter 32
UTF8
  about 278
  superset, choosing 279

V

version control software 61, 62
Very Large Database (VLDB) 11

W

wrc 13

Thank you for buying
Oracle Database 11g—Underground
Advice for Database Administrators

About Packt Publishing

Packt, pronounced 'packed', published its first book "*Mastering phpMyAdmin for Effective MySQL Management*" in April 2004 and subsequently continued to specialize in publishing highly focused books on specific technologies and solutions.

Our books and publications share the experiences of your fellow IT professionals in adapting and customizing today's systems, applications, and frameworks. Our solution based books give you the knowledge and power to customize the software and technologies you're using to get the job done. Packt books are more specific and less general than the IT books you have seen in the past. Our unique business model allows us to bring you more focused information, giving you more of what you need to know, and less of what you don't.

Packt is a modern, yet unique publishing company, which focuses on producing quality, cutting-edge books for communities of developers, administrators, and newbies alike. For more information, please visit our website: www.packtpub.com.

Writing for Packt

We welcome all inquiries from people who are interested in authoring. Book proposals should be sent to author@packtpub.com. If your book idea is still at an early stage and you would like to discuss it first before writing a formal book proposal, contact us; one of our commissioning editors will get in touch with you.

We're not just looking for published authors; if you have strong technical skills but no writing experience, our experienced editors can help you develop a writing career, or simply get some additional reward for your expertise.

Oracle 10g/11g Data and Database Management Utilities

ISBN: 978-1-847196-28-6   Paperback: 432 pages

Master twelve must-use utilities to optimize the efficiency, management, and performance of your daily database tasks

1. Optimize time-consuming tasks efficiently using the Oracle database utilities

2. Perform data loads on the fly and replace the functionality of the old export and import utilities using Data Pump or SQL*Loader

3. Boost database defenses with Oracle Wallet Manager and Security

4. A handbook with lots of practical content with real-life scenarios

Getting Started With Oracle SOA Suite 11g R1 – A Hands-On Tutorial

ISBN: 978-1-847199-78-2   Paperback: 482 pages

Fast track your SOA adoption – Build a service-oriented composite application in just hours!

1. Offers an accelerated learning path for the much anticipated Oracle SOA Suite 11g release

2. Beginning with a discussion of the evolution of SOA, this book sets the stage for your SOA learning experience

3. Includes a comprehensive overview of the Oracle SOA Suite 11g Product Architecture

Mastering Oracle Scheduler in Oracle 11g Databases

ISBN: 978-1-847195-98-2 Paperback: 240 pages

Schedule, manage, and execute jobs that automate your business processes

1. Automate jobs from within the Oracle database with the built-in Scheduler

2. Boost database performance by managing, monitoring, and controlling jobs more effectively

3. Contains easy-to-understand explanations, simple examples, debugging tips, and real-life scenarios

Oracle Warehouse Builder 11g: Getting Started

ISBN: 978-1-847195-74-6 Paperback: 368 pages

Extract, Transform, and Load data to build a dynamic, operational data warehouse

1. Build a working data warehouse from scratch with Oracle Warehouse Builder.

2. Cover techniques in Extracting, Transforming, and Loading data into your data warehouse.

3. Learn about the design of a data warehouse by using a multi-dimensional design with an underlying relational star schema

Please check **www.PacktPub.com** for information on our titles

Breinigsville, PA USA
01 June 2010
239010BV00003B/8/P